A NEW
CONSTITUTIONALISM

A NEW
CONSTITUTIONALISM

*Designing Political Institutions
for a Good Society*

EDITED BY

Stephen L. Elkin and Karol Edward Sołtan

THE UNIVERSITY OF CHICAGO PRESS
Chicago & London

Stephen L. Elkin and Karol Edward Sołtan are, respectively, professor and associate professor of government and politics at the University of Maryland. Among Elkin's books is *City and Regime in the American Republic* (1987), and among Sołtan's, *The Causal Theory of Justice* (1987).

The University of Chicago Press, Chicago 60637
The University of Chicago Press, Ltd., London
© 1993 by The University of Chicago
All rights reserved. Published 1993
Printed in the United States of America
02 01 00 99 98 97 96 95 94 93   1 2 3 4 5
ISBN: 0-226-20463-4 (cloth)
         0-226-20464-2 (paper)

Library of Congress Cataloging-in-Publication Data

A New constitutionalism : designing political institutions for a good society / edited by Stephen L. Elkin and Karol Edward Sołtan.
   p. cm.
Includes bibliographical references and index.
   1. Public interest.   2. Common good.   3. State, The.
4. Constitutional law.   I. Elkin, Stephen L.   II. Sołtan, Karol Edward, 1950–   .
JC330.15.N48   1993
320'.01'1—dc20   92-38703
                                                                 CIP

⊚ The paper used in this publication meets the minimum requirements of the American National Standard for Information Sciences—Permanence of Paper for Printed Library Materials, ANSI Z39.48-1984.

CONTENTS

Preface   vii

PART ONE
Introduction to a New Constitutionalism   1

1. KAROL EDWARD SOŁTAN: *What Is the New Constitutionalism?*   3
2. STEPHEN L. ELKIN: *Constitutionalism: Old and New*   20

PART TWO
Varieties of Constitutionalist Theory   39

3. JAMES W. CEASER: *Reconstructing Political Science*   41
4. KAROL EDWARD SOŁTAN: *Generic Constitutionalism*   70
5. CHARLES W. ANDERSON: *Pragmatic Liberalism, the Rule of Law, and the Pluralist Regime*   96
6. STEPHEN L. ELKIN: *Constitutionalism's Successor*   117

PART THREE
The American Regime   145

7. THEODORE J. LOWI: *Two Roads to Serfdom: Liberalism, Conservatism, and Administrative Power*   149
8. CASS R. SUNSTEIN: *The Enduring Legacy of Republicanism*   174
9. EDWIN T. HAEFELE: *What Constitutes the American Republic?*   207

Contributors   233
Index   235

PREFACE

The essays in this book seek to direct the focus of political study to the improvement of political institutions. The study of politics, the authors contend, should be neither a solely empirical enterprise, cut off from the service of the most fundamental human interests, nor a disembodied normativism, indifferent to limits on the possibilities of political design. In many ways, these essays argue for a return to the best in political study—to the ancient Greeks' concern with classifying and creating good political regimes, and to the great constitutionalist visions of Locke, Montesquieu, and Madison. The essays also show a kinship with an older tradition of political economy whose greatest luminary many consider to be Adam Smith.

These theorists—from the ancient Greeks to moderns such as Locke and Smith—thought that a political science divorced from an examination of political practice would leave human beings prey to the forces of chance and brute power. A fully just commonwealth might be beyond the capability of humankind, they thought, but significant improvement in political life was possible. Some political ways of life are better than others, they said, and we need not settle for whatever fortune hands us.

Recent political study, especially in its manifestations in post–World War II America, has not been kind to this older vision of political science. It has, for the most part, marched down paths defined by a taste for chewing over and digesting ever more refined bits of political data. In the law schools—those products of an unhappy divorce between political and legal theory—things have not been much better. There, students are taught the arts of close reading and rhetoric, and made to remember legal doctrine as propounded in leading cases. Only a few students emerge from their schooling as more than resourceful technicians, prompted perhaps by the good luck of having encountered one of a handful of teachers who remember that legal and political theory were once joined.

And then there are the students of political philosophy, alternatively in the grip of a desire to wring the last drop of political knowledge from the corpus of the great political thinkers, or bedazzled by the shiny goods of a revived moral philosophy. Yet the gap between an inquiry into the sources of moral value and one into the foundations of attractive and well-functioning political regimes is large enough to suggest that these are not siblings, but, at best, cousins. No doubt a certain modesty is called for in the matter of contemplating the design of good regimes, and the reticence of students of political philosophy is thus not wholly inappropriate. And, while it is salutary to be reminded that the deepest understanding of political life and its place in nature may be timeless, still time does march on—and many a corporate behemoth now commands more resources than all the ancient cities taken together.

The authors of the essays assembled here think that there must be a way to theorize about politics that takes its bearings from the enduring concern with political value and gives due attention to the way the political life of modern polities works and might work. Although all the authors may not care to hang out a shingle that says *constitutionalist theorist,* their essays all contribute to a definition of the constitution of good political regimes. The authors are not perhaps pathbreakers in the study of politics; nor are they so prideful as to ignore on whose shoulders they stand. Still, they are set off from many of their peers at least by this: the conviction that something systematic can be said about how political institutions work and can be made to work, how they may be assembled into the larger wholes of political regimes, and why some regimes are better than others.

A political science and legal theory that has these questions at its center would, the essays suggest, be a compelling enterprise. It would, if properly pursued, not only prompt a remarriage of political and legal theory but give humankind at least some chance to flourish in the face of its own unattractive qualities. Perhaps the burden of these essays might be summarized in the following fashion. At their best, political institutions make it harder for people to do what is cruel and foolish. And they may even make it more likely that the political right and the political good will not always be unwelcome orphans.

Aiming to join theory and practice over the past few years, we have combined the preparation of this book with efforts to establish the Committee on the Political Economy of the Good Society (PEGS), a new organization of theorists, activists, and policy professionals concerned with the kind of "constitutional" questions this volume addresses. Multidisciplinary and politically nondenominational, the organization includes on its founding board lawyers, philosophers, economists, political scientists, and policy activists. We think of the present volume as the first scholarly product of PEGS, and consider it volume one of the *PEGS Papers*.

For various kinds of help received along the way we would like to thank Rogers Smith, Fred Alford, Diana Elkin, Jyl Josephson, Manabi Majumdar, Kim Schepple, Anna Sołtan, and Margaret Sołtan. For assistance with organizing the footnotes and bibliography we would like to thank Judith Pellerin, who has opened up for us whole new vistas of computerized indexes and catalogues.

Stephen L. Elkin
Karol Edward Sołtan

PART ONE

Introduction to a New Constitutionalism

The papers in this section introduce a "new constitutionalism." Each approaches the subject in a different way: Karol Edward Sołtan focuses on how a new constitutionalism fits into the several frameworks of social science and social theory; Stephen L. Elkin provides an overview of a wide range of constitutionalist thinking. Both see the principal concern of a new constitutionalism as developing a body of theory concerned with institutional design that will be helpful in the constitution of desirable political orders. The underlying aim, both say, is to create a practical political science, one of use to citizens and anyone else who wishes to think of political matters from a designer's point of view. Sołtan and Elkin argue that a crucial task of social science is to enhance the ability of political actors to design institutions to achieve valued political ends.

Sołtan argues that it is now time to shift direction from the central concerns of much recent political and social theory, with its concern for unmasking the hidden realities of our collective life, to a constructive emphasis—analysis from a designer's perspective. He argues that such analysis is the precondition of responsible empowerment, which he characterizes as a form of understanding necessary to transform a subject or petitioner into a citizen. He shows why this practical focus must be centrally concerned with institutions, and he explicates the role of constitutionalist thinking in developing a design-oriented social science. In the principal sections of the paper, Sołtan discusses "reconstructive" theory—the new constitutionalism being an exercise in the development of such theory—and presents a critique of several important efforts to develop a design-oriented social science.

Elkin sets out the two principal strands of constitutionalist thinking on which new work can be built. The first, which he characterizes as the classical tradition, takes its bearings from a perceived need to limit the arbitrary exercise of political power. The second, which builds on the work of Kenneth Arrow, takes, as the central task of institutional design, how to combine a concern for economic efficiency and democratic control. Elkin discusses variations on each of these themes and concludes by listing a set of questions that must be addressed if the new constitutionalism is to develop into a powerful body of theory.

The papers that follow this introductory section are of two kinds. Part 2 contains several views of the central issues in a constitutionalist social science that centers on institutional design. Part 3 presents three different views of the American regime, each of which argues for a view of the central design questions that need to be faced in order that the regime's promise may be more fully realized. Overall, the aim of the papers in all sections is not to develop a new school of constitutionalist thinking but to illustrate what a political science might look like that is oriented to practice-minded institutionalist thinking.

CHAPTER ONE

What Is the New Constitutionalism?

KAROL EDWARD SOŁTAN

THE NEW CONSTITUTIONALISM is based on a constructive impulse: it contributes to the current institutionalist turn in social science and builds in large part on the recent revival of political economy. It is a program for the study of political and economic phenomena from the perspective of an institutional designer.

The new constitutionalism responds, in part, to a felt need for a deeper rethinking of traditional political programs of the left, the center, and the right. It is an answer to the dramatic shift in the political and economic realities that surround us: the collapse of communism and the general weakening of the socialist ideal, the much slower, but nonetheless noticeable, decay of many capitalist and democratic institutions, the developing recognition of the seriousness of the ecological constraints within which we must work. These developments require a realignment of social and political thinking.

We have, then, strong political grounds now for thinking deeply and *constructively* about institutions, but we have intellectual grounds as well. The intellectual history of the last century has been marked by the questioning, doubting, and weakening of human ideals, under the influence of Marx, Nietzsche, and Freud, and of a social science free of normative commitments and often doubtful about the capacity of human beings to act freely and responsibly. Such was the price we paid for understanding more deeply the causes of human behavior and the nature of the human mind.

But we have come a long way from the daring doctrines of Marx, Freud, and Nietzsche to the pedestrian debunking common in contemporary political science and sociology, or to its arcane and scholastic counterparts in literary theory. In social and political thinking we are also coming to a point of crisis, an opportunity to search for depth in new directions, or perhaps to abandon the search in a postmodernist spirit. The intellectual impulses that have dominated the last 150 years may well be running out of creative energy. Those that have been submerged and relegated to the margins may now take a more central role. It is a good time to try something new or to give new form to old ideas.

Thus the essays in this volume elaborate one promising old idea in new form, a "new constitutionalism." They contribute to our understanding of human institutions from a "designer's perspective," and to an account of the "competence of an ideal citizen" (see the discussion of Chomsky and Anderson below). This effort can be seen as a culmination of an evolution in the social sciences from social theory in the shadow of the masters of suspicion (as Ricoeur [1970] calls Marx, Freud, and Nietzsche), through various forms of rational reconstruction, to the constitutionalist concern with the competence of an ideal citizen. I sketch below the key stages of this development, focusing on some early work of Habermas and some more recent efforts in rational reconstruction.

When we talk about a "designer's perspective" on institutions, we are in danger of sounding too much like social engineers, determining the shape of institutions the way other engineers design bridges and ships or the way architects design buildings. The design problem for institutions is clearly quite distinctive, so adopting a designer's perspective need not lead us to the grand constructivism that Karl Popper (1962), Friedrich Hayek (1973–79), and many others have rightly criticized, and whose dangers are obvious. It is simply a perspective of those who seriously attempt to reform institutions (or to start new ones), whether the reforms are minor or major, whether the institutions are large or small. Those in positions of power have this task, hence social science from a designer's perspective should be included in the education of the powerful—in curricula of schools of public policy and public administration, law schools, and business schools. But the responsible exercise of power is also, more broadly, the task of citizenship.

Social science from the designer's perspective is thus a useful tool not simply for those in power, but for those who aspire to be powerful. It is also a precondition of responsible empowerment open to everyone, a form of understanding necessary to transform a subject or a petitioner into a citizen. This form of constitutionalism is, therefore, or ought to be, an instrument of citizen education most broadly conceived: not instruction in how a particular political system operates, but in how institutions can be made to operate in general. Citizenship in this broadest sense is a form of responsible membership in institutions, whether these are states, corporations, unions, or parties (cf. Selznick 1969).

We call this perspective "constitutionalist" for a variety of reasons. Some derive from the meanings of words: to constitute is to create or to bring into being; the constitution of something is the basic character of that thing as a whole. There are also reasons of continuity with the constitutionalist intellectual tradition, though the name is not meant to connote a more narrowly legal or historical conception of constitutions and constitutionalism. In fact a polemic against narrow conceptions of constitutionalism is one of the subthemes of the essays collected in this volume. They argue against the narrowly legal conceptions, against the approaches that see constitutionalism as a matter of institutional and intellectual history, and—finally—against the view of constitutionalism as aiming only to protect individual liberties by limiting the scope and power of government (see, esp., the essay by Elkin, chap. 6 below).

The designer's perspective extends from design on the smallest scale to the largest. In social life the smallest scale "design" involves individual actions, like a football pass. To look at such individual action from the designer's point of view is to take a "voluntaristic" position (Parsons 1937), according to which actions are artifacts, products of human creativity, no matter how the underlying causal laws operate. Actions are an exercise of our skills, not just an outcome of environmental forces. Social design on the largest scale, by contrast, involves stable *institutions* for large collectivities, as in the writing of constitutions. Here the full complexity of the design perspective is most fully articulated and most clearly visible. The essays in the present volume focus on this most complex level.

Critique of Rational Reconstruction

I would like to suggest two somewhat unusual, but especially illuminating, ways of locating this new constitutionalism in the intellectual terrain. The first traces an evolution from critical theory, through rational reconstruction, to a concern with the competence of an ideal citizen. The second contrasts the new constitutionalism with some other recent attempts to revive and broaden the tradition of political economy.

Contemporary social science has been deeply influenced by the hermeneutics of suspicion as represented by Marx, Nietzsche, and Freud. Their basic strategy for the interpretation and understanding of human phenomena is now widely believed to be the main way to achieve some form of depth. The goal of the hermeneutics of suspicion is to show an institution, a pattern of behavior, or any text or text-analogue as a mask that hides the more lurid reality behind it. Institutions and actions are less than they appear; high motives and moral principles are an illusion, a rationalization, an ideology. The real moving force of human life is elsewhere: in class struggle, in the will to power, in the chaotic impulses of the id.

A good way to trace the move away from an exclusive preoccupation with this kind of theory in the shadow of suspicion is to look at some early work of Jürgen Habermas, an intellectual deeply steeped in the tradition of Marx and Freud. In *Knowledge and Human Interests* (1971) Habermas distinguished three types of theory, the empirical-analytic, the hermeneutic, and the critical, each based on a different knowledge-constitutive interest. The main examples of critical theory were Marxian critique of ideology and Freudian psychoanalysis. Aiming to build on their work, Habermas at this stage identified himself clearly with the tradition of the masters of suspicion.

But only five years after *Knowledge* first appeared in Germany, in a "Postscript" to the second German edition, Habermas (1973) introduces some new elements into this account. He writes there that the book suffers "from the lack of precise distinction . . . between reconstruction and 'self-reflection' in a critical sense" (182), and he traces the problem to the ambiguity in the meaning of the concept of "reflection" in the tradition that goes back to German idealism. He now distinguishes the reconstructive from the critical sciences. In Gilbert Ryle's (1949) terms, a reconstructive theory is the translation of a "knowledge how" into a "knowledge that," from a knowledge expressed only in actions and in inarticulate judgments (e.g., "This is just wrong") to one expressed in a fully systematic theory (in which a judgment of wrongness is derived from an explicitly stated set of rules).

Generative grammar (Chomsky 1965) is perhaps the best example of a reconstructive science, in Habermas's sense. Its goal is to give an account of the linguistic competence of an ideal speaker-hearer. Its data are (mainly) judgments of grammaticalness made by fluent speakers of a language. Generative grammar attempts to provide a set of fully explicit rules that could generate the judgments found among such speakers. The resulting theory does not explain actual linguistic *performance* (i.e., what is *actually said*); it identifies instead the set of rules that makes successful performance possible. It is an account of linguistic competence, not performance, and it is reconstructive since it attempts to make fully explicit the normally tacit understanding of grammatical rules that constitutes such a competence.

The precise nature of Habermas's conception of rational reconstruction in his "Postscript" need not detain us here. It is an early work, later corrected and elaborated (see, e.g., Habermas 1979; McCarthy 1978). In any case "A Postscript to *Knowledge and Human Interests*" serves us here only to locate the new constitutionalism in a larger intellectual setting. For that purpose it is only important to stress the one way generative grammar is *not* typical of rational reconstructions: it does not aim to prescribe, and it cannot be used to improve anyone's language. But other rational reconstructions *do* have normative force.

Examples of reconstructive theory with a prescriptive content can be found in law, in ethics, and in the philosophy of science. One case is the account of law from a judge's point of view given by Ronald Dworkin (1977, 1986). It is in part an explanation of the institutional facts, including the legal precedents, rules, and principles. But it is an explanation of a very special kind, one that can be also used as a partial justification of those facts, showing how the institutional facts could be the product of good reasons. But the goal of such an account is not only to reproduce the institutional "givens" by deducing them from a more explicit and systematic theory; the goal is to guide the development of law, to suggest *changes in,* or at least *additions to,* those institutional givens. The reconstruction of law needed by a judge in hard cases (and in judge-centered legal systems, such as that found in the United States) must have prescriptive force.

This form of reconstruction can be found in ethics as well as in law, as in the method of reflective equilibrium articulated by John Rawls (1971) and Norman Daniels (1979, 1980*a*, 1980*b*). Here, too, we begin with some givens—not the institutional givens of a legal system, but the considered moral judgments of an individual or a group. The goal, as a first approximation, is to find an explicit and systematic theory that can generate those judgments, but we must also allow for the possibility that the systematic theory will change the judgments. Indeed we *welcome* such a possibility as the basis for moral growth. The reconstructive theory is not supposed to leave everything unchanged; it *is* supposed to have normative force.

A final example comes from the philosophy of science. Many philosophers (Lakatos 1978; Newton-Smith 1981) distinguish the internal from the external history of science. Within internal history, only those explanations of scientific change are accepted that can also be taken as justifications of that change. So, for example, we explain (in internal history) the transition from Newtonian to Einsteinian physics by citing the valid reasons (theoretical arguments, evidence, etc.) scientists had for making the transition. External history might, by contrast, see the move to general relativity as one more product of the breakdown of turn-of-the-century bourgeois society. Internal history can succeed only to the extent that it reconstructs the rational standards that scientists themselves rely on when evaluating their theories. Lakatos, Newton-Smith, and others do in fact offer such reconstructions, and we can use these to explain many features of both current scientific practice and the direction of scientific development. The reconstructions can be used prescriptively as well, and they are often used in this way by social scientists.

These three examples of rational reconstruction allow prescription based on the reconstructive theory. They also share a restrictive condition, which may be the defining characteristic of rational reconstruction (as Habermas, among others, suggests). In all three cases, the judgments that make up the data for reconstruction are considered to be in some sense authoritative. They are expressions of a tacit *competence*, a tacit understanding of the proper standards of validity and rightness. Our main task is to make those standards explicit; the standards may change in the process of being made explicit, as we have seen in some of the examples above, but other sources of possible change of standards are excluded.

For many purposes rational reconstruction is too narrow; it is better to see the articulation of tacit knowledge as only a partial account of competence, which we improve and complement by further investigation. On this broader view, we take a designer's perspective on the relevant object (sentences of a language, laws and other institutions, moral and scientific theories). From that perspective we certainly would want to take advantage of the tacit competence concerning the object that is already found in the relevant population, but we need not assume that this competence cannot be improved. We should not be satisfied with rational reconstruction alone.

Chomsky gave as the task of generative grammar the (fully explicit) description of the linguistic competence of an ideal speaker-hearer (Chomsky 1965). By way of analogy we can consider it the task of a constitutionalist social science to describe the political competence of an ideal citizen. A citizen in this formulation is simply anyone who takes a designer's perspective on an institution. The task is to describe a citizen's *competence*.[1] We are not interested in the actual behavior ("performance") of citizens, but only in their capacities (their

---

1. Charles Anderson (1988) makes a similar suggestion about the central task of political science.

skills and knowledge). The capacities we are interested in, furthermore, are those of an *ideal* citizen, one without the usual intellectual and moral limits. An ideal citizen will of course understand the importance of such limits in *real* citizens for institutional design, but that is quite a different matter.

This parallel formulation of the tasks of generative grammar and of constitutionalist social science should not blind us, however, to the fundamental differences between them. Since fluent speakers of a language can be assumed to be competent judges of the grammaticalness of sentences, the description of linguistic competence can rely on the strategy of rational reconstruction to the exclusion of all others. Concerning institutional design, however, we cannot assume a full though tacit competence in any population. The strategy of rational reconstruction must be complemented by building a broader social science from the designer's perspective.

Critique of Political Economy

The new constitutionalism builds on a number of established traditions.[2] There is, first, the continuing development of "traditional" constitutionalism, with various efforts to incorporate the findings of contemporary social science. The most important work in this group is that of Charles McIlwain (1947), M. J. C. Vile (1967), and Carl Friedrich (1968).[3] In a very different vein there are contributions emerging out of a general concern with social planning and administration. The range of these can be shown by citing two very different classics: Robert Dahl and Charles Lindblom's (1953) *Politics, Economics, and Welfare* and Herbert Simon's (1969) *Sciences of the Artificial.* There is also a considerable amount of more specialized work in legal theory (Ackerman 1984), policy analysis, and "policy science," as well as in organizational theory developed from a designer's perspective (see, esp., Mintzberg 1979). And there are other efforts worth noting, especially various Polish works concerned with human practice and design by the philosopher Tadeusz Kotarbiński (1969) and by the "sociotechnics group" led by Adam Podgórecki (1966, 1970).

Still, perhaps the strongest precedents come from the recent revival of interest in political economy. The old tradition of political economy differed from its successors (economics, political science, and sociology) in two main ways. First, it was not restricted by the

---

2. A far more detailed account of these traditions, focusing on political science, may be found in Stephen Elkin's complementary introduction to this volume.

3. A collection of important recent contributions is in Elster and Slagstad (1988).

intellectual specialization that came later; from our contemporary vantage point it appears to have been "interdisciplinary." Hence both the old political economy and its more recent revivals are better able to recognize and study the various forms of complex interdependence among major political and economic institutions (the state, the corporation, and the market chief among them) than the more narrow disciplines of economics and political science. They are also in a better position to study and to understand the fundamental social processes central to both political and economic institutions. Such processes include "the allocation of scarce means to competing ends," as well as bargaining and the exercise of power.

The second distinctive feature of political economy, in contrast to much of contemporary mainstream social science, is the aspiration to prescribe as well as to describe and explain. The old political economy was a moral science and did not worry about the more recent injunctions of "value neutrality" and "fact-value" distinction; in the old political economy as well as the new, normative conclusions were and are welcome. The aspiration to unity of theory and practice in some form—not necessarily the Marxist form—is accepted.

Works in political economy written from a designer's perspective range from the libertarian contractarianism of James Buchanan (e.g., Buchanan 1975; Brennan and Buchanan 1985) through the institutionalism of Charles Lindblom (1976) to the detailed design of a socialist politico-economic system by the Marxist Branko Horvat (1982). A more detailed consideration of the works of these three political economists, representative of the three main traditions of political economy, is perhaps the best way to show both what social science from a designer's perspective might look like and its current deficiencies.

All three are concerned with the proper goals of a politico-economic system and the various institutional means available to achieve them. The goals are left somewhat underspecified by Lindblom but are quite explicit in the two others: a contractarian liberalism for Buchanan, and egalitarianism in all central spheres of modern life for Horvat. The means to achieve these goals are taken to be various instruments of social control (exchange, authority, and persuasion) and the institutions constructed out of those instruments (Lindblom). Or the means are constitutional rules capable of effectively restraining the ordinary politics of self-interested bargaining (Buchanan). Or, finally, the means are specified in a detailed blueprint for a socialist society (Horvat).

These are among the best models so far of a political economy from the designer's perspective, and we can learn much from them.

But we can also find in them important weaknesses, some of which can be traced to insufficient clarity about the form of knowledge such a perspective requires. This is perhaps clearest in the awkward relations these works have to established traditions of prescriptive theory and in the uncertainty concerning the level of specificity that the designer's perspective requires.

Prescription is plainly needed in a design perspective, but it is not easy to find its most appropriate form. One might consider political economy as a field in which political and moral philosophy is applied, but our three authors do not do this. Lindblom simply ignores normative theory; in the manner popular among economists he takes certain ends as given (e.g., popular control) without even clarifying what they are or considering potential internal contradictions within them (as shown in Arrow's theorem, for example; cf. Oppenheimer 1980). Horvat does not ignore philosophical normative theory entirely, but he discusses it very briefly and awkwardly, and then proceeds in a way almost totally independent of his discussion. He talks first of Rawls, but then builds his design on the principle of equality of citizens, producers, and consumers, which is independent of Rawls. Finally, Buchanan constructs his own, contractarian, normative theory; but it is almost certainly too simple to do all the work that such a prescriptive theory must. These works fail to identify, in short, the form of prescription appropriate for a social science written from the designer's perspective.

They also have some trouble choosing the appropriate degree of specificity. Horvat comes close to one extreme, made notorious by the early ("utopian") socialists: the construction of detailed blueprints. Political economy written in this vein will almost certainly dramatically underestimate the dependence of proper design on the real-world environment within which the designed institution will function, an environment all but impossible to predict. The other extreme, represented by Lindblom, does not even identify, as such, the designer's perspective. This leaves unclear the central purpose of the account of politico-economic systems put forward. So Lindblom's (1977) *Politics and Markets* shifts from the basic categories of exchange, authority, and persuasion through the central problem of the privileged position of business to the contrast between two models of the role of reason in social life—all without sufficiently explaining how each of these stages contributes to one coherent view of politico-economic systems.

The different forms of incompleteness from which these works suffer can be usefully summarized through a brief discussion of their contribution to the critical and constructive aspects of political economy. To put the distinction crudely: the constructive aspect of political economy is concerned with tendencies that we believe ought to be reinforced by institutions, the critical aspect with tendencies that institutions ought to counteract.

It is the great virtue of these authors that they pay *some* attention to the constructive side of political economy. But surely they do not pay enough. Buchanan's constructive side consists of an identification of constitutionalism with contractarianism and a proposal for a distinctive contractarian ethic. Horvat's consists of a generalized egalitarianism applied to the spheres of production, consumption, and citizenship. Both are far too simple as a specification of goals for institutional design. Lindblom specifies the goals even less; he is preoccupied almost exclusively with means and with building blocks: with exchange, authority, and persuasion at one level, and with the role of reason as a means to institutional design and policy-making (model 1 vs. model 2) at another.

The critical side of these works also seems too short. It is likely that the institutions of a politico-economic system will need to counteract more than the simple pursuit of narrow self-interest, which is the single preoccupation of Buchanan and of the Virginia school of political economy. Surely the privileged role of business is not the *one* key problem in the development of a constitutional democracy combined with a market economy. The critical aspect of political economy needs to be made more complex.

The notion of a designer's perspective implicit in these works is in a variety of ways too simple. The burden of the essays that follow is to try to move us toward a more complex view, one that could provide us with a reasonably clear statement of theoretical goals different from both the application of traditional political and moral philosophy and from the construction of detailed blueprints. The approach represented by the constitutionalist writers in this volume can be distinguished from that of Buchanan, Horvat, and Lindblom (as different as these are from each other) perhaps chiefly in its more detailed attention to the nature and, especially, the complexity of the designer's perspective. The main goal of the present volume is to make that complexity more explicit.

If we are to develop the view of institutions from a designer's perspective we must perform three quite distinct tasks. The first elaborates our understanding of what is required for such a perspective, and the message we must deliver is one of the complexity and interdependence of design. In one way or another we will be vindicating tacit knowledge in practical affairs; we will urge greater concern with political judgment and wisdom. But all interesting forms of complexity can be disaggregated, and the study of complex wholes can be supplemented by the analysis of the basic units that compose them. Such is the second task of the study of institutions from a designer's perspective. Finally, the value of such a study must be demonstrated in the only way it can, by a broad range of applications across institutions and across cultures.

The essays of this volume concentrate on the first of these three tasks. Not all the authors, in fact, would accept the full list of tasks as given here, but all contribute in various ways to a better understanding of the complex nature of the institutional designer's perspective.

Main Themes of the New Constitutionalism

Though no one coherent doctrine emerges from these essays, some shared intellectual sources are clear: "traditional" political science (including—especially—the Madisonian tradition), pragmatism, and certain branches of legal theory (Selznick 1969; Ackerman 1984; Dworkin 1986). Some widely shared themes emerge as well. These sources and themes can be taken as a kind of preliminary characterization of a constitutionalist social science.

Theme 1: The inadequacy of various narrow conceptions of institutional design. An appreciation of the complexity of the designer's point of view supports a number of conclusions, including some straightforward (though important) distinctions, such as the contrast between constitutional choice and policy choice within a given constitution. Others concern more pervasive questions of the appropriate standards of evaluation. Contrary to a view common in public policy, organization theory, and management, we are urged that institutions are more than instruments. In designing institutions we are not only concerned with the choice of the best means to some established end; we are also concerned with something more, though it is not so easily agreed what that is, and what follows for institutional design. Still some form of a "critique of instrumental reason" (Horkheimer and Adorno [1947] 1972; Horkheimer 1974; Held 1980) is a common theme in constitutionalist social science, as reflected in the essays of this volume.

Institutions also need not be neutral among human interests, as is required by many of the dominant forms of liberal political theory, especially the contractarians and utilitarians. They can do more than simply maximize the aggregated interests of the individuals they affect, without favoring any of those interests (as in utilitarianism), or serve as a neutral instrument for multiple individual purposes (as in "rights-centered" theories of Dworkin, Hayek, and others). In opposition to the ideal of interest neutrality, the authors of the essays in this volume emphasize the role of rational deliberation as a way of discovering the public good, which may or may not favor some interests over others (see esp. the essays by Anderson, Elkin, and Sunstein). They ask us to consider institutions as preference formers, and not as mere instruments of existing preferences, as communities of inquiry and as deliberative bodies, and not simply as interest aggregators.

Theme 2: The inadequacy of the simple application of prescriptive standards, especially those of moral and political philosophy. The idea of prescription as application of moral standards obtained independently is rejected on at least two grounds: insufficient realism and neglect of the internal point of view. The idea is insufficiently realistic because it does not take into account problems of regime maintenance (as Ceaser argues). The ideal regime is not necessarily the one most closely in agreement with some abstract standard of justice and right. Institutional design must take into account the basic limits of human nature: the human tendency toward error and fallibility, the strength of self-interest against the public good, the power of passions against reason. Institutions ought to be the best they can be (as Dworkin and the U.S. Army would say), given these serious constraints.

James Buchanan and the Virginia school of political economy direct this argument against economists who apply prescriptive standards of welfare economics in their policy recommendations, without concern for the motivations of the government officials expected to choose those policies. In this volume it is an argument James Ceaser directs, in the name of a "traditional political science," against simple applications of moral and political philosophy.

The simple application of moral philosophy also fails to the extent that it prevents the recognition of a legitimate diversity of evaluative standards, according to which some aspects of evaluation may be institution specific as well as culture specific. And it also fails as a way to formulate standards of institutional *redesign* (*re*form), a task more common than beginning from scratch. Redesign requires a special consideration of the existing institution in a way that the simple application of moral philosophy does not allow. We need for this purpose an understanding of institutions from the internal point of view (cf. Dworkin 1986), a point of view that combines appreciation and expertise.

The internal point of view is *loyal* to the institution, the point of view of those who appreciate and accept the purpose and value of the institution at least in general outline. It is *developed through deliberation,* by those who *participate in the making* (or designing, or "framing") of the institution, or perhaps by those who simply wish to participate in this way. We do not use it simply to defend the status quo, but to propose reforms and to direct the continuing development of the institution. The study of institutions from the internal point of view will typically include some account of them as they are, combined with an attempt to see the purposes they serve and the general values they express. Both elements are necessary to make well-supported proposals for changes in those institutions, changes that would transform them into better instruments and more accurate expressions of shared ideals.

Theme 3: The importance of American politics as an example. Perhaps the best example of large-scale institutional design is the making of political constitutions. The U.S. Constitution is in many ways the best case to study, and the defense of that constitution in the *Federalist* papers is a model for social science from the designer's perspective. If our goal is to understand better this perspective in its full complexity, then we ought to look carefully at the making of the U.S. Constitution and at *The Federalist.* Hence the essays that follow pay special attention to the American case, and to the more narrowly political aspects of the American regime in particular. But American politics is simply a strategically appropriate area within which we can develop our understanding of the designer's perspective, not more than that. The final product of constitutionalist social science ought to be not simply a better understanding of politics in the United States, or of the American political system, but rather a distinctive *constructive* form of social theory (cf. Ackerman 1984).

Theme 4: The inadequacy of various narrow conceptions of human motivation. We engage here in a double polemic. First, we have an argument against institutional design that neglects the dark side of the human soul or—more prosaically—against design that neglects the power of self-interest as a dominant motive. This is a polemic against contemporary forms of utopianism, such as the frequent calls for a radical participatory democracy often invoking the old republican tradition (e.g., Barber 1984) or the ideal of a permanent revolution in the form of continuous context smashing (Unger 1987).

But we also engage in a polemic, on the other side, against design based on the assumption that self-interest is the only motive, as proposed in some of the writings in public choice. In those writings, institutions and collective decisions are largely seen as products of shifting balances of interests, and politics is a matter of bargaining, coalition building, and exchange. Much of politics, of course, is that way; but not all of it is. Another kind of politics, or another aspect of politics, centers on deliberation rather than bargaining and involves something more akin to the search for the right answer to a question or the best solution to a problem. Attempts to understand and promote this more principled aspect of politics play a central role in a constitutionalist social science.[4]

Conclusion

A designer's perspective on institutions is a foundation for a principled politics. Those who adopt it do not simply manipulate institutions for their narrow purposes: they also try to improve them. The improvement is achieved in part by making institutions more immune to manipulation, in part by articulating more fully ideals implicit in them. Such a task requires a well-developed constructive social theory, which accepts the relevance of the practical test for theories and attempts to go beyond the undermining and debunking of appearances.

The intellectual history of the last century and a half has left us with insufficient resources for these constructive efforts. The masters of suspicion, their students and epigones, have dominated, and it may legitimately now seem that all intellectual depth is on that side. We find there both the great masters of the past and many of the dominant thinkers of contemporary intellectual life (e.g., Foucault and Derrida). The constructive side has been, by contrast, represented by the bromides of humanistic psychology or the peculiar constructions of utopian socialists, and much less rigor or depth has been seen on this side. But the situation may be changing. The tradition that derives from the masters of suspicion faces intellectual exhaustion, as we see in its increasingly hysterical tone, obscure form, and repetitive content, as well as in the loss of its ability to shock and surprise. Add to that the increasingly urgent *practical* necessity of a constructive social theory, and we can see strong reason to shift intellectual resources. There are signs of new life on the more constructive side of social science: in the growth of the "reconstructive

---

4. The argument for more complex conceptions of human motivation has recently been gaining in popularity. The best overview can be found in Mansbridge (1990).

sciences," in the reemergence of the designer's perspective in political economy and elsewhere, and in an increased interest in a morally committed social science (Selznick 1969; Haan et al. 1983; MacRae 1976; Phillips 1979, 1986). The idea of a new constitutionalist social science is another way to promote such a shift.

REFERENCES

Ackerman, Bruce. 1984. *Reconstructing American Law.* Cambridge, Mass.: Harvard University Press.
Anderson, Charles. 1988. "Political Theory and Political Education: A Consumer's Report, a Modest Proposal, and a Tribute to Lane Davis." Paper read at the meetings of the Midwest Political Science Association, Chicago.
Barber, Benjamin. 1984. *Strong Democracy.* Berkeley and Los Angeles: University of California Press.
Brennan, Geoffrey, and James Buchanan. 1985. *The Reason of Rules.* Cambridge: Cambridge University Press.
Buchanan, James. 1975. *The Limits of Liberty.* Chicago: University of Chicago Press.
Chomsky, Noam. 1965. *Aspects of the Theory of Syntax.* Cambridge, Mass.: MIT Press.
Dahl, Robert, and Charles Lindblom. 1953. *Politics, Economics, and Welfare.* New York: Harper.
Daniels, Norman. 1979. "Wide Reflective Equilibrium and Theory Acceptance in Ethics." *Journal of Philosophy* 76:256–82.
———. 1980*a*. "On Some Methods of Ethics and Linguistics." *Philosophical Studies* 37:21–36.
———. 1980*b*. "Reflective Equilibrium and Archimedean Points." *Canadian Journal of Philosophy* 10:83–103.
Dworkin, Ronald. 1977. *Taking Rights Seriously.* Cambridge, Mass.: Harvard University Press.
———. 1986. *Law's Empire.* Cambridge, Mass.: Harvard University Press.
Elster, Jon, and Rune Slagstad, eds. 1988. *Constitutionalism and Democracy.* Cambridge: Cambridge University Press.
Friedrich, Carl. 1968. *Constitutional Government and Democracy.* 4th ed. Waltham, Mass.: Blaisdell.
Haan, Norma, Robert Bellah, Paul Rabinow, and William Sullivan, eds. 1983. *Social Science as Moral Inquiry.* New York: Columbia University Press.

Habermas, Jürgen. 1971. *Knowledge and Human Interests.* Boston: Beacon Press.
———. 1973. "A Postscript to *Knowledge and Human Interests.*" *Philosophy and the Social Sciences* 3:157–89.
———. 1979. *Communication and the Evolution of Society.* Boston: Beacon Press.
Hayek, Friedrich A. von. 1973–79. *Law, Legislation, and Liberty,* 3 vols. Chicago: University of Chicago Press.
Horkheimer, Max. 1974. *Critique of Instrumental Reason.* New York: Seabury.
Horkheimer, Max, and Theodor Adorno. (1947) 1972. *Dialectic of Enlightenment.* New York: Herder & Herder.
Horvat, Branko. 1982. *The Political Economy of Socialism.* Armonk, N.Y.: Sharpe.
Kotarbiński, Tadeusz. 1969. *Traktat o dobrej robocie* [Treatise on Good Work]. 4th ed. Wroclaw: Ossolineum.
Lakatos, Imre. 1978. *The Methodology of Scientific Research Programs.* Vol. 1 of *Philosophical Papers,* edited by John Worrall and Gregory Currie. Cambridge: Cambridge University Press.
Lindblom, Charles. 1977. *Politics and Markets.* New York: Basic Books.
McCarthy, Thomas. 1978. *The Critical Theory of Jürgen Habermas.* Cambridge, Mass.: MIT Press.
McIlwain, Charles. 1947. *Constitutionalism: Ancient and Modern.* 2d ed. Ithaca, N.Y.: Cornell University Press.
MacRae, Douglas. 1976. *The Social Function of Social Science.* New Haven, Conn.: Yale University Press.
Mansbridge, Jane. 1990. *Beyond Self-Interest.* Chicago: University of Chicago Press.
Mintzberg, Henry. 1979. *The Structuring of Organizations.* Englewood Cliffs, N.J.: Prentice-Hall.
Newton-Smith, W. H. 1981. *The Rationality of Science.* London: Routledge & Kegan Paul.
Oppenheimer, Joe. 1980. "Small Steps forward for Political Economy." *World Politics* 33:121–51.
Parsons, Talcott. 1937. *The Structure of Social Action.* New York: McGraw-Hill.
Phillips, Derek. 1979. *Equality, Justice and Rectification.* London: Academic Press.
———. 1986. *Toward a Just Social Order.* Princeton, N.J.: Princeton University Press.
Podgórecki, Adam. 1966. *Zasady socjotechniki* [Principles of Sociotechnics]. Warsaw: Wiedza Powszechna.
———. 1970. *Socjotechnika* [Sociotechnics]. Warsaw: Ksiazka i Wiedza.
Popper, Karl. 1962. *Conjectures and Refutations.* New York: Basic.
Rawls, John. 1971. *A Theory of Justice.* Cambridge, Mass.: Harvard University Press.

Ricoeur, Paul. 1970. *Freud and Philosophy*. New Haven, Conn.: Yale University Press.
Ryle, Gilbert. 1949. *The Concept of Mind*. London: Hutchinson.
Selznick, Philip. 1969. *Law, Society and Industrial Justice*. New York: Sage.
Simon, Herbert. 1969. *The Sciences of the Artificial*. Cambridge, Mass.: MIT Press.
Vile, M. J. C. 1967. *Constitutionalism and the Separation of Powers*. Oxford: Clarendon Press.

CHAPTER TWO

Constitutionalism: Old and New

STEPHEN L. ELKIN

POLITICAL SCIENCE ORIGINATES in an effort to evaluate political life and its place in nature. Its first practitioners did not only ask: Why do various political regimes work as they do? They also asked: How shall the various types of regimes be judged and improved? And, perhaps most important of all, they considered whether it was possible to construct political regimes that would be better than those currently in place. Thus, from the beginning, political science has been concerned not just with explanation and evaluation, it has also focused on the practical matter of constructing good political regimes and improving existing ones.

The heart of such a practical political science must be the design of the formal and informal institutions that compose a desirable political regime. A practical science that is adequate to political life cannot assume a background of political institutions to which advice is directed in the manner of much contemporary policy analysis. It is the workings of the institutions themselves that are crucial—for what they do as a matter of course and over time is what gives the political regime its character.

It is to the development of such a practical political science that the papers in this volume are devoted. Since institutional thinking in the past has often proceeded under the heading of "constitutionalism," and since this is a long-honored and valuable tradition of institutional thought, we employ its name in the characterization of the work presented here—a new constitutionalism. The term *constitutionalism* also points to a central feature of this institutional thinking: it is oriented to the design or constitution of whole political orders and to their reform—and this too is a central concern of the papers.

And by talking about a *new constitutionalism* we want to emphasize that its foundation should not just be in the traditional concern for limiting the exercise of political power.

Discussion of the new constitutionalism can profitably begin by a consideration of its predecessors, starting with the classical tradition of constitutional thought. This review will help identify the central questions that must be addressed in the development of such a practical political science.

Strands of Constitutional Thought

The Classical Tradition

The dominant theme of Western constitutional thought has traditionally been the design of political institutions to limit the exercise of political power. Political institutions are conceived of as the means by which some seek to gain advantage over others. But when institutions are properly arranged, they can prevent such attempts from sinking into arbitrariness and domination. Thus, classical constitutional thinking has traditionally concerned itself with maximizing "the protection of members of society from one another . . . while minimizing opportunities for government itself to harm its citizens." Its goal has been "the avoidance of tyranny" (Gwyn 1986, 66). As McIlwain (1940, 21) puts it, constitutionalism meant simply "the legal limitation on government . . . [whose] antithesis is arbitrary rule" (see also Kraynak 1987; Gwyn 1986; Vile 1967; and Mansfield 1991).

An early and powerful expression of the underlying rationale of classical constitutionalism can be found in the Royal Writ that called the Model Parliament of 1295 and declared that "what affects all should be approved by all" (as quoted in Einzig 1959, 39). The basis for these constitutionalist formulations is a view of human nature nicely stated by Hume (1882, 117–18): "Political writers have established it as a maxim, that, in contriving any system of government, and fixing the several checks and controuls of the constitution, every man ought to be supposed to be a *knave*, and to have no other end, in all his actions, than private interest."

The emphasis then is protective, securing the choices that individuals may make from the incursions of officials and fellow citizens. Locke states the rationale for the separation of powers, the classic device for achieving these objectives.

> It may be too great a temptation to humane frailty, apt to grasp at Power, for the same Persons who have the power of making Laws, to

have also in their hands the power to execute them, whereby they may exempt themselves from Obedience to the Laws they make, and suit the Laws, both in its making and execution, to their own private advantage. (Locke 1960, 12, para. 143)

Perhaps the most extensive and penetrating expression of classical constitutional theory is to be found in *The Federalist*, which sets out the rationale and principles of action for the American political regime. Here we may find all the central ideas of the tradition, including the importance of limiting the power of those chosen by the people to rule and of the people themselves; an emphasis on dividing and separating powers; a suspicion of direct democratic rule; and a sense of the need to deflect the passions of ordinary people away from those they have chosen to be their rulers.

Orthodox reformulations. Classical formulations find contemporary expression in the work of Michael Oakeshott, James Buchanan, F. A. Hayek, and Theodore Lowi. Whatever their differences, they are all haunted by the specter of government becoming simply the exercise of discretion. If government officials have great latitude, there can and will be arbitrariness, and with arbitrariness will come the decline of individual freedom, which is the most important of political values. All turn to some version of government according to law as the principal means by which arbitrariness can be restrained.

Thus Oakeshott (1975, pts. 2 and 3) considers what association through law means. He highlights his understanding of such association—civil association as he terms it—by contrasting it with what he calls enterprise association. An enterprise association has goals and thus requires management, which is understood by Oakeshott to concern the choice of means to further the association's ends. Civil association, on the other hand, has no goals; it is association in terms of subscription to norms of conduct that are to be taken into account when citizens go about their self-determined pursuits.[1]

Buchanan seeks the foundations of association through law in the sorts of rules self-interested and rational citizens might agree upon in forming a political society.[2] He believes that they would agree to rules that would allow full scope for people to conduct their own affairs through market and private cooperative arrangements, much

---

1. Compare Lippmann's (1943, 267) comment that "in a free society the state does not administer the affairs of men. It administers justice among men who conduct their own affairs."
2. An early and clear statement of Buchanan's views can be found in Buchanan and Tullock (1962).

in the fashion of Oakeshott's citizens who join together through civil association. With Buchanan, as against Oakeshott, we get a more explicit statement that purposive, active government cannot be free government since individual desires are diverse, and any effort to amalgamate these desires into a collective choice will result in the imposition of some people's preferences upon others.

This theme—that purposive government cannot be free government—also finds strong expression in the work of Hayek. He argues that law—what he calls the Rule of Law—must take the form of general rules whose effects on particular classes of individuals cannot be known beforehand. If ruling occurs through law thus understood, then arbitrariness can be avoided, since the essence of arbitrariness for Hayek is a set of government officials who have the power to issue commands to known individuals in the pursuit of specified projects. All regimes that allow significant instances of such planning are tyrannies.[3]

In the work of Lowi, the problem of discretion wielded by government officials reappears.[4] For Lowi this is principally the problem of administrative officials who operate under laws that are insufficiently precise. But Lowi, in contrast to Hayek, takes for granted that a modern democratic state will address a wide range of policy questions, and will thus find itself trying to alleviate the plight of many of its citizens. Thus, while in sympathy with Hayek's views, Lowi replaces Hayek's Rule of Law with "good law," which is law with standards. Law must say with precision what lawmakers wish to see done and how it is to be accomplished—which is to say that law can and likely will be an instrument of the planning that Hayek abhors. According to Lowi, law must not simply announce that there is a policy problem and create the powers to deal with it, while, for Hayek, law at its best should not deal with policy problems at all. Hayek would like to eliminate the administration that comes with planning and policy-making if that were feasible (and he realizes it is not). Lowi wants to make administrators party to better planning by getting them to elaborate the rules that lawmakers hand them.

The focus on law and lawmaking by these reformulators of orthodox theory distinguishes them from their predecessors. The crucial problem for classical theorists was to show why any claim to an unlimited right to rule could not be sustained and how limits on ruling might be achieved. Classical theorists could reasonably assume that

---

3. For a clear statement of Hayek's initial position, see Hayek (1944); later formulations can be found in Hayek (1960, 1973).
4. The most detailed statement of Lowi's views can be found in Lowi (1979).

the making of law by a legislature would not be a continuous affair and that therefore the essential problem of limiting government lay elsewhere. The principal danger was in the concentration of all governmental powers in a single person or body of persons, and thus the task was to establish the independence of the various branches of government.

But for contemporary theorists like Hayek, lawmaking is, in fact, not only a crucial activity of modern government but also the principal means by which good government is perverted. The reality is an interventionist, policy-oriented state driven by a demos anxious to use public authority to improve its lot. The remedy, say such theorists, must therefore lie in either reining in the tendency to pass ever more laws or in setting out principles that enable a distinction to be drawn between real (or good) law and the mere imposition of the preferences of some sectors of the society upon others. For theorists like Hayek, the heart of modern constitutionalism must then be a theory of law and lawmaking.

Orthodoxy Transformed

Classical and orthodox theorists focus on formality. The arrangement of formal political institutions and the forms that lawmaking must follow prevent the arbitrary use of political power. In the work of some contemporary theorists the focus shifts—to the informal means by which power is controlled, the ways in which these informal means may fail, and the manner in which they may be improved. The best known of such theorists are Charles E. Lindblom and Robert Dahl. Lindblom looks beyond formal political institutions to the economic institutions of market and enterprise for additional methods of control. Dahl looks instead to the sociology of interests, elite beliefs, and organizations for the means by which political power may be kept within bounds.

Lindblom takes the orthodox problem of limiting political power and restates it as an analysis of control processes. These processes are the means by which people attempt to alter the behavior of others. Lindblom distinguishes three elementary ones—authority, exchange, and persuasion—out of which more complex processes are built. The basic problem of political life, for Lindblom, is that the welfare of the mass of people depends on the choices made by a relatively small number of leaders—who, he argues, are inclined to consider only a limited range of policy alternatives. The general problem of constitutional design is then to devise means by which leaders can control one another, subordinates can control leaders, and followers can control leaders—all in the service of widening the range of considerations in the making of social decisions.[5]

The relation between businessmen and public officials in the political economies of the West, argues Lindblom, poses the constitutional design problem in acute form. Markets, he contends, are the preferred device for tying the choices of producers to the desires of consumers. But markets have limits as control processes, notably that they must give to producers considerable discretion over investment and other important matters. The result is that public officials, who are naturally worried about economic performance, are drawn into inducing producers to use their discretion in ways that will promote economic growth. Producers, however, also require things from officials, for example, property rights guarantees. The relations between officials and producers that arise out of these mutual needs work to restrict the public agenda and, with it, democratic control. The crucial task for constitutional design, argues Lindblom, is to find ways around this difficulty.

Dahl's reformulation of classical arguments takes its bearings from his conception of political equality, which he defines as the equal opportunity to have fully informed preferences that are to be taken into equal account in the formulation of the binding decisions of the polity.[6] Arbitrariness is thus to be reduced, not by dividing power—and, as a consequence, reducing the value of gaining any particular office—but by insuring that there is equality in the voices to whom officeholders listen.[7] Indeed, Dahl argues that the traditional devices for limiting political power are, in any case, largely in the service of preserving undeserved privilege. Institutional arrangements, such as the separation of powers, make it harder for the demos and its representatives to do what they may legitimately undertake. And worries about whether such a relatively unrestrained demos will trample rights are misplaced, says Dahl: historically, the spread of democracy has proceeded apace with respect for rights.

For Dahl, the real guarantors of limits on the use of political

---

5. The most extended statement of Lindblom's views on these matters is found in Lindblom (1977); see also Lindblom (1965).

6. Relevant arguments can be found in several works by Dahl (1956, 1961, 1967, 1985). His summing up is in Dahl (1989). Dahl's work, starting with *A Preface to Economic Democracy*, is substantially less concerned with the control of the powerful and more nearly concerned with the design of institutions that will make political equality a reality.

7. To paraphrase John Taylor of Caroline (1814, 51) no interest should be able to cook others in the modes most delicious to its appetite.

power are not, in fact, to be found in the internal arrangements of government. Not only do these tend to foster arbitrary distinctions between acceptable and unacceptable majorities, they are almost certainly too weak to do the job. Effective sources of restraint on the arbitrary exercise of power are instead to be found in some combination of the commitments of political elites to limiting the use of power, the pluralism of interests, and, most important of all, the pluralism of autonomous organizations. The real guarantors of limited government, for Dahl, are sociological rather than narrowly political. The overall problem of constitutional design is how to meet the objectives of political equality and limited government, where the latter has its roots in sociological facts like autonomous organizations, elite attitudes, and social pluralism.[8]

For both Dahl and Lindblom, just as much as for classical and orthodox constitutionalists, the control of political power is then the essential institutional design problem. But for them and many other contemporary theorists, the arbitrary exercise of power occurs when powerful leaders subvert the realization of democratic preferences, not when the formalities of the separation of powers or the rule of law are evaded. It is not the control of power per se that concerns these theorists but the control of those who would subvert the (considered?) views of the people. Formalities are thus of little interest to theorists like Dahl and Lindblom, for the people have shown that they can govern without lapsing into tyranny. And it is *in*formalities that are of the greatest importance since it is in the workings of social power that democratic rule may be thwarted.

The work of Dahl and Lindblom also teaches the lesson that constitutional design requires a consideration of economy and society as well as state. It is a whole regime that is being constituted—a government whose workings depend on, among other things, how productive assets are controlled and the belief systems of political elites. This focus on the whole complex of social interactions is not in and of itself a major departure: the same emphasis can be found in the work of the greatest classical constitutional theorists. But the substantive changes in the make-up of market and society in the modern world require a restatement of constitutional theory, and this Dahl and Lindblom go some way toward providing. In doing so, they make clear just how far constitutional theory must reach in the modern

---

8. Strangely, Dahl (1956) thinks that in emphasizing such factors he is departing substantially from Madison. What makes Madison a great constitutional theorist is precisely that he is not given to placing too much faith in "parchment barriers." In his way, he is as much a political sociologist as Dahl.

context if it is to give a compelling answer to its central question: How may we insure that political power is not misused?

Social Choice Theory

Another whole strand of constitutional thinking grows out of welfare economics. The roots of this newer constitutionalist theory are in the utilitarian tradition, in which the question of how to secure the rule of law and individual rights gives way before the problem of how to maximize social welfare.[9] Insofar as arbitrariness enters into the discussion, it is largely a matter of making sure that institutional arrangements do not lead to needlessly forgoing increases in social welfare. Although work in this tradition is not often characterized as being constitutionalist, its concern with the design of political institutions and systems makes it appropriate to describe it as such.

The canonical text in this tradition is Kenneth Arrow's (1963) *Social Choice and Individual Values*.[10] The problem that Arrow sets for himself is the reformulation of the standard problem of welfare economics; that is, how to construct a social welfare function that can be used to choose among all the possible states of society.[11] He starts from the proposition that, for a given set of resources and technologies, there are an infinite number of possible states that can result from their combination. One desirable property of any social decision process is that it choose efficient states only. But since there are an infinite number of such states, the problem can be restated as how to rank the states on the welfare frontier. This problem, in turn, is understood by Arrow as involving an inquiry into the logical coherence of various sets of social decision rules that can structure the process of choosing among such efficient states. Arrow can thus be understood as saying that the problem of social choice is one of devising the decision rules that will determine which state is socially superior among those that are economically equal.

In designing this social decision process, Arrow starts with preferences held by individuals about the desirability of various social states. The decision rules determine just how these preferences are to be aggregated into the social choice that defines which state is socially preferred. Arrow offers what he considers to be a widely agreed upon

---

9. If social choice constitutionalism finds its ultimate justification in Bentham, modern reformulations of classical constitutionalism can be said to look to Kant.

10. On Arrow as a constitutional theorist, see his own comments (1963, 106); see also Luban, n.d.

11. My understanding of Arrow's work owes much to conversations with Edwin Haefele.

set of decision rules—and then points to the difficulties, indeed the impossibility, of combining them in such a way that a social choice will emerge. Thus even with seemingly undemanding rules—such as (1) the outcome cannot be dictated by one person and (2) if everybody in the society prefers X to Y, then society must reflect this preference also—the outcome is unstable. There is no ranking of the states under consideration; the constitution does not work.

In principle, there is no reason why constitutional theory of this type should only concern itself with the choice among economically efficient states (see, e.g., Sen 1970). But there is considerable analytic power in Arrow's way of looking at constitutional matters. He says, in effect, that the task of constitutional design is to successfully combine the pursuit of economic efficiency and democratic social choice. This is not an implausible view of the problem.

But what *is* difficult to accept—it is a consequence of Arrow's work being rooted in welfare economics—is that constitutional design should start from a given set of efficient social states and take as its central question how to choose among them. In the design of any actual constitution, such a starting point is useless since we do not and cannot choose among social states, efficient or otherwise. What we might plausibly try to do is design institutions that will *reach* an efficient social state—not choose among those that are in some sense supposed to preexist the fact of choice.

This is one of the tasks that those who might be called aggregators have set themselves.[12] These theorists are interested in the design of institutions whose choices will be efficient, where efficiency is typically understood as the maximum possible increase in the aggregate of the preference satisfaction of individuals. As a student of aggregative views puts it, "Society is rightly ordered and therefore just, when its major institutions are arranged so as to achieve the greatest net balance of satisfaction summed over all individuals belonging to it" (Rawls 1971, 24).[13] Following Arrow, aggregators focus on decision rules—both those that should guide the choice of representatives in a democratic system and those that should determine the outcomes of legislative deliberation. The term *aggregators* seems especially suitable because the analysis of voting, which is the principal focus for these

---

12. The most notable text is probably Mueller (1979); see also Mueller (1989).
13. Rawls is here talking about utilitarianism. As noted, there are deep affinities between social choice theory and utilitarian thought.

theorists, is understood as an inquiry into the proper aggregation of voter preferences.

An aggregative view of political institutions rests on an understanding of political life as essentially cooperative. Conflicts among political actors are restated as a problem of how best to combine preferences. Institutional arrangements are valued insofar as they resolve differences in opinion in ways that are potentially or actually beneficial to all concerned (Olson 1968).

Effective political institutions for aggregators are economically rational. The key to such rationality is the ability to treat all means as common, that is, with no characteristics that make them incommensurable. This similarly must also be true of ends: none can have a privileged status, and each is simply a means to other ends. The inner logic of economic rationality is to homogenize: to make everything comparable to everything else in order to facilitate calculation. Aggregators are thus drawn to focusing on preferences. Instead of looking at the substantive features of means and ends, they look instead at preferences for them. Preferences are, at least in principle, more amenable to combination through various institutional processes. Good political institutions then are those able to register and combine preferences in a manner that produces an efficient outcome.[14] These institutions are understood as complex bits of machinery that take fixed inputs, perform computations on them according to a set of operating rules, and serve up a set of results that—if the proper rules are at work—are socially efficient.[15]

Aggregators are like policy analysts who evaluate the alternatives before decision makers: they are economizers who understand the state to be a "productive-commercial or a development corporation under the management of a government" (Oakeshott 1975, 219–20). Political life is simply the extension of economic life by other means: the same matters need to be decided, and the institutions for deciding

14. For aggregators, preferences are typically taken as "given." They are exogenous in the sense that they are the stuff on which institutions are presumed to operate. These preferences may change, but the sources of change, including any effects of the institutional method for aggregating them, are deemed to be of little interest. As an acute student of aggregative views puts it, to treat the origins of preferences as outside the question of how to design institutions "makes it natural to see existing wants as starting points when the aim is to try to promote desirable states of affairs, and to define desirable states of affairs solely in terms of the degree to which . . . these preexisting wants are satisfied" (McPherson 1985, 110).

15. For aggregators, the favored definition of efficiency in this context is Paretian efficiency. For a particularly clear discussion of Pareto judgments, see Calabresi and Bobbitt (1978).

them must be judged by the same criteria.[16] The principal difference between policy analysts and aggregators is that the analysts assume they are talking to an existing decision maker while aggregators assume that the problem is to design one.

Aggregative theorists have proceeded down several paths, including an examination of a wide range of voting rules with an eye to their efficiency properties; a reconsideration of the definition of social efficiency itself to include less restrictive versions than have been traditionally used;[17] and the introduction of equality considerations into analyses hitherto dominated by efficiency concerns. This last effort complicates the constitutional design problem since institutions that may be fine at making efficient choices may be terrible at making equitable ones. This is the problem, for example, with the market, and the question does not get any easier in the political realm.

While aggregators are typically economists whose aim is to extend their concern for efficiency to the realm of collective choice, another set of theorists, who also draw inspiration from Arrow, have moved down different paths. They are, for the most part, people trained in political theory. For them, the charms of efficiency may remain ample, but they are not so alluring as to drive out other considerations. These theorists might appropriately be called public choice theorists—to distinguish them from aggregators for whom, as noted, political choice is simply an extension of market choice.[18]

A variety of differences between these public choice theorists and Arrow and the aggregators[19] may be noted. For example, Edwin Haefele (1973) has argued that Anglo-American political practice has found a way out of the instability that so worries Arrow through the device of a two-party system that structures the choice set. Haefele might be read as saying that, in constitutional design, it is perfectly appropriate to modify the conditions of choice to avoid chronic instability. Persons skilled in the political arts have always sought to do

---

16. Thus, the preferred institutional arrangements from an aggregative viewpoint are those that rely on exchange and economizing. These are thought to be the most effective in combining individual preferences into collective choices. See Elkin (1985).

17. The effort here is to go beyond Pareto efficiency, which is far too restrictive to be of much use. See the discussion in Calabresi and Bobbitt (1978).

18. It is worth noting that this label has come to mean too many things—not least, the designation of a certain kind of methodology and a set of assumptions about social behavior, neither of which is a necessary part of any compelling theory of public choice. Nevertheless, the label seems too valuable to discard, and insisting on its proper use may reduce confusion.

19. Aspirants to a career in rock music take note.

this since stability is as much a political value as a transparent registering of preferences in public choice—possibly even more so, given the way the world continues to operate. In a similar vein, it might be argued that, while efficiency may be desirable, there is no reason why it should claim our exclusive attention. As A. K. Sen (1970, 22) has said, a society can be Pareto efficient and perfectly disgusting.

In the hands of William Riker, Arrow's insights have been developed in yet other directions. Concern for efficiency has been reformulated as a problem in finding equilibrium choices—in other words, choices that, once made, provide no one with an incentive to look for a different result.[20] This concern for equilibrium choices has led Riker to investigate the properties of majority voting systems—in particular, to consider whether the "will of the people" may be said to have any meaning (see, e.g., Riker and Weingast 1988). Given the problems of voting cycles—that is, a lack of equilibrium—Riker doubts that it does. Voting choices are essentially arbitrary in his view. They are simple arithmetic artifacts that have no moral standing since they could just as easily have come out in some other way. This conclusion has led Riker to consider what functions majority voting for the selection of rulers and policies *can* play and to examine the merits of various forms of judicial review that may turn out to be less arbitrary than voting.

Public choice theory as it has been developed by Riker reinforces the central proposition of classical constitutionalism: democratic control of authority is in and of itself no guarantee against arbitrariness. Since Arrow's original work, this has been a prominent theme in social choice theory generally, if often an implicit one. The burden of much social choice theorizing seems to be that, once we actually try to design institutions for registering democratic preferences, substantial irrationalities and impossibilities emerge. But there is also a less pessimistic side to social choice theory that reflects its roots in utilitarianism: government is also potentially an engine for increasing aggregate welfare. In this view, an active policy-making government will not be arbitrary if it works to serve the public interest. Whether any defensible conception of the public interest can be offered is another matter, but the idea of government as an engine of welfare at least provides a clue as to why, given a chance, the mass of citizens attempt to so use it. This is no small fact, and any constitutional theory must digest it. Social choice theory, in its optimistic guise, reminds us that the meal cannot be put off.

20. That is, assuming as given the preferences of the actors involved and the decision rules operating.

The Extension of Constitutional Thinking

The preceding review suggests a number of questions the new constitutionalism must address if it is to develop. For a start, how can a utilitarian and democratic concern for advancing social welfare through the exercise of governmental power be joined to the long-standing concern for reducing arbitrariness in the exercise of that power?

The principal theorists of classical constitutionalism were largely concerned with designing a political regime that provided a framework within which citizens should administer their own affairs. Social problem solving was largely to occur through the private interactions that law and markets made possible. Increases in social welfare were to come through private exertions, not governmental action. The democratization of politics has, however, led to a substantial increase in governmental efforts to alleviate the distress of particular sectors of the society and to deal with the collective dilemmas of the whole community. Democratic governments now not only administer the justice that is the foundation of private interactions but make policy as well. Short of denying that the democratization of political life in constitutional regimes is a good thing, the new constitutionalism needs to show how democratic government can be both limited and purposive—that is, engaged in the active promotion of social welfare without collapsing into the arbitrariness of merely distributing benefactions to its best-organized citizens.

A second question for the new constitutionalism arises from the implicit view that political institutions are essentially practical devices. That is, according to much existing constitutional thought, these institutions are designed to limit power, increase popular control, and promote intelligent policy-making. But political institutions also have an educative dimension, as a long line of political theorists, beginning with Plato, have argued. The question naturally follows, What sort of individual character should political institutions foster?

For constitutional theorists the answer is, the kind of character that is necessary for the proper functioning of a constitutional regime.[21] This being so, the constitution of a constitutional regime must make provision for the education of citizens. This phrasing highlights the various meanings of "constitution": (1) a constitution is that which results from an effort to constitute; (2) a constitution is that which

---

21. This is an instrumental answer to the question. A noninstrumental answer would contend that some human types are simply better than others and should be fostered by all political regimes, constitutional or otherwise.

gives a regime its form, by defining its governmental offices and powers and the character of its citizens; (3) a constitution is that which limits the powers of government. The new constitutionalism must attend to these several meanings. Its guiding question must be, How shall a constitutional regime be constituted?

If this is to be the guiding question, it follows that the new constitutionalism must address the full array of political and social institutions that give it its particular form. What principles shall guide the combination of the various institutions into a workable constitutional whole? This is a third question that the new constitutionalism must address.

There is, in fact, a strong temptation to avoid the whole question of how to combine institutions and to proceed one institution at a time, indicating how the institution might be designed and assuming that the various institutions that compose the political regime can be made to cohere. It is, after all, difficult enough to think through the design of even one institution. But what looks like a desirable feature of an institution treated on its own may be pernicious in the context of trying to create a workable political whole. And it is the latter that is the point of constitutional theory. Thus, for example, it might be argued that local political institutions should be designed so that they encourage the habit of democratic deliberation—since, as Tocqueville argued, such institutions are an essential part of a constitutional regime. But it is not possible to stop there and leave until later the possibility that a local political life of this kind could prove inhospitable to the individual rights that are also a crucial part of constitutional regimes.

So much perhaps is obvious. What is less clear is how constitutionalist thought should proceed instead. If political institutions are living modes of association, this will set limits on how, and indeed whether, they can be combined. But the nature of these limits is not apparent. What *can* be said is that the new constitutionalism must be an exercise in practical rationality, which is the reasoning appropriate to how the political and social practices that are institutions can and should be combined. And perhaps its overall task is to define the substance of that rationality.

Perhaps the most fundamental question the new constitutionalism must address is whether its very concern for political design and the creation of good political regimes can be defended.

To begin with, are human beings even capable of such large-scale designs? Doubtless any one person at a single point in time is not. But the more important question is whether many people over a long time period are. They can approach the question iteratively, repairing what has gone wrong and making additions as it becomes possible to do so. Even thus described, however, it seems a far from easy task, but the alternative seems worse. As Hamilton said long ago, it would be a "general misfortune of mankind" if it turned out that "good government" cannot be established "from reflection and choice" and that human beings "are forever destined to depend for their political constitutions on accident and force."[22] Even those who doubt that human beings are capable of synoptic rationality agree that large-scale design is possible as long as the limits on human rationality are taken into account both in the design process itself and in the amount of knowledge required by those who will operate the institutions.[23]

Just as pressing for the new constitutionalism is the question of whether constitutionalism as an effort to improve political life is simply a sham. By its very nature, constitutional theory aims at political construction, and, as such, it will be subject to the critiques of political life that see it as a tragedy of domination and futility. Constitutional theory must in the end find a way to confront criticisms of the value of political life that can be traced back at least to Marx and Nietzsche. Without a reply to such arguments, the project of developing a new constitutionalism can seem jejune or worse. In replying to such charges, the new constitutionalism must join hands with political theory more generally in the quest to provide a secure basis on which questions of political value may be discussed.

The point of departure for any such undertaking is that the task of constitutional theory is to design good political and social institutions *in the face* of the fact that politics can easily become a form of organized domination. The possibilities of domination set the problem, they do not rule out all possible solutions. At its best, constitutional theory will acknowledge these possibilities by making provisions against their occurrence. It may even be able to make use of the desire to exercise power over others in the service of more benign causes.

Though they may not be the final words on the subject, the comments of E. P. Thompson say much of what needs emphasizing in this context. Thompson is a historian who need not concede pride of place to anyone in his understanding of the ways that law and consti-

---

22. *The Federalist* no. 1 (Cooke 1961).
23. In pursuing institutional design, Hayek argues that we must focus on general rules of conduct rather than set out particular destinations (see Hayek, 1973; see also Lindblom 1977, chap. 5). Hayek also argues that use must be made of localized knowledge by disaggregating decisions in the manner of a market system.

tution can be the means for the exercise of illegitimate power. But he simply says that "the notion of the rule of law is itself an unqualified good" (Thompson 1975, 267). Along the way to this conclusion, he argues that "the essential precondition for the effectiveness of law, in its function as ideology, is that it shall display an independence from gross manipulation and shall seem to be just" (263).

Even as it is used to mystify and mask the exercise of arbitrary power, law then offers more, and so does constitutional design. To resist this conclusion is, in its way, as foolish as the error of assuming that political power will always be used for good ends: feckless optimism meets fashionable nihilism. Political power needs form and direction in order to be in the service of political good. However halting and misguided our efforts in this respect may be, to attempt anything less is to mistake metaphysical musings for deep acquaintance with concrete political endeavor.

REFERENCES

Arrow, Kenneth. 1963. *Social Choice and Individual Values.* New York: Wiley.
Buchanan, James, and Tullock, Gordon. 1962. *The Calculus of Consent: Logical Foundations of Constitutional Democracy.* Ann Arbor: University of Michigan Press.
Calabresi, Guido, and Philip Bobbitt. 1978. *Tragic Choices.* New York: W. W. Norton.
Jacob Cooke, ed. 1961. *The Federalist.* Middletown, Conn.: Wesleyan University Press.
Dahl, Robert. 1956. *A Preface to Democratic Theory.* Chicago: University of Chicago Press.
———. 1961. *Who Governs?* New Haven, Conn.: Yale University Press.
———. 1982. *Dilemmas of Pluralist Democracy: Autonomy vs. Control.* New Haven, Conn.: Yale University Press.
———. 1985. *Preface to Economic Democracy.* Berkeley and Los Angeles: University of California Press.
———. 1989. *Democracy and Its Critics.* New Haven, Conn.: Yale Press.
Einzig, Paul. 1959. *The Control of the Purse.* London: Secker and Warburg.
Elkin, Stephen L. 1985. "Economic and Political Rationality." *Polity* 18(2): 253–71.
Gwyn, William P. 1986. "The Separation of Powers and Modern Forms of Government." In *Separation of Powers—Does It Still Work?* Edited by Rob-

ert A. Goldwin and Art Kaufman. Washington, D.C.: American Enterprise Institute.
Haefele, Edwin T. 1973. *Representative Government and Environmental Management*. Baltimore: Johns Hopkins University Press.
Hayek, Friedrich A. 1944. *The Road to Serfdom*. Chicago: University of Chicago Press.
———. 1960. *The Constitution of Liberty*. Chicago: University of Chicago Press.
———. 1973. *Law, Legislation, and Liberty*. Vol. 1: *Rules and Order*. Chicago: University of Chicago Press.
Hume, David. 1882. "On the Interdependency of Parliament." In *Essays Moral, Political and Literary*. Edited by T. H. Green and T. H. Grose. London: Longmans, Green.
Kraynak, Robert P. 1987. "Tocqueville's Constitutionalism." *American Political Science Review*. 81(4):1175–95.
Lindblom, Charles Edward. 1965. *The Intelligence of Democracy*. New York: Free Press.
———. 1977. *Politics and Markets*. New York: Free Press.
Lippmann, Walter. 1943. *The Good Society*. New York: Grosset & Dunlap.
Locke, John. 1960. *Two Treatises*. Edited by Peter Laslett. Cambridge: Cambridge University Press.
Lowi, Theodore J. 1979. *The End of Liberalism: The Second Republic of the United States*. 2d ed. New York: Norton.
Luban, David. N.d. "A Public Law Approach to Two Paradoxes of Liberalism." Institute for Philosophy and Public Policy, University of Maryland.
McIlwain, Charles. 1940. *Constitutionalism: Ancient and Modern*. Ithaca, N.Y.: Cornell University Press.
McPherson, Michael S. 1983. "Want Formation, Morality and Some Interpretive Aspects of Economic Inquiry." Edited by Norma Haan et al. *Social Science as Moral Inquiry*. New York: Columbia University Press.
Mansfield, Harvey. 1991. *America's Constitutional Soul*. Baltimore: Johns Hopkins University Press.
Mueller, Dennis. 1979. *Public Choice*. Cambridge: Cambridge University Press.
———. 1989. *Public Choice II*. Cambridge: Cambridge University Press.
Oakeshott, Michael. 1975. *On Human Conduct*. Oxford: Clarendon Press.
Olson, Mancur. 1968. "Economics, Sociology and the Best of All Possible Worlds." *The Public Interest* 12 (Summer): 96–118.
Rawls, John. 1971. *A Theory of Justice*. Cambridge, Mass.: Harvard University Press.
Riker, William, and Weingast, Barry. 1988. "Constitutional Regulation of Legislative Choice: The Political Consequences of Judicial Deference to Legislatures." *Virginia Law Review* 74(2):373–402.

Sen, Amartya. 1970. *Collective Choice and Social Welfare.* San Francisco: Holden-Day.
Taylor of Caroline, John. 1814. *An Inquiry into Principles and Policy of the United States.* Fredricksburg, Va.
Thompson, Edward Palmer. 1975. *Whigs and Hunters.* London: Allen Lane.
Vile, M. J. C. 1967. *Constitutionalism and the Separation of Powers.* Oxford: Oxford University Press.

PART TWO
Varieties of Constitutionalist Theory

The four papers in this section—by James W. Ceaser, Karol E. Sołtan, Charles Anderson, and Stephen L. Elkin—are programmatic statements that outline some of the essential features of a designer's perspective that is focused on institutions. The opening paper by Ceaser addresses some of the metatheoretical questions that the new constitutionalism must address. In particular, Ceaser presents a critique of behavioral political science and what he terms the new normativism. He argues that these newer and deficient forms of political inquiry should be replaced by a kind of theory modeled on the old political science with its focus on whole regimes. The concern of this traditional political science with the creation, maintenance, and corruption of regimes, and its focus on practical knowledge—theory useful for those who take a legislative or citizen perspective—are precisely the concerns of the new constitutionalism.

For Sołtan and Anderson, the designer's perspective ought to focus first and foremost on the reduction of arbitrariness. This should be the heart of the desirable regime that is Ceaser's concern. Sołtan and Anderson draw on both meanings of the term *constitution,* that which pertains to questions of creating political orders and that which points to the desirability of impartial standards, minimization of tyranny, and the like. It is worth emphasizing how expansively Sołtan and Anderson treat the question of the reduction of arbitrariness and the development of impartial standards. Neither thinks that the constitutional task is exhausted by encouraging the rule of law. For

Sołtan, both the public and private domains can be constitutionalized, and arbitrariness can be reduced in a number of ways other than by reference to law. For Anderson, communities of practice across the full range of social activities provide, with their public standards, criteria for the judging of performance.

Elkin provides the conclusion to this section. He is more explicit than Ceaser in linking good regimes to the design of their component institutions. And he reinforces the arguments of Sołtan and Anderson that political institutions are more than just potential means of domination and devices for restraining these activities. His principal argument is that we must move beyond this perspective, which is the heart of traditional constitutional thought, and assimilate its insights into a more expansive view of institutions that takes account of their problem-solving and educative dimensions. Elkin's chapter also serves as a bridge to the next section of the book. His arguments concerning the essentials of a constitutional regime provide a theoretical perspective through which to view American practice as that is analyzed by Lowi, Sunstein, and Haefele. Of particular importance is the role he says deliberative ways of lawmaking must play in a constitutional regime. In various ways, this theme is picked up by the authors in the third section, who wonder whether to lament its absence, reinforce its necessity, or indicate how it might be fostered.

CHAPTER THREE

Reconstructing Political Science

JAMES W. CEASER

STUDENTS OF THE DISCIPLINE of political science, if not all of its practitioners, have been saying for some years now that political science is in a state of crisis. According to Gabriel Almond, there is an "uneasy separateness" in the discipline in which "the various schools and sects of political science now sit at separate tables, each with its own conception of proper political science" (Almond 1988, 828). One problem, which political science shares with the other social sciences, is a disagreement about the character of social scientific knowledge. Does knowledge consist in elaborating cause-effect laws, in grasping meaning in diverse contexts, or in articulating abstract theoretical proofs? Another problem, which is specific to political science, is the inability to agree on the discipline's subject matter and on the ends or purposes for which political knowledge is sought. This concern has been summed up by the simple query, "Knowledge for what?"

Although these two problems are connected, the question of the content of the discipline is clearly more fundamental. It is necessary to have an idea of what one wishes to know before considering how one can know it. In this chapter, I will accordingly look at some of the ways in which the question of "knowledge for what" has been treated in the discipline over the past quarter-century. The analysis is designed not just to survey recent approaches, but to discuss them critically as a way of preparing the ground for a reconstruction of political science, a reconstruction that Stephen Elkin and Karol Sołtan refer to as a "new constitutionalism."

Constitutional Political Science

When I began to study political science in the mid-1960s, news was just reaching the provinces that the great war for the soul of the discipline had ended. The forces calling for a genuine science of politics, which were marching under the banner of "behavioralism," had defeated and dislodged an older approach dismissed for being "value laden," "legalistic," and "metaphysical" (see Dahl 1961). All that remained were a few mopping-up operations to eliminate the last pockets of resistance. Behavioralism was clearly the wave of the future, embraced by all sophisticated researchers seeking foundation grants and by nearly all of the nation's major graduate programs.

Yet waves, as we now know, can recede almost as quickly as they arise. It is important, therefore, to reconsider the older approach, which was known as traditional or constitutional political science. There are five elements to this approach, which we present here not always as it was practiced but as it can be reconstituted according to its major tenets.

First, traditional or constitutional political science is distinguished not by a normative or legalistic mode of reasoning, but by a certain approach to the *analysis* of political affairs. Under this approach, the subject matter of the study of politics derives from a commonsense encounter with the political world. Although people's particular political concerns vary with time, place, and objective, these concerns reflect certain abiding questions, the study of which informs an understanding of the fundamental political problems.

The focus of political science under the traditional conception is on the study of "constitutions" or "regimes" or "forms of government."[1] A constitution is characterized by who rules, by the basic principle of justice or overarching belief that moves those who hold the preponderant influence in society, and sometimes by the spirit or passion that dominates in the society. The focus on the study of forms of government emerges initially from political life itself. The regime is the thing that appears most important to those acting in the political world. It is perceived as the largest whole that structures the way of life in a developed human community, and its ruling principle or idea of justice is perceived to determine the core of the whole structure. Thus, when most observers identified the fall of communist systems in the last decade—that is, a regime change—as the most

---

1. The term Aristotle uses is *politea*, which is usually translated as "regime" or "constitution" (as the British use that term). Montesquieu refers to the fundamental political unit as a "form of government" (see *The Spirit of the Laws*, bk. 2, chap. 1).

significant political development of our era, this claim was perfectly consistent with what traditional political science defined to be the proper focus of the discipline. This focus is not, as behavioralism claimed, "metaphysical" but empirical.

Second, traditional political science holds that politics supplies its own motive of action. People are moved in politics—not of course, exclusively—by a concern for the character of the constitution, in particular for its principle of justice. A claim of justice cannot be computed either as "altruistic" or as self-interested. It must be understood on its own terms, as a distinctly political motive directed to a concern for the character or shape of the community in which one lives. It is as distinct to the political realm as individual self-interest is said to be to the economic realm.

Third, the term *constitution* or *regime* is not a narrow or legalistic concept. In an age of written constitutions, there is a tendency to identify a constitution with a written document, especially in the United States, where the Constitution enjoys such an exalted status. But a constitution, according to traditional political science, has an earlier and more primary meaning. It refers to how a society is constituted, not just by its governmental institutions, formal or informal, but more generally by its way of life. What is political in the broadest sense is not always exhausted by what governments are empowered to do, for what governments may or may not do is itself determined by the regime and constitutes one of its most important characteristics. The constitution thus cannot be identified with "the state," which in a strict sense is only a part of the regime.

That which helps to shape a regime, including its principles of justice and arrangements of public offices, often originates from influences beyond the political acts (narrowly conceived) of those holding office or political power. These influences come from realms we refer to as cultural, religious, economic, and intellectual. The study of the influence of these realms on the regime opens up another understanding of the concept of a regime that goes beyond the concrete idea defined thus far. The realms of civil law, religion, and philosophy can constitute bodies of influential doctrine ("regimes") that help to shape regimes in the conventional sense. It is in this respect that one can speak metaphorically of the "regime" of the enlightenment, or of modern commerce, or of technology. This usage of the concept clearly complicates the discipline of political science by opening it to the study of forces beyond "power acts" in the ordinary sense. This complication, however, derives from the character of political life itself and to the full set of factors that influence it.

Fourth, constitutional political science has both an empirical and a normative aspect. In its empirical or analytic aspect, political science focuses on the factors that support or undermine various regimes or types of regimes. The elaboration of a body of relationships between these factors and the regimes constitutes the central concern of the practical study of politics. In its normative aspect, political science is concerned with ranking regimes—with determining the character of the best regime, the best regime generally practicable, and the best form of each regime.[2]

Fifth, traditional political science is at one and the same time the least theoretical and the most theoretical of the social sciences. It is the least theoretical because it developed in large part to assist in a practical activity of handling political affairs, of instituting constitutions, and of supplying advice for how to maintain or destroy them. The connection of political science to the practical world differentiates it, for example, from anthropology and sociology, which were invented as theoretical disciplines to satisfy an intellectual project for understanding man and society. There is a political sphere that consists of a real human activity independent of the discipline that studies it; there is no comparable anthropological or sociological activity. The knowledge political science seeks is not only for the sake of knowing, but also for the sake of being put to use by citizens and legislators. Even the criteria of what makes for a good explanation in political science arguably should have reference not just to how much is explained, but also to how an explanation might assist in the handling of political affairs.

Yet it turns out that the very fact of its practicality makes political science the most theoretical of all the social sciences. Political science is the most theoretical of the social sciences because it is the only one that must consider the status of things that humans assert that they know to be fundamental to the human situation, like the importance of justice. What is the status of these political things—what kind of "beings" are they—and what is the character of a "science" that is designed to treat them? To answer these questions, political science had to ask a completely new series of philosophical questions that pertained to the status not just of physical things but of human opinions as well. Political science also had to become autoreflective in the sense of being conscious of itself as a discipline that influences the subject matter from which it emerges. Since the discovery of political science political life has never been the same. The place that political

---

2. See Aristotle *Nichomachean Ethics* 1181b16–23. See also *Politics* 1288b–1289a25 and 1319b35–1320a15.

science should occupy in society is a question that political science, by virtue of its own idea of its subject matter, is obliged to pose.

The Science of Politics in the 1960s

According to the conception of social science I encountered in my first undergraduate course in political science, knowledge in the social realm had nothing to do with such "given" categories. Genuine scientific knowledge consisted in the elaboration of causal connections among social phenomena. Social science—the formulation was Max Weber's—seeks "to order empirical reality in a manner which lays claim to validity as empirical truth," with the ordering intended to explain "the relationships . . . of individual events in their contemporary manifestations and . . . the causes of their being *so* and not *otherwise*."[3]

Beyond causal knowledge of this kind, social science could not go. For all its precision, social science left much up in the air. As expected, it could not instruct us directly about normative questions, however much it might help to clarify implications by showing causes and consequences. But neither could it offer us guidance about which social phenomena to study, for it provided no internal criteria of significance. What political science investigates had to be determined by a standard external to this pure conception of social science.

Among political scientists of the day, there were two schools of thought offering guidance about what should be studied. One school sought to derive criteria of importance from a model of knowledge deriving (supposedly) from the hard sciences. In this understanding, the quest for knowledge begins by demarcating the phenomena under purview and then proceeds to look for laws that explain either the greatest *amount* of phenomena in the field or that achieve the greatest *certainty* in what is explained. The usual approach in the 1960s consisted of breaking down political matter into a basic political unit or atom—"acts performed in power perspectives" (Laswell and Kaplan 1947, 240) or relationships "that involve, to a significant extent, control, influence, power, or authority" (Dahl 1984, 10)—and then looking for various connections that covered great parts of this data. From this perspective, it might be just as useful to study "private clubs, business firms, . . . clans, perhaps even families" (Dahl 1984, 10) as political regimes.

---

3. The quotes are taken from Weber's famous program for social science, " 'Objectivity' in Social Science and Social Policy" (see Natanson 1963, 364, 378).

A second school of thought held that the scholar seeks scientific knowledge of things that experience with the political world reveals to be humanly important or interesting, either to the scholar or to his culture. In this view, importance is not a function of the quantity of political phenomena explained, but of what *we* take to be significant—we being human beings who project significance according to changing human values.[4] What is studied will thus differ from culture to culture, from generation to generation, and from scholar to scholar. The content for political science is more malleable than for the first school, but it is no less scientific: one can be systematic in what one chooses to study without choosing what to study on the basis of what can be made most systematic.

Although these two schools differed in regard to the criteria establishing significance, all scientific scholars saw themselves engaged in the same struggle, bordering for many on a crusade, to rid the discipline of the traditional approach and to establish a genuine *science* of politics. The two scientific modes of determining importance were thus declared to be complementary. Concepts derived from efforts to systematize knowledge could be brought to bear in understanding humanly important problems, while scientific findings of the important human questions could be incorporated into general theories. At some point the "top-down" and "bottom-up" approaches would meet to form a grand general theory.

What was the focus of political science as judged by those in the 1950s and 1960s who relied on this human standard for determining importance? What did they deem to be significant? One question clearly stood out as preeminent: how to maintain liberal democracy. As Sidney Verba recently explained, "We were concerned [in the 1960s] with the question of why some democracies survive while others collapsed" (see Almond and Verba 1980, 407).[5] This concern resulted from the fact that these scholars had lived through an age in which the fate of liberal democracy was still very much at issue.

The important question for these scientists—how to sustain liberal democracy—thus turned out to be a case or instance of the central empirical question of traditional political science: What maintains different regimes? Yet according to the strict logic of science, this correspondence was only accidental, as the regime question had no

---

4. According to Weber, "The very recognition of the existence of a scientific problem coincides, personally, with the possession of specifically oriented motives and values" (as quoted in Natanson 1963, 367).

5. This question was the central concern of such leading scientific scholars as Gabriel Almond, Seymour Martin Lipset, and Robert Dahl.

privileged status. Furthermore, there was—or would shortly be—a growing uneasiness over the apparent commitment to liberal democracy that seemed implicit in the scientists' concern for discovering what led liberal democracies to survive or fail. Although many scientists openly proclaimed a preference for liberal democracy (unrelated, they insisted, to anything that could be justified by political science), others began to turn against liberal democracy and claim that they were only describing it, never in any way supporting it.

The particular model or theory of liberal democracy that these scientists originated became known as "pluralism."[6] To bolster the claims of novelty and originality for this model, the scientists relentlessly attacked the prescientific views of liberal democracy, chiding its proponents for beginning with unscientific notions like "larger political units" (regimes) and for inquiring into "how men ought to act"; a genuine theory, it was said, had to begin from the only real empirical data available to us: the observable behavior of individuals.[7] The scientists prided themselves on a kind of no-nonsense realism, as if the tougher they appeared, the more scientific they must be. Their descriptions of liberal democracy purported to uncover its hitherto unknown, and shockingly low, foundations. Major studies found that voting behavior had little rational content and that political stability relied in large measure on political apathy. The most celebrated book of the decade, *The Civic Culture,* argued that liberal democracy depended for its existence on an elite's false belief that voters can discipline leaders and the voters' false belief that the elites can be checked by the public. Political leaders "must believe in the democratic myth that ordinary citizens ought to participate in politics and they are in fact influential"—a view that at best has only "some truth to it." Fortunately, "whether true or not, the myth is believed" (Almond and Verba 1965, 352–54).

This conclusion raised a question: Might not science uncover findings which, though admittedly circulated in an almost unreadable prose, could prove harmful to liberal democracy, whether by "liberating" citizens from certain beneficial myths or by encouraging leaders to act on dangerous or cynical premises? For foes of liberal democracy, this question posed no difficulties. Yet for most, who were its friends, the issue could not be entirely dismissed. One group of scien-

---

6. See Joseph (1981), in which he rightly points out that it is a mistake to collapse all pluralists into one mold.
7. See Dahl (1961, 766, 768). In some of these characterizations, he is citing (approvingly) David Easton and David Truman.

tists denied that this conflict ultimately was very serious—a position that seemed to undercut earlier claims of how radical their discoveries were. Another group sketched a "role theory" for social scientists under which one's duties as scientist and as citizen were to be kept scrupulously compartmentalized. As a political scientist, one's highest commitment must be to science, with the scientific chips being left to fall where they may, without any supervision or interference for political reasons. As a citizen, one had a right to pursue one's political preferences, including a right to help undo any damage science might inadvertently have created.

The issue involved here, which role theory did no more than restate, concerns the nature of political science as an enterprise in society. As an important form of human knowledge, political science is part of social reality with potentially significant political consequences. Can a political science be said to fully account for its own subject matter if it fails to consider its own effect on society or to reflect on its potential function as a political force?

Political Science Today

What might the student today, curious about the same question of what constitutes political knowledge, discover from his or her education? The dominant theoretical view today, as in the 1960s, derives from the scientific idea. Thus most political scientists probably subscribe to the idea that social science establishes the method of inquiry but not the standard of relevance. This view has encouraged growth in the number of questions pursued, while at the same time casting doubt on any attempt to define a substantive core to political science—other, that is, than the sum total of interests of those working in the field. A glance at the roster of panels at recent meetings of the American Political Science Association quickly confirms that the profession today displays a range of interests that could be described as catholic, if not undiscriminating.

Yet those of a scientific persuasion do not choose their subjects of study randomly or in isolation. The direction of scientific research today appears to be set ultimately by the same two types of schools that operated in the 1960s: one that looks to maximize the amount of political data explained (or the certainty with which it is explained) and another that looks for scientific answers to humanly important questions. Only both of these schools today have a different orientation than they did twenty years ago. The first relies on a new technique (rational choice), while the second asks a new question: not what maintains political systems, but rather how specific policies in a political system measure up against various standards of justice. Let us examine each of these.

Rational Choice

Among those political scientists who exhort their colleagues to build "powerful" scientific theories, there has been a decided shift in the last decade. The new approach favors models which, given their assumptions, can make clear and indisputable deductions from stated premises. These deductions can then be checked against actual behavior. This approach goes by the name of rational choice. Although rational choice can be regarded merely as a technique for investigating questions humanly important to us—and some use it modestly in this fashion—its most ardent champions also contend that it provides a solid foundation on which to build a full and systematic political science.

Rational choice has replaced behavioralism as the preferred scientific method in the discipline. This fact can be ascertained not only from a casual observance of the major journals, in which symbolic equations increasingly crowd out statistical presentations, but also from the allocation of teaching positions in political science departments at major universities. Yet if the utility of rational choice for professional advancement has become apparent, its theoretical import for the discipline is less clearly understood. Behavioralism, as the dominant type of scientific approach of the 1960s, had two basic meanings. Rational choice challenges it on both counts.

In one sense, behavioralism was used synonymously with empirical political science—albeit an empirical political science that privileged one kind of empirical fact: the repeated, visible, and quantifiable acts of individual behavior. The behavioral approach seeks to explain "the empirical aspects of political life by means of the methods, theories, and criteria of proof that are acceptable according to the canons, conventions, and assumptions of modern empirical science"; it "aims at stating all the phenomena of government in terms of observed and observable behavior of men."[8] Under this approach, the effort is to observe human behavior and then, on the basis of these observations, derive statistical generalizations ("laws") of behavior. These laws are in effect the tallies of observed regularities in actual human behavior.

Rational choice conceives of the scientific project quite differently. It begins with a simple assumption about human behavior—

---

8. See Dahl (1961, 766–68). In one case Dahl is citing David Truman on a point with which he "wholeheartedly agrees."

that man is a utility maximizer, ideally where utility can be expressed in terms of a common unit of measurement. This starting point allows one to deduce logical conclusions about what behavior is (or would be) without having to deal directly at every point with observed behavior. Rational choice thus involves a good deal of abstract theorizing—modeling and game playing—that has no immediate empirical dimension. The "power" of the approach inheres precisely in the fact that it is not directly tied to empirical phenomena or limited to what can be seen or measured. Rational choice can draw precise conclusions from its own axioms. Not only is it less expensive and more reliable than behavioralism, but it can also offer speculations about hypothetical situations of what would happen if such and such were the case.[9]

Rational choice is not, however, antiempirical. Its underlying premise is that the initial assumption (and thus deductions drawn from it) is sufficiently accurate to throw a good deal of light on actual human behavior. Although nowadays there are more than a few practitioners who become spellbound by the sheer "elegance" of arguments and proofs—as if truth were beauty and beauty truth—so pure a formalism has yet to win the day. (It is also a wonder how such a highly developed aesthetic sensibility emerges from a view that posits calculating self-interest as the guiding principle of human behavior.) In any event, for most rational choice advocates today, the worth of its assumption of self-interest must be validated in the final analysis by some sort of test of the fit between its models and observed human behavior. Such tests obviously must rely on methods other than rational choice.

In its second meaning, behavioralism was equated with modern political psychology. According to this view, human behavior is motivated by the individual's pursuit of selfish gratification, which can be understood either as a straight concern for safety and income or as a search to gratify certain unconscious needs and desires. The latter idea, which emphasizes the nonrational or irrational sources of behavior, was introduced into political science by Harold Laswell (1961) and became a prominent assumption in the behavioral movement. Behavior, it was argued, originates either from deep subconscious drives in the individual's own psyche (as, e.g., in "a passion to dom-

---

9. I am simplifying here. The rational choice approach can in fact be divided into a "hard" and a "soft" variant depending on whether the utility that drives human behavior is posited in advance (the hard variant) or whether it is derived empirically (the soft variant). I have discussed these in more detail elsewhere (Ceaser 1990, 79–87) and the full issue is explored in *Beyond Self-Interest* (Mansbridge 1991).

inate") or from psychic needs, reflective of subconscious fears or desires, that are stimulated from the outside by socialization or by techniques of mass persuasion. In the latter case, the individual is conceived as being acted upon, subject to control or manipulation from advertising or propaganda.

These motivations of human behavior, even though they could never literally be observed, were taken to be "real" and constituted the foundation of the realistic understanding of political behavior found in the pluralist models of liberal democracy and in much voting research. These studies brought together the two meanings of behavioralism. They sought observable patterns of regularity and then explained or grounded them in a "behavioral" explanation of human psychology.

Rational choice postulates a different understanding of human motivation. It assumes an individual who acts on the world and brings to it a faculty for calculating his or her own utility. The individual is not regarded as driven by irrational impulses or as being easily controlled or manipulated from outside. The individual is rational, albeit in a purely instrumental sense. The model for behavior is thus not modern psychology, but economics. The differences between these two approaches would seem to point in very different directions, although the analysis of such problems as information costs has brought rational choice theory a bit closer to behavioralism in some of its practical conclusions. For example, rational choice models of voting now note that a healthy dose of "rational ignorance" can often be expected, as voters may find it more cost-effective in many situations to economize by relying on superficial information and by employing simplifying devices like party labels. But this practical convergence on a few points does not alter the fundamental difference in perspective between the two approaches.

Rational choice, while touted as being a more powerful scientific approach than behavioralism, probably owed part of its initial attraction to another fact. It managed to avoid or overcome some of the tensions that began to grow up in the 1970s between behavioralism and a new group of normative critics (discussed below) who began calling for a more "human" form of democracy that was egalitarian and socialistic. Behavioral models came under attack for their emphasis on irrationalism. Man was now widely declared to be good and capable under the proper conditions of profound "human development." Against this onslaught, only rational choice seemed able to hold its ground and—for those concerned—to rescue liberal democracy from the charge of being grounded in false myth. Rational choice achieved this advantage not by abandoning itself to an idealistic psychology, but by relying on a highly realistic view of human behavior in its own right. Its premise of self-interested calculation had nothing to be embarrassed about in front of behavioralism's claims of irrational impulses and manipulation. Still, it is not clear if liberal democracy is much safer when grounded in narrow calculation than in irrationalism. The choice here would seem to be between citizens and politicians as either mercenaries or fools, where the fool at least can sometimes be tricked into believing in a common good.

Observing the bitter disputes today between adherents of rational choice and of behavioralism, one might get the impression that both sides believe that they are debating the two great alternatives of human psychology. From the perspective of traditional political science, however, the battle is little more than a family quarrel. Both are heirs of an individualistic-hedonistic psychology, differing only in their views of what constitutes gratification and how the individual seeks it. Neither of these approaches takes seriously the view that a motive of political action—in fact, the most important motive—derives from a distinctly political or social source, from ideas and beliefs about what is just or what is theoretically (or theologically) right for the regime. In this century, this point has been made most forcefully by the famous Marxist theorist, Antonio Gramsci: "One may speak separately of economics and politics and speak of 'political passion' as an immediate impulse to action which is born on the 'permanent and organic' terrain of economic life but which transcends it, bringing into play emotions and aspirations in whose incandescent atmosphere even calculations involving the individual human life itself obey different laws from those of individual profit."[10]

The premise of traditional political science that there is a political source of political action has been widely misunderstood. It is not at all affected by the observation that claims about justice are often (though not always) linked to people's economic situation. Thus it did not require the advent of rational choice to know that the poor and many tended to press democratic arguments, while the wealthy and few often advanced oligarchic arguments. (Critics of rational choice, incidentally, fall into a foolish trap if they try to contest rational choice by proving that people must act altruistically; altruistic behavior is no more political than is self-interested behavior.) The basic point, then, is not that there is no link between people's situation and their view of justice; it is rather that assertions about justice are not the same

10. See Gramsci (1971, 140). A more developed view of this kind of political psychology is found in Aristotle's treatment of sedition in the *Politics* 1301a19–1302a35.

thing as—and are not explained by or reducible to—assumptions deriving from individual calculations of self-interest.

This difference can be seen in the different kinds of behavior to which each premise gives rise. Rational choice theory itself proves this point, when it shows that its own logic cannot explain why people vote or why people engage in some of the most significant kinds of collective political action. Even in what look like some of the easiest cases for explanation by rational choice—when, for example, the oppressed struggle for the rights of the oppressed, or when working people fight for working people's rights—the self-interested premise often cannot account for the actions of individuals, who themselves are often risking far more economically than they are likely to gain. This behavior, as Gramsci indicates, is accounted for by considering a different kind of logic. Nor is the basic assumption of rational choice saved by arguments that political actors often follow strategies of calculating and "economizing" to maximize their goal. This too is hardly news, and in any event it provides no insight whatsoever into the kinds of goals being pursued in the first place.

The idea that there are distinctly political (or political-theological) sources of behavior has also been attacked by some adherents of modern political science on the grounds that it leads to "idealistic" assumptions, where idealism refers to instincts identified with being "nice," "helpful," or "safe." This criticism is false. Traditional political psychology is highly realistic in its own way, accounting for behavior that is harsher than that explained by rational choice, which misses motivations related to intense anger, to a desire for retribution connected with feelings of injustice, and to passionate reactions stemming from alternative understandings of customs and gods. Traditional political psychology does not thereby share the behavioral view that political action is fundamentally irrational in the sense of flowing from individual psychological needs for gratification. Rather, it holds that collective political behavior flows from a political motive. The concern for justice gives rise to certain passions that sometimes make it difficult for people to calculate deliberately their own interest, whatever that interest might be. It also gives rise to instances of public-spiritedness, for a concern for justice is also a concern for the common good.

These disputes over psychology, however, take us away from the central question of inquiring into what political science studies and why. Rational choice, insofar as it has been put forward not just as a tool of analysis but as the cornerstone for a science of politics, has had to define the criteria of significance for the discipline. It has done so by advocating analysis of that which promises to provide us with the greatest certainty in what we study. This point was recently reiterated by a leading rational choice theorist from Harvard University. Speaking at a time when his audience was concerned with the fate of the transformation of the former communist states, this theorist had the purity of commitment to urge researchers to focus their attention on topics having real potential importance for political science, such as decision making in the Harvard faculty club.[11]

The New Normativism

If one school of modern political science seeks to determine importance by the quantity or certainty of what is explained, recall that a second school insists that importance be determined by whatever we deem to be significant. By this criterion, as noted, the question that dominated much of political science in the early 1960s was, What sustains liberal democracy? By the end of the decade, however, there was, as Sidney Verba explains, a change in mood: "The concerns expressed in *The Civic Culture* [the focus on democratic survivability] were products of their times.... Just as political beliefs change, so do the concerns of political scientists" (in Almond and Verba 1980, 408–9). Such shifts are properly viewed as governing the focus of the discipline, as they supply the only criteria of relevance.

With this change in mood has come a new question for political science. That question, according to Verba, centers on the policy performance of governments. The new project frequently proceeds by analyzing and judging specific policy performances (again performances in liberal democratic systems) in light of certain standards or values. Any value might conceivably be chosen as a subject for investigation, but researchers naturally emphasize the values they somehow deem highest—values such as "equality," "substantive justice," "human development," or "rights." The researcher then proceeds to consider, in Robert Dahl's (1986) words, "the gap between criteria and performance."

Why did this change of mood occur and this new focus for political science emerge? A complete explanation is not possible, but three reasons have been suggested to help account for the change.

First, liberal democracy by the mid-1960s began to look safer to most political scientists, in the sense that it did not appear to be in jeopardy of succumbing to retrograde forces, either from within or without. This situation provided the luxury of substituting a new

---

11. Related by Kenneth Shepsle at a lecture at the University of Virginia, November 1991.

concern (How does liberal democracy measure up to certain standards?) for the old concern (What sustains liberal democracy?). Yet it would be a mistake to say that political scientists argued that liberal democracies in the 1970s and 1980s were free of crisis. On the contrary, they tended to play up the idea of crisis, only now the underlying attitude toward crisis was different. In contrast to the mood of the early 1960s, when crises seemed to be regarded with deep anxiety, the crises of the new era were depicted, sometimes almost gleefully, as a logical result of (if not a punishment for) the failure of this system to live up to certain values or standards of justice. A crisis of liberal democracy was thus something almost to be hoped for. According to Charles Lindblom (1983), "Our best, yet dismal, hope for structural change is through a transitory catastrophe."

Second, some political scientists consciously saw that by changing the central question from what sustains liberal democracy to how it measures up to certain criteria, they could enlist the discipline as an agent of change to help "overcome" liberal democracy (see, e.g., Bay 1965). These political scientists had recourse to the tactic of using the previous scientific pluralist model against itself. If, as the pluralist model said, liberal democracy was a mere struggle among self-interested groups, if voters were deluded, if the system rested on patently false myths of which intelligent statesmen had no inkling, on what basis could this form of government be defended? Critics had a field day, taking the stark "realities" of the pluralist model and exposing them to the light of day. Here stood Frankenstein's monster naked before its creator's eyes. The scientists who had made pluralism were now accused of being conservative and deficient in their enthusiasm for such values as equality and "human development." In response, many scientists found it easier to slip that criticism by insisting that their effort to describe liberal democracy had never had anything to do with a project to aid it, but that its real aim was—or should have been—to lay a foundation for the critique of liberal democracy and to prepare the way, in Charles Lindblom's (1983, 384) words, to put "both pluralism and democracy under socialism."

Third, the most sophisticated of the scientists began to develop a new relationship with normative theory. If scientists in the 1960s had rejected political theory as being unhelpful or metaphysical, now, according to Robert Dahl (1984, 126–27), "the normative orientation has become a rapidly expanding frontier of political science, just as empirical analysis had become earlier." Normative theory could now be looked to to supply the criteria of importance for the empirical enterprise by providing the standards or norms for judging policy performance. Empirical scientists—often blithely unaware of whom they were serving—were being sent to fetch the data to illustrate the "gaps" between performance and standards.

Yet here it is essential to note that the theory on the "frontier" that developed this new "normative orientation" was not traditional political science. For this reason, and to distinguish this approach from constitutional political science, I shall call it "the new normativism." By this broad label, I mean a kind of analysis that first posits certain values or norms derived from abstract analysis, such as theories of justice, and then proceeds to apply these values to the political realm without serious consideration of whether they could be incorporated into any workable political regime. The emphasis is on the values or norms, not on a systematic analysis of constitutions and how different factors maintain or undermine them. It is this form of theorizing, whether on the left or on the right—and there are variants today on both sides—that now supplies the agenda for much of the discipline. Although the ascendancy of this "normative orientation" in theory is often celebrated as a return to political philosophy, it might be more accurately characterized as an application of academic philosophy or ethics to politics. Arguably, the term political philosophy should be reserved to systematic thought about politics itself.

Constitutional Political Science and the New Normativism

Although constitutional (or traditional) political science and the new normativism both have a normative component to them, the two are distinguished, and distinguished sharply, by the way each applies values to political life. Traditional political science addresses normative issues in a way that tightly limits the direct application of norms and values and that opens up a wide range for an empirical determination of such issues. Traditional political science begins its analytic inquiry with the question of what supports or undermines regimes, whereas the new normativism begins with the question of how discrete policies measure up against chosen values, like equality or justice or rights. Traditional political science addresses the question of values in political life not directly, but in the first instance in terms of a choice among constitutions. It weds the value question to a consideration of regimes and what maintains them. The new normativist, by contrast, poses the question of values directly, with the regime issue often ignored, treated cosmetically, or introduced as an afterthought. The aim of the inquiry is to ask how "every law and constitutional clause" or every policy measures up to certain norms (Bay 1965, 49). The worth of a regime is judged more or less by a summation of these responses.

The difference between these two approaches profoundly affects the character of concrete political analysis. As the choice of the form of government is the most important political question for constitutional political science, all other questions must be considered initially in their relation to this one. Thus the first issue in policy analysis is how each policy affects the form of government, not how each policy measures up to certain norms.

The choice of regime in any particular case involves asking which regimes in that context are within the realm of reasonable possibility, what is their rank order, and what might be prudent to attempt under the circumstances. Abstracting here from the question of prudence, it stands to reason that among the possible regimes in any case, the choice should go either to the regime that is highest in rank or to one which, though not the highest, is less prone than those that outrank it to degenerate into a lower type. Hence ranking regimes is fundamental to traditional political science and constitutes its more theoretical dimension, although a theoretical dimension linked to practical concerns.

To rank regimes clearly involves consulting standards beyond the forms of government. It is here that the traditional political scientist must consider pure values, like fairness, virtue, or human development. The ranking proceeds by measuring the degree to which different regimes contain the best mix of such standards. In making this ranking, however, it is necessary to include what is actually needed to establish and maintain each regime. Those things that make each regime hold together and function are essential to judging regimes. Regimes, in other words, must be considered as "wholes" or complete systems, which means taking account not just of their aspirations, but of the things needed to sustain them. The fundamental political choice is not one among standards, but among forms of government, for it is the form of government (with the standards contained in it), not the standards themselves, that actually orders the life of a society.

The political scientist must therefore investigate what makes each regime a whole or a system. The things that serve to maintain a regime have a certain justification, the more so as they are essential to its survival. What is needed to sustain any regime, not under exceptional circumstances but on a regular basis, will be considered "just"—relative, of course, to that regime (see Strauss 1983, chap. 6). At the same time, even in the best regimes, certain of these things will not be considered right or conducive to human development when they are judged independently in light of some general standard. This fact deserves not just to be noted, but underlined, as it marks a limit to the possibilities of political life. It shows the inadequacy of making the direct application of pure standards to individual policies the decisive criterion for investigating normative questions and requires the development of a *political* approach to ethical or normative questions.

The fundamental political choice always relates to the form of government. Any issue having a significant effect on maintaining or undermining a regime must first be considered politically, which is to say by reference to its influence on preserving or destroying the regime. There may, of course, be alternative means for maintaining a regime, and to this extent, the means may be judged not only in light of the concern for maintenance, but also in light of an abstract value standard. But in so doing, the application of the abstract value must first be sanctioned by a prior political judgment.

For traditional political science, the distinction between regime issues and policy issues is fundamental. The regime refers to how a society is constituted or what it is, while a policy refers to what a government decides to do (or, more broadly, allows to be done). Thus, how much money the federal government provides for roads and rails is a policy matter, for whatever decision the government reaches, the United States would still "be" the same form of government. This example seems to suggest a neat compartmentalization between policy and regime questions, in which regime questions are matters of "high" politics, like a revolution, and policy questions are matters of "low" politics, like auto emission standards. But reality is not so simple. Issues that are not dramatic, that appear to be parts of "low" politics, may importantly affect the form of government. Regimes can often be changed without revolutions, or a revolution can be the final stage of a process that has been prepared long in advance by what looked to be insignificant steps; and strategies can be devised to alter the character of a regime (usually in its civil aspect) before directly redefining the public principle of rule—or in rare cases without ever directly confronting it.

These subtleties make the distinction in practice between regime questions (how a society is politically constituted) and policies (what the government decides to do) difficult to ascertain. What is presented publicly as a mere policy change might in fact be a measure that is designed to change—or that will have the unintended effect of changing—the form of government. To the degree that a policy has the effect of precipitating a change in regimes, it is in reality a regime question, no matter whether it is offered (or even consciously perceived) as such. Constitutional political science seeks to identify developments that fall into the category of substantial regime questions and distinguish them from policy questions. It thereby helps us to know what is truly important politically, regardless of how matters are actually presented in political discussions or how they are presented as products of the times.

Nothing I have said about traditional political science thus far should be taken to mean that value questions are confined only to the initial choice of regimes and never raised thereafter. Such a position would inappropriately limit the scope of normative concerns. Not every political action or problem bears in any significant degree on regime maintenance. For matters that are substantially neutral in regard to regime maintenance—that is, policy questions—political analysis will have recourse to other grounds for making judgments, consulting general principles of right or justice or efficiency. The realm of policy issues is both enormous and enormously important.

What applies to policy questions, in the sense of the distribution of resources, applies as well to the goal of human development. Traditional political science investigates the relations of regimes to human development, ranking regimes in large part by what promotes human development. Once a selection of regimes is made, however, political logic holds that the focus should turn largely to what is needed to maintain (or destroy) the form of government, and no longer only to what promotes human development. Traditional political science recognizes that even in a regime defended for enhancing human development, what sustains the regime will not in every instance be the same as what promotes human development.

Traditional political science is not thereby lacking in a normative dimension. Even when investigating what maintains regimes, it seeks to keep as close to the surface as possible the broader point that regimes are to be chosen by their worth as measured against certain standards. And after the choice of regimes is made, traditional political science urges that standards should be directly consulted where no substantial regime effects are involved or where latitude exists in what maintains the regime. Each regime should be made as just as it can be; but it can only be made so just and still remain itself.

Traditional political science would lead to the same form of reasoning as the new normativism under either of two suppositions: if inquiry into what promoted a standard like "substantive justice" on matters of policy involved posing the same concrete questions as what maintains regimes and if no tension existed between what promotes such standards and what maintains a viable regime. But neither of these suppositions holds for any abstract principle of justice. What maintains any real regime cannot be fully known by asking what maximizes an ideal principle of justice, and what is needed to maintain any real regime will not correspond in each case to ideal principles of justice. This conflict exists in some form in every regime, including the best regime. The maintenance of political regimes always exacts a "price" in the world of moral concerns.

Criticisms of Constitutional Political Science

Constitutional political science has been criticized on two substantive grounds: its conservatism (used in a pejorative sense) and its "apriorism."

By focusing attention on the analytic question of what maintains (or undermines) regimes, traditional political science is said to lead to an unreflective bias for existing systems (in our case, to liberal democracy). Yet it is difficult to see why posing the analytic question of what creates or destroys a regime works in favor of maintaining it. The choice for or against any regime is a different question, which is prior in importance to this analytic question. Moreover, if anything, the question of what maintains regimes seems to challenge a soft-headed reformism and forces one to confront the fundamental issue of the defensibility of the constitution as a whole.

Another aspect of the charge of conservatism applies to the attitude traditional political science is said to foster "after" a regime is chosen. By stipulating that policies should first be judged politically in light of what maintains the system, traditional political science provides an excuse for delay by imposing a "double test" on any policy; policies must be checked for their regime effects as well as for their justice or efficiency. This, it is said, impedes the progressive movement toward a just society, which ought to proceed by the "single test" of judging each policy proposal by some preferred standard of right. The response here is simple. Although a "double test," if applied with a covert partisan aim, could serve an unjustified end, applied honestly it introduces a conservative check in the best sense of the word. It demands that the consequences of actions be judged in light of what is most important to conserve or destroy. All "single tests" necessarily make unexplored assumptions of what holds a society together.

Finally, the charge of conservatism rests on a confusion that equates the question of what maintains a regime with the question of what maintains the status quo or promotes short-term stability. These are distinct matters, having only a limited bearing on each other. What protects the status quo may or may not help maintain the regime. Dismantling segregation in the South in the 1960s, for example, clearly upset the status quo, but it hardly ran counter to any general propositions of what maintains liberal democracy. Traditional political science, because it is analytic and not descriptive, always holds the status quo up to a model of the regime. As for the question of stability, it is largely a consideration of prudence that must be addressed in particular circumstances. Promoting stability may have something to recommend it where one seeks to maintain the existing regime, for the simple reason that instability opens the door to accidental possibilities for a regime change. But this judgment is only a rough rule of thumb and is subordinate to an analysis of how well or how poorly the status quo works to maintain the regime.

The second charge made against traditional political science is that it is guilty of apriorism. It presents us, the argument goes, with a closed matrix of regimes that it has artificially constructed and then asks that we define or understand existing regimes without seeing how they actually perform.

Traditional political science proceeds on the basis that in each society there is a deeper structure—or struggle over a deeper structure—that aims to or has the effect of forming or defining society, including its policies or performances. Traditional political science further posits that the actual regimes can be grouped or analyzed in terms of a limited number of general regime types, even though each actual regime has its own unique properties; these groupings or classifications into general types serve, however, not as ends in themselves, but as instruments to be translated back into particular cases in a way that will be able to serve legislators and citizens.

Nothing in this way of looking at politics amounts to saying that the matrix of regimes is closed. New things may be discovered about particular regimes or general regime types, and certain characteristics may manifest themselves differently in the course of history. Moreover, new regime types on occasion emerge—for example, liberal democracy in the eighteenth century or Marxist-Leninist regimes in the twentieth century. The objects on which political science concentrates are thus not fixed a priori in number, and we are constantly learning new things about them. Political science is a body of knowledge that can never be completed.

The charge of apriorism also relates to the claim that traditional political science does not take policies seriously enough. It defines the regime by its structure without looking first at its specific policies, whereas (it is said) it is the sum of the policies or performance that best defines any regime. A regime, in this view, is what it does, and what it does is best determined by a summation of its policies, not by some a priori idea of its structure or nature.

Answering this objection requires one to distinguish between general regime types and the specific policy output of specific regimes and to understand the overall purpose of speaking of general types. It is clear that one of the objects of studying regime types is to understand the logic of how each type tends to perform. Performance is analyzed as a set of general tendencies of the regime or the regime type, relating to such matters as its principles of distribution (e.g., that a democracy tends to an egalitarian standard of distribution, an oligarchy to an inegalitarian standard), its policy-making capacities or characteristics (e.g., that democracies are often mutable or unstable in their policies, aristocracies patient and fixed in their objectives), and its foreign policy orientation (e.g., that a fascist state will tend toward expansion, a traditional monarchy to caution).

The study of regime types is not, however, designed to predict each and every policy output. A given regime type may almost dictate certain kinds of policies, but it may provide only minimal constraints for others. Thus to say that a regime is a liberal democracy does not tell us specifically what policies it will adopt in every field. When we look at particular regimes, therefore, we find that the policies undertaken by a certain government are not always constrained by its general form, and that in specific cases they may even vary considerably from the norm. Policies, moreover, are made by individuals, who are never fully determined by a regime structure and who, under certain circumstances, may act in ways highly uncharacteristic of it. Situations where the leadership acts in conflict with the normal tendencies of the regime—for example, a Brasidas in Sparta or a Gorbachev in the Soviet Union—are, almost by definition, unusual, but they are certainly not unknown. Whether such cases are merely instances of conflict—that is, instances wherein the regime outlasts the situation—or whether these conflicts become the source of a full regime change is the fundamental question. Traditional political science focuses on this question and prevents us from analyzing politics simply at the level of policy.

Traditional political science does not equate the regime with its policies. The regime represents a "structure" that goes deeper than specific policies. The regime gives rise to general policy tendencies, not to each and every policy. The regime does not change with every major policy shift, including policies that are at variance with its own tendencies. The form of government is the cause which, more than any other cause that humans can deliberately choose, gives immediate shape to the society. But there are other causes at work in specific cases that can change or alter a "predicted" outcome.

It follows that there are two levels of analysis—one dealing with the form of government, the other with policy. These two levels are linked. The form of government creates general policy tendencies, while specific policies at variance with the regime can unloose consequences to change the regime. The links between these two levels may be tighter or looser according to the character of the regime. The failure to understand the distinction between these two levels and to give each its proper weight leads to two different kinds of errors. One is to overinterpret the significance of the regime and to hold that every major policy must reflect its principles or logic. Under this approach it is almost impossible to conceive of change, other than by overt revolution, or to take advantage flexibly of mechanisms that might eventually lead to a regime change. The other error is to underestimate the significance or influence of the regime and to identify the immediate policies as the only real element of political analysis. Under this approach, the risk is that one will exaggerate change and rush to identify temporary or ostensible signs of movement with a fundamental change of regimes.

Constitutional Political Science and a Science of Politics

Traditional political science, while it relies heavily on empirical observation, differs on many points from the modern scientific approach. According to the scientific view, we live in a world in which we know nothing other than that there are certain data ("power acts") that constitute political reality. These data have no structure or meaning that can reliably be grasped by direct human perception. We construct our concepts by discovering connections and interrelations through scientific tests, or we impose certain tentative boundaries on the data in order to learn about something we know to be important to us.

For traditional political science, the human perception of the concept of the regime and its primacy is the starting point for the discipline. This perception, confirmed by the repeated experience of knowledgeable people after a certain stage in human development, is not something to be mistrusted, but accepted and built on. It is a fact established or known phenomenologically. Since human beings are part of reality, and since politics is an activity of human beings, the way we perceive and structure the world is part of the "data" of reality, indeed its most important part.

There is something curious in the repeated practice in modern political science of chasing constitutional analysis out the front door (when one offers a formal definition of political science) only to bring it in the back door, when one begins to speak of an important "frame of reference" or of "differences that make a difference" (Dahl, 1984, 66). If the regime is the important "frame of reference," and if its principle of justice constitutes the "difference that makes a difference," it would hardly seem unscientific to say so and then investigate these matters. At least, however, the duplicity of bringing regime analysis in the back door allows the political scientist to focus on what is important. This is a far better situation than when researchers actually follow the formal definitions of the modern scientific view, for they are then apt to end up engaged in trivial pursuits like studying the decision making of faculty clubs.

Knowledge of regimes and what works to maintain or undermine them is the principal aim of the empirical part of traditional political science. The political scientist here searches for general relationships or laws of causality that state whether the presence of a certain factor—be it physical, economic, cultural, or political—tends to promote (or undermine) a given type of regime. These relationships are not merely legal. It is in this context that political science may indeed be interested in clubs, families, international trading "regimes," and the like. But it does not focus on these things as the final objects of analysis, but in terms of their relationship to undermining or maintaining regimes. Far from limiting the importance of political science, this approach actually asserts its centrality. By studying other social units in light of the regime, which is the deepest human structure for which we can provide by deliberate human action, we insist on the importance of the political and prevent the discipline of political science from being swallowed up by sociology, anthropology, or economics.

The question of regime maintenance can, of course, be set aside or bracketed when studying other matters, such as the efficiency of different policies or arrangements. But these other questions can only be properly studied *after* one has "checked" on the regime issue and determined how (or whether) it affects the matter at hand. To consider other matters independently of the regime is to take them out of their most important context. A study of the most efficient administrative arrangement, or the ideally competitive party system, even the perfectly competitive economy, is at best an abstraction, at worst an absurdity. Administrative arrangements, party systems, even economic systems do not exist by themselves but within regimes. The regime is prior in importance to any of these other systems.

The search for the causal relationships between factors and regimes involves, but is not limited to, the study of observed cases. Observed cases can sometimes be too particular to be useful in forming a general body of knowledge. The perspective that allows for generalities derives from speaking of regime types. One normally proceeds by looking at the available cases (e.g., liberal democracy as it appears in the United States, Great Britain, or France) with the end or object of drawing inferences about general types (liberal democracy). The particular cases are the concrete instances through which one attempts to "see" the general type. Where no actual cases exist of a certain phenomenon, it is still possible to construct a type by delineating in thought what its characteristics would be if and when it existed.

Analysis of cases by statistical means (i.e., counting each case equally and using this data base to establish or disconfirm hypotheses), while often the soundest point from which to begin, does not always enable one to capture fully the character of the general idea or to ascertain genuine causal relationships between forms of government and the various factors. The cases (forms of government) are systems of the most complex sort in which the number of variables usually exceeds the number of cases, making the introduction of statistical controls often implausible or impossible. Moreover, as each case is found in a particular historical context, it is "tainted" by the particular and the accidental, so that certain cases may be of less value than others in developing general theory. The aim of classifications and theory is not just pure knowledge, but a body of thought that might prove helpful to people acting in politics. This is why particular cause-effect relations in particular places must be "translated" first into general categories, which in turn can then be used by being "translated" back into different particular contexts.

The political scientist naturally welcomes more cases in order to increase the likelihood that statistical information will prove helpful. Yet because the numbers of examples is often so limited, it is difficult to establish many genuine causal relationships between factors and regimes without going beyond statistical analysis. The political scientist will therefore introduce commonsense criteria that allow certain cases to be excluded and others to be considered as more revealing of the nature of a form of government. The aim is to strip away from existing cases factors that are artifacts of the particular case in an effort to comprehend the type at the most general level.

Existing cases, moreover, do not contain all of the possibilities. The fact that certain factors have in the past helped maintain a certain type of regime does not mean that other factors, untried or unobservable at the present time, might not support that regime as well or better while at the same time further promoting a standard like human development. For traditional political science the object is not descriptive but analytic; it is to penetrate to the logic of the types and deduce causal relationships between factors and types in a way that would enable one to say how they relate, even where no existing cases can prove or disprove the deduction. These relationships, where they cannot be tested by observation or by facts currently known, must stand as tentative hypotheses.

A descriptive political science that looks only at existing cases and does not abstract to regime types might well be too "conservative." It is clearly part of the task of constitutional political science to seek out the best possibilities for different regimes, the best practicable regime in a given time or under given circumstances, and in some way the best possible regime. This task—pursued, for example, in a classic work like Tocqueville's *Democracy in America*—looks to indicate the principles, the laws, and the mores, not yet fully realized in any existing regime, that would contribute to the maintenance of a given system and that, within that system, would do the most for human development. In leaving immediately observable acts, there is always a danger of slipping into naive idealism by positing relations that could not exist. Fanciful relations of this sort, advanced by weaker theorists, have rightfully provided targets for attacks by those who call themselves realists. Yet the fact that a technique can be misused does not make it invalid. The aim of traditional political science is to explore *genuine* possible relations, even if they are not actual. Exploring hypothetical cases can be an entirely realistic pursuit, if the spirit in which the analysis is undertaken is realistic.

Traditional political science also differs from the scientific approach in the intended use of its knowledge. Advocates of the scientific approach have conceived the ultimate aim of knowledge in two radically different ways: either as an enterprise that guides massive social engineering and/or as an activity that is detached and academic. The first view was espoused by a few of the early pioneers of the scientific approach like Harold Laswell (1961, 513), who called for "nothing less than the drastic and continuing reconstruction of our own civilization, and most of the cultures of which we have any knowledge." Political science would not only provide the knowledge for this enterprise, but also supply the personnel, in the form of trained political psychologists, who would replace the traditional statesman as the source of real political power. The generation of scientists of the 1960s renounced this grandiose enterprise, settling instead on the more modest academic goal of explaining variance. Pure political scientists today tend to write mostly for other political scientists. Perhaps for the first time in human history, the profession is large and wealthy enough to supply adequate material and professional incentives to motivate and reward its members, regardless of any considerations of practical utility.

Traditional political science has a different aim than either of these two scientific views. It differs from the Laswellian approach, not in renouncing a practical intent, but in pursuing that practical intent by working through actual or potential statesmen, legislators, and citizens. It works with and through politics rather than attempting to displace it, because it denies the possibility that the "matter" of politics can be manipulated and rearranged like so many atoms. It prefers to present the political world in terms of regimes having a certain shape or integrity that can be directed and guided, but not fully mastered.

Traditional political science differs from the academic view, which insists that the sole aim of the discipline is to "understand variance." Traditional political science holds that its own understanding of its subject matter provides validation for a discipline that is engaged in society and that makes itself available to serve the human good. If traditional political science has a purely academic aspect to it, abstracted from its practical enterprise, it consists of the internal discussion of how much this enterprise might reasonably hope to accomplish and of how best to insert this enterprise into society.

Insofar as political science has the practical or human end of aiding legislators, it favors certain kinds of explanations. Although it is concerned with attaining the most comprehensive knowledge of the relationships of factors to regimes, it seeks to connect physical and economic correlations to explanations that legislators feel they can use and that relate to their experience with the world. The explanations legislators seek, while they may have a physical or economic component to them, are those expressed finally in terms of human, that is, cultural, political, or psychological, motivations. The human motivation is the immediate or closest cause of action. While it may be found to covary with certain physical and economic factors, it usually has some independence or autonomy: no physical or economic cause is likely to produce a unique result in respect to any important human motivation, and no important human motivation will be found only under one set of physical or economic circumstances.

As a result, no legislator could ever rest content with an explanation of the sort that substantial national wealth correlates highly with liberal democracy. The practical actor will want to know the human reason why a relationship holds in order to be able to make practical judgments in specific cases about whether the case at hand follows the rule or the exception. No correlation can supply the basis for making this determination. Furthermore, since a legislator might not be able to change certain physical or economic facts, the most useful explanation is one expressed in terms of human motivation, for it alone can provide guidance about the possibility of attaining a political result in the absence of the usual physical conditions which which it is associated. The quality of explanation in political science is thus not solely a function of the amount of statistical variance accounted for, but of its political utility in assisting practical deliberation. In the world of traditional political science, not all variance is equal (see Eckstein 1961, 21).

Political science is not a science in the modern sense, but a body of knowledge that makes use where appropriate of certain modern scientific techniques. Political science is also a human activity that takes place in society and that has very important consequences for political life. The mode of engagement of political science in society is therefore a proper object of inquiry for political science. The analysis of political life shows that there is always some mode of thinking—whether it be customary, dogmatic, ideological, or pseudoscientific—that must play a major role in shaping the character of political regimes. Political science holds that the systematic study of regimes can help improve the quality of political regimes. Political science cannot therefore be indifferent to being replaced or diminished in its influence by other disciplines, such as ethics, academic philosophy, or economics, that do not hold the same promise for guiding political life.

REFERENCES

Almond, Gabriel. 1988. "Separate Tables: Schools and Sects in Political Science." *PS*, fall.

Almond, Gabriel, and Sidney Verba. 1965. *The Civic Culture*. Boston: Little, Brown.

——, eds. 1980. *The Civil Culture Revisited*. Boston: Little, Brown.

Bay, Christian. 1965. "Politics and Pseudopolitics: A Critical Evaluation of Some Behavioral Literature." *American Political Science Review* 59:42–50.

Ceaser, James. 1990. *Liberal Democracy and Political Science*. Baltimore: Johns Hopkins University Press.

Dahl, Robert. 1961. "The Behavioral Approach in Political Science: Epitaph for a Monument to a Successful Protest." *American Political Science Review* 55:763–72.

——. 1984. *Modern Political Analysis*. 4th ed. Englewood Cliffs, N.J.: Prentice Hall.

——. 1986. "On Removing Certain Impediments to Democracy in the

United States." In *Moral Foundations of the American Republic,* edited by Robert Horwitz. Charlottesville: University Press of Virginia.

Eckstein, Harry. 1961. *A Theory of Stable Democracy.* Princeton, N.J.: Center of International Studies.

Gramsci, Antonio. 1971. *Selections from the Prison Notebooks.* New York: International Publishers.

Joseph, Lawrence. 1981. "Democratic Revisionism Revisited." *American Journal of Political Science* 25:160–87.

Laswell, Harold. 1961. *The Political Writings of Harold D. Laswell.* New York: Free Press.

Laswell, Harold, and Abraham Kaplan. 1947. *Power and Society.* New Haven, Conn.: Yale University Press.

Lindblom, Charles. 1983. "Communications to the Editor." *American Political Science Review* 77:384–86.

Mansbridge, Jane, ed. 1991. *Beyond Self-Interest.* Chicago: University of Chicago Press.

Natanson, Maurice. 1963. *Philosophy of the Social Sciences.* New York: Random House.

Strauss, Leo. 1983. *Studies in Platonic Philosophy.* Chicago: University of Chicago Press.

CHAPTER FOUR

Generic Constitutionalism

KAROL EDWARD SOŁTAN

THE CONSTITUTIONALIST TRADITION builds on two themes implicit in the double meaning of the word *constitution*. Constitution can refer to a process of creation and to a limit or a boundary on power. The fundamental themes of constitutionalism are, then, the themes of creation and limitation. "Generic constitutionalism," as I call it in this essay, is distinctive in its effort to make these themes both more general and more abstract.

Constitutionalism understood in this way refers to more than the study or the writing of constitutions. It is not simply a perspective within what is quaintly known as public law in American political science, nor is it just another way to understand American politics. It has a new form, different from the traditional constitutionalism that survives mostly in a few unreconstructed corners of political science. It is instead part of an attempt to change social and political thinking, without much respect for disciplinary boundaries, through new research questions and a moderately novel political program.

The main concern of the research is to study a set of socially significant and general forms of human competence, those required for institutional design. Constitutionalism takes the perspective of the designer (or framer) of institutions, with the understanding that such design is neither a one-shot affair (like the construction of a bridge) nor achieved only by the few (the social engineers). Design of institutions (their creation and reform) is a continuing business in which anyone can, in principle, participate.

The political program of "generic constitutionalism" takes in new directions the basic idea of limiting power in the service of moral and political ideals not just within the state, but also in private organizations and bargaining, as well as revolutionary and reform movements. It also presses into new areas the contrast between the ideals of limited and popular sovereignty, including an environmentalist ethic based on the limited sovereignty of the human species on earth.

The generic constitutionalist perspective cannot be satisfactorily explained in a single chapter.[1] My only goal here is to give a sampling of the different strands of thought that enter into it, including a preliminary section on the intellectual and political background, some consideration of the study of human competence in general, and of its most distinctively "constitutionalist" aspects, as well as an outline of a generic constitutionalist political program.

The Intellectual and Political Background

Science versus Autonomy

In developing generic constitutionalism I would like to draw on elements of both the intellectual and the political legacy of the Enlightenment. The intellectual legacy includes a basic contradiction. We inherit, on the one hand, an aspiration to extend the scientific forms of understanding to human behavior, leading again and again to various forms of biological or situational (e.g., Becker 1976) determinism. People appear as puppets, helpless weaklings at the mercy of forces entirely outside their control. Human behavior is explainable and predictable only to the extent it is determined by some externally observable causes.

This kind of scientific view of human nature goes hand in hand with the development of institutions and organizations that *make* human behavior more predictable and more fully determined by external constraints (as in B. F. Skinner's *Walden Two* [1976]). Taylorism and the scientific management movement (Taylor 1947) have been among the most extreme expressions of this tendency, which aims to make human behavior as machinelike as possible, to reduce both discretion and autonomy. But rationality does not equal Taylorism. The intellectual legacy of the Enlightenment also incorporates an ethic urging us to treat everyone with equal respect as an autonomous agent. This ethic is articulated most fully in the Kantian tradition, but its appeal is felt more broadly.

The conflict between determinism and the appeal of autonomy has a cultural importance far beyond the more narrowly philosophical questions of free will (Unger 1987). It gives the boundary between facts and values a key role, protecting these two commitments from

---

1. I am preparing a book version tentatively entitled *The Ideal Citizen*.

each other. But because the protection is imperfect, we encounter people who disparage morality as unscientific and human autonomy as a chimera, as well as others who attack science and turn against it, thinking it devalues and undermines morality and virtue. We can easily see how science, especially some forms of social science, can undermine and distort important moral commitments, but we can also see the opposite situation, in which moral commitment undermines science.

If we take Galileo as the symbol of the intellectual transition from a basically Aristotelian world to one in which rationalism takes a modern scientific turn, then we can see that Galileo's revolution is incomplete. Our understanding of actual human behavior in the scientific spirit has developed with some success. But an ethics and a normative political theory in the same spirit are really yet to be born.[2] Hence the common theme of intellectual hostility between science and morality, between a scientific understanding of human nature that often denies autonomy and a morality that affirms it.

We need a more stable resolution of this enduring contradiction, in the form of a scientific but respectful understanding of humanity, for which human nature and behavior are more than playthings of their internal biological nature and their external environment. It must be a view consistent with *human creativity* and capable of describing and appreciating it. Institutions, personalities, characters, actions must all be seen as human *artifacts* (see Giddens 1984; Unger 1987) created by men and women, not products of some impersonal forces. From this perspective the human species would appear above all as a community of makers and designers. Instead of predicting human behavior on the basis of external clues, we would try to give an account of human capacities to create or constitute. We are led along this path toward a form of *constitutionalism*.

This intellectual contradiction in the legacy of the Enlightenment is especially strongly felt in contemporary social sciences, where the front lines have been most clearly drawn and the important and bloody battles fought. The main protagonists of this war are determinists of various kinds on one side, and interpretivists on the other. The purest form of situational determinism is represented by the behavioral schools in psychology (Skinner 1953) and in economics (Becker 1976). But there are also many more diluted and mixed forms: behavioralism in political science or "social exchange theory" in sociology (e.g., Homans 1974). Situational determinism requires only the simplest models of the human mind. Its goal is to explain

---

2. Unless we count here utilitarianism and some of its social scientific offshoots.

even the most complex patterns of behavioral change exclusively by changes in the situation. The mind is a passive instrument, hence simple models of utility maximization and of learning by association are sufficient. We see here an image of mankind as a collective of simple minds preoccupied with adapting to the external situation, hardly worthy of our respect.

The most prominent and clearly articulated alternative to this view in the social science community is put forward by the interpretive or hermeneutic tradition. It aims to understand the human mind and its products in all their complexity, diversity, and uniqueness. Instead of constructing a social science in the spirit of the Enlightenment, thereby extending the scientific understanding of human nature and behavior, it pursues a scholarship based on the model of the humanities and centered on the interpretation of texts and text analogues, hence on hermeneutics.

In political science this basic methodological conflict of all the social sciences is reinforced by the contradiction between the aspiration to promote good institutions (and democratic institutions in particular) and the aspiration to study them scientifically. To the extent the latter undermines the former, political science faces what we should perhaps recognize as a tragic dilemma (this is Ricci's view [1984]). Here again, the promotion of the good comes in conflict with science, a respectful understanding of mankind comes in conflict with a scientific one.

The two extremes of determinism and hermeneutics do not exhaust the set of alternative methodological and theoretical stances available in the social sciences. There is also a large mainstream, full of attempts to construct some form of a mediating position. We find here the sociology of Max Weber (1949) and the Weberians, the voluntarism of Talcott Parsons (1937), various "moderate" versions of structuralism (Merton 1957; Stinchcombe 1968; and others), as well as those theorists of rational choice who try to develop more complex views of human competence (as in game theory, e.g., or in the work of Elster [1979], Margolis [1982], Sen [1977], and others), rather than serving as a front for situational determinism. Constitutionalism, as I see it, belongs among those mediating positions, but extends them to include a more systematic study of normative questions relevant to the development of institutions.[3] It is part of a larger effort aiming to vindicate the hope that a respectful understanding of mankind can be accessible to science as well as to the humanities, that respect for

---

3. Questions about the development of character, and the construction of actions, are also in many ways closely related.

human autonomy does not require rejecting the scientific tradition or the intellectual legacy of the Enlightenment more broadly conceived.

Constitution versus Revolution

Some form of the political legacy of the Enlightenment is also worth preserving. This legacy can be described in many ways, but for my purposes it is best to distinguish two grand themes: the revolutionary and the constitutional.

The theme of revolution has its own internal logic of development, which has come to define the left-to-right spectrum in politics. There is a right-to-left pattern through which individual revolutions typically move. More important, from the French to the Bolshevik revolutions (and well into the twentieth century) the general developmental tendency of politics has been well described by this right-to-left pattern. Marxist theory codified it into a sequence of stages of socioeconomic development, with revolutions as crucial transition points.

Nineteenth-century politics was in many ways dominated by the memory and the model of the French Revolution. One side saw it as the great threat, the other as a basic "engine of history." In the twentieth century the Bolshevik Revolution has played a somewhat similar role. In both instances the "Great Revolution" is the awesome event in the shadow of which, fear mixed with fascination, ordinary politics plays itself out.

The experience of revolutions has also been a great source of inspiration and ideals, as well as some practical lessons of how to reach them. Revolutions showed that large masses of people can be awakened from their slumber. Given the right moment and the right organization they can be willing to risk suffering and death for a larger cause. The ordinary limits of interest and vision can be lifted.

Again and again since the French revolution "the people" rose up in the service of a larger cause. Again and again, the revolutionary movement of the people spontaneously organized itself in the same way, in councils of workers, peasants, or soldiers (Arendt 1963; Horvat 1982). Inspired by this experience, many political theorists attempted to make this pattern permanent and to institutionalize its organizational form. The slogans "permanent revolution" and "all power to the people" were the basic guidelines. Such has been the core of a broad range of movements in modern radical politics, from communists, through many shades of socialists, to radical and participatory democrats, from the radicals of the French Revolution, through Marx and the Marxists, Lenin and the Leninists, to Roberto

Unger's (1987a, 1987b) contemporary call (made in the modernist spirit of transgression) to smash all contexts.

The legacy of revolution demands the smashing of contexts, the crossing of boundaries, and the elimination of limits—in part as an end in itself, but in part also as an instrument to activate an otherwise passive people. Within the constitutional legacy, by contrast, limits and self-limitation are a cherished ideal and an aspiration. Limited government has been, for the last 200 years, the most basic demand of the constitutionalists. It is a worthy cause, to be sure, but hardly sufficient for great sacrifices. As a carrier of political idealism the constitutional legacy has been far weaker than that of the revolution. It has not had the same general and passionate appeal.[4]

The main causes can be found, I believe, in the powerful narrowing tendencies within the constitutionalist tradition. The result is a form of constitutionalism preoccupied with (and distorted by) *interests*, a bourgeois constitutionalism, as its enemies would call it. Constitutionalism came to be distorted by the forces of narrow interest when it developed into the political instrument of the propertied classes. The task of limiting government came to coincide with protecting the rights of property. The more general and abstract aspirations to limit power, and to put it in the service of a self-limiting morality, have had a difficult time emerging from this variant of interested constitutionalism.

The Relative Decline of the Revolutionary Legacy

In the twentieth century we have seen two striking political developments: the slow decline of the legacy of revolution and the parallel development of constitutionalist tendencies beyond the narrow confines of "bourgeois" constitutionalism. The threat of organized power, whether revolutionary or counterrevolutionary, whether held by a state or a corporation or an interest group, has become far more pervasive than before. The increasingly clear perception of this threat is a key factor behind the growing interest in constitutionalism.

The parallel intellectual changes have been much slower in coming. The revolutionary tradition, inspired by the French Revolution and the writings of Marx, Sorel, and others, is still more influential.

---

4. Except, perhaps, in the United States. The contrast between the revolutionary and the constitutional traditions derives in many ways from the contrast between the French and the American revolutions. The latter was doubtfully a revolution, but was certainly a great "constitutional event." The former was a revolution all right, but rather a failure on the constitutional front.

Constitutionalism has nothing comparable. As Arendt (1963) has noted, on the intellectual front the French Revolution has been a triumph, while the American Revolution has had little impact. This is still basically true, and it is one reason for developing a more general and abstract understanding of constitutionalism.

The Bolshevik Revolution has been the central event in the political decline of the revolutionary tradition. Its beginning and triumph were an inspiration for many idealists across the world. But as the communist regime has evolved, first in the Soviet Union, and then elsewhere, and as its nature became increasingly clear, massive disillusionment and cynicism followed. The revolutionary heroes of the twentieth century who died early remain heroes. Those who lived long have left a more ambiguous legacy. The revolutionary tradition is certainly not dead, but it is weaker today than it has been for a long time. It is difficult now to see a revolution as a source of idealistic inspiration.

The decline of the revolutionary tradition is most vivid when we look at what is left of communism. It is not just its final collapse that is striking. For a long time these were regimes in the midst of a continuing and deep crisis. Normally revolutionary movements and organizations develop in such settings, yet none did as communism was collapsing. This was so, I believe, because communist regimes were the *products* (for the most part) of organized revolutions. Their founding experience was the easy corruption of such revolutions. Those who would have to organize and plan a revolution in a communist country had before their eyes every day the possible consequences. A call to *another* revolution had limited appeal. Various elements of a constitutionalist program, by contrast, had strong support, including a renewed respect for the rule of law, the separation of powers, freedom to speak and to organize, and a free market (Kaminski and Sołtan 1989). Montesquieu and Madison were read with renewed interest throughout the communist world. With the collapse of communism the interest in constitutionalism has only intensified.

Montesquieu and Madison are also read with new interest in the West, where the revival of constitutionalism responds to the growth of the state and of the corporation and to the increasingly clear inadequacies of the contemporary versions of pluralism and neocorporatism as methods of organizing politico-economic systems.

Perhaps the most striking feature of the contemporary social world, when compared with the situation 100 or 150 years ago, is the dominant role played by formal organizations. The most powerful of these is the modern state, which throughout the twentieth century has taken on an increasing number of tasks and functions, employed an increasing number of officials, and dominated both the domestic economies of most countries and the international economic system. Close behind the growth of the state has been the growth of corporations, many of which have become highly diversified multinational giants.

The modern state has grown and increased in power, but it has not become more effective. Controlling the state's power can be, therefore, only a partial solution: we need also to make it work better. Efforts to do so have led many scholars toward a more critical view not just of the state, but of the pluralist political system, within some version of which the contemporary democratic state operates.

Under pluralism, decisions are divided, so that instead of a few big decisions, we have many small ones. Rapid and broad shifts in policy are replaced by piecemeal, gradual changes. Furthermore, control over these small and gradual changes tends to be highly decentralized. In the United States, congressional subcommittees, administrative agencies, and groups of experts monopolize small, specialized areas of decision-making authority. Within each such area the influence of special interest groups may be considerable.

There are many advantages to this way of running government, but recently the disadvantages have become more noticeable (see e.g., Olson 1982; Dahl 1982; Lowi 1979; Lindblom 1977). A decentralized, piecemeal decision-making system tends, first of all, to suffer from collective action problems (Olson 1965). Each special interest gains advantages from the state in its area of concern, but the effect of granting such advantages to a broad range of groups is to make all of them worse off. Furthermore, a decentralized pluralist system of this kind favors decisions whose benefits are concentrated and costs dispersed, even if the total costs outweigh the benefits, and it blocks decisions whose costs are concentrated and benefits dispersed, even if the benefits outweigh the costs. The only antidote to these tendencies seems to be a centralization of decisions, that is, an increase in the power of central authorities relative to the various specialized groups.

This is the main argument in favor of authoritarianism in countries where democracy is not fully institutionalized. In more stable democracies this argument has been used to support strengthening the executive (the presidency in the United States), strengthening and centralizing political parties, and strengthening the corporatist tendencies in the process of interest articulation. Similar arguments are also often used against the democratization of private corporations. Corporations organized in a more democratic fashion will approximate more closely the pluralist model and suffer the consequences.

An alternative to these various proposals, one form of which has been put forward by Lowi (1979), is to constitutionalize more fully both the state and the processes of pluralist bargaining, restraining them by law, impartial standards, and rules. The propensity of the state to give in to the myriad specialized interests will thus be limited without resort to authoritarianism. The power of government officials to do what they want will *decrease* thanks to the restraining force of rules.

This is the main solution to the pluralist troubles of the democratic state proposed and elaborated by the various new forms of constitutionalism. Central authorities are not to be given additional power to act as they will, and thus there is no question of promoting authoritarian tendencies. But central authorities are given resources (the impartial restraints) that can allow them to resist more effectively the narrowly specialized pressures of organized groups. Such restraints are needed, and must be made more effective (as Lowi has urged), in administrative agencies. But surely not only there. The entire apparatus of the modern state, and of many modern corporations, can benefit from this kind of constitutionalization.

The new forms of constitutionalism require a broadening of the constitutionalist tradition. Much of this broadening has already occurred, but it remains mostly hidden and typically understood in different and diverse political categories. Thus, to take just one example, changes in management, and in labor-management relations, have gone far toward the constitutionalization of private enterprises (Selznick 1969). But they have done so mainly in the guise of organizational rationalization, the human relations school of management, and collective bargaining. The underlying unity of these various tendencies has gone largely unnoticed, except in the work of a few social scientists, Selznick prominent among them.

But to really understand the shifting fortunes of the two sides in the larger battle between the revolutionary and constitutional legacies of the Enlightenment, we need to pay special attention to the first steps in the constitutionalization of revolutionary movements themselves. It is here that the shift from the revolutionary to the constitutionalist tradition is most explicit. And it is here that we can *really* see the birth of a constitutionalism freed from its association with propertied interests.

In the twentieth century, revolutions have been disappointing, and attempts to abandon the Enlightenment tradition (as in fascism and Nazism) have been a disaster, but one new political invention has been a source of considerable hope and some faith in the possible (if only occasional) effectiveness of human ideals: the development, by Mohandas Gandhi more than anyone else, of a nonviolent mass social movement, a self-limiting (constitutionalized) revolution. In the hands of Gandhi, Martin Luther King, Jr., Lech Wałęsa, Corazon Aquino, and others this invention has emerged as perhaps the greatest gift of twentieth-century politics to future generations.

Gandhi-style social movements are not commonly seen as a stage in the development of constitutionalism, and indeed Gandhi's main sources of inspiration lay elsewhere. Constitutionalism is normally narrowly understood, making it difficult to see the profound analogies between a self-limiting government and a self-limiting revolution. There is much to gain, therefore, by looking at Gandhi's work as a stage in the constitutionalization of protest and revolt. The earliest revolts (such as medieval and postmedieval peasant rebellions or early worker protests) had a large component of random and aimless violence, of pure expression of anger. They were in their own way examples of tyranny, short-lived but ruthless in the extreme: brutal killings and mass destruction of property were common.

The revolutionary tradition represents the first stage of the constitutionalization of revolt. Violence is now guided by a purpose and is therefore more rational and restrained. But the violence continues, and it does not choose its victims with any elaborate concern for justice. The revolt is still a "tyrannical moment," though now the violence is purposeful. Gandhi's nonviolent mass social movement is an important second stage in the constitutionalization of revolt. Now the limits on violence are more serious, and the ideal of self-limiting revolution more explicit. Revolutions, like states and corporations, are forms of socially significant power. They now come to be limited in their powers and restrained by self-imposed rules. This is perhaps the most dramatic step forward in the political broadening of the constitutionalist tradition. What I call "generic constitutionalism" is an effort to push forward this broadening on the intellectual front.

Generic Constitutionalism as a Research Program

The Study of Competence

The research goal of this generic constitutionalism is to study human institutions (but also human actions and individual character) from the perspective of a designer. Predicting and explaining what people will do, the common interest of mainstream social science, is at best a means to this research goal. The creativity and unpredictability of human behavior is an accepted given. The subject of our study is therefore not the behavior itself, but the various skills that are required to make the behavior succeed. The motive, at least in part, is a purely scientific one—to find the most orderly aspect of the phenomena under study. The chaos of human performances contrasts with more orderly patterns of human competence. There are other motives as well: the pursuit of an understanding of mankind that is respectful as well as scientific, the development of a broadly based practice-oriented social science, and the urgency of a certain kind of political reform, reflected in the developments described above.

The classic example of the distinction between competence and performance comes from the study of language. When we study *performance*, we observe what people actually say. When we study *competence*, we reconstruct the linguistic rules they have adopted implicitly or explicitly. The data look different. In the first case, they are spoken or written sentences, or other sequences of linguistic symbols. In the second case, they are judgments of what is grammatical or acceptable. What people actually say is difficult to predict, and subject to many ad hoc influences, distortion, and errors. The hidden order in language is more likely to be found through the study of competence. This, indeed, was one of the breakthrough ideas that allowed the development of generative grammar and the theoretical awakening of linguistics. The larger lesson of this development is that an empirical social science need not be a science of behavior, except in the very special sense that certain *kinds* of behavior are used as evidence for competing theories of the underlying object of study—the various forms of human competence.

Generative grammar studies one kind of human competence, that involving the mastery of language. But there are many different types of objects that human beings master, and this mastery takes many different forms. One way to distinguish among the forms of mastery is to consider the signs or symptoms we accept as evidence of an underlying competence, the different ways we know that we know. Some of these symptoms are purely subjective; they are mental states of a particular kind, such as the absence of confusion or the *feeling* of understanding. Others are more objective, but still not very reliable, such as the capacity to answer questions about something. We have this capacity to answer questions when we understand something well, but we also have it when we have elaborate delusions. The fact that we can answer questions (articulately, in detail, and with confidence) does not guarantee that we know what we are talking about.

Other symptoms of knowledge, however, are both more objective and more reliable. Three of these seem most important: successful prediction, successful manipulation, and successful redesign. If we can predict the behavior of an object, we have evidence of understanding it. Similarly, if we can use it successfully for our purposes, or if we can redesign it in a way that improves the object in the eyes of others who have mastered it, we also have evidence of understanding the object.

Consider two simple examples that involve our knowledge of a radio and of the game of chess. When we can predict the effect of pushing various buttons, or when we learn to *use* the radio for our purposes, we have an elementary mastery of the radio. In this case, but not for all other objects, the ability to predict and the ability to use are closely connected. Finally, if we can improve a radio we have shown an even deeper mastery of it.

When we consider the game of chess (or most other games), the situation is not much different. The ability to predict moves is a sign of understanding chess. Far more important, however, is the ability to win the game, which is a way of using it for one's own purposes. We do not doubt our mastery of chess just because we cannot predict the moves of all players, especially of those who do not know how to play, as long as we can win the game. Winning is a clear signal of competence for chess players. For chess officials and referees the signals of competence take the form of the acceptability within the "chess community" of the changes in the rules of the game which they suggest. These need not be large changes, but a referee's decision in a hard case, to the extent it sets a precedent, will transform the rules of chess to some degree (see Dworkin 1977). A good decision will show a distinct type of mastery of the game.

We can test our mastery of a system of law in the same way. First, we demonstrate our mastery by predicting the moves of players, especially of judges (see Holmes 1897). Second, we show that we can use the law to our advantage, as lawyers are trained to do. And, finally, our mastery is evident by our reformulating law in ways acceptable to the legal community, which is (as Dworkin would have it) what judges should aim to do in hard cases.

We cannot develop all three types of competence, the predictive, the manipulative, and the developmental, for every object. We need to distinguish, for example, between natural and artificial objects and between natural and artificial sciences. Artificial objects are products of human design, or at least open to human redesign; natural objects are not (see Simon 1969). Developmental competence, whose external sign is the acceptable and successful redesign or reform, can arise only with artificial objects, not with natural ones. We have here a likely source of important differences between social sciences, where many objects are artificial, and natural sciences, where few are (cf. Vico 1948).

But in *any* field the confidence we have in our mastery of something is likely to be greatest when the signals of competence are many and *diverse*. Technological success and experimental use, as well as predictive success, reassures the natural scientist (Hacking 1981). Success in redesign and reform should have an equally reassuring effect on the social scientist. If knowledge is more reliable to the extent its symptoms are more diverse, then social science ought to aim for theories that are predictively accurate, but which also produce the other, basically normative, signals of understanding and competence (winning and improving the game).

We can identify a continuum of forms of mastery of social institutions, from the purely passive to the purely active. Purely passive competence expresses itself in predictive success; active competence shows itself either in successful manipulation of an institution, or in successful reform. Mixed forms of competence should generate predictions of how the institution (or other object) will behave, and they should suggest prescriptions for successful use and for improvement. The mixed type of mastery of a social institution can take two forms, depending on the nature of its normative component. It can be manipulative (when successful use is the standard) or developmental (when successful reform is the standard). A theory of manipulative competence will explain behavior and institutions to the extent that they are products of successful manipulation by self-interested parties. We see this in most of rational choice theory, game theory, and in public choice. A theory of developmental competence can explain the behavior of individuals, and the nature of institutions, to the extent that they are products of the appropriate reform efforts, accepted as improvements by those with a commitment to the institution.

In bargaining, for example, we can distinguish two points of view, one of the players, governed by a desire to do as well as possible in the game, and one of the referee (see Luce and Raiffa 1957), governed by a desire to resolve the conflict cheaply, fairly, and effectively. Schelling's (1960) study of the convergence of expectations on the obvious or conspicuous point and Fisher and Ury's (1981) emphasis on the role of objective standards in bargaining give some content to our conception of a referee's impartial perspective. The task of the referee is to constitutionalize bargaining by applying a developmental understanding of the bargaining situation.

This contrast between two perspectives, one manipulative and the other impartial, can be seen also at a macroinstitutional level in the study of politico-economic systems. Such systems can be seen as nothing more than products of battles among conflicting interests. Some pluralists, and much of the public choice literature, take this view. Politico-economic systems are seen from the players' perspective, with each player aiming to win. But political economies can also be seen from the "referee's" perspective, in which the point is not to win, but to develop institutions acceptable to those with a strong commitment and a deep understanding of them. We see collective decisions in these systems more as exercises in impartial problem solving than as products of manipulative politics.

Both for bargaining and for politico-economic systems we can distinguish two basic perspectives that reflect the two forms of active competence, one manipulative, the other developmental. For both forms of competence we can further establish a continuum from the most local to the most general. Local competence involves the mastery of unique institutions and historical situations. It is a mastery that does not travel: playing chess well does not guarantee that we will succeed in any other game and mastering organizational politics in one setting may not be useful in another. Local competence is the usual subject of citizen education—the goal is to explain the local institutions among which the educated citizen will live and in which she might participate. But not all competence is local in this way. Some lessons do travel well. There are general skills of game playing, of bureaucratic politics, and much more. The most generic aspects of manipulative competence make up a general mastery of power. The most generic aspects of developmental competence, on the other hand, consist of the least institution-specific lessons in institutional design, a kind of generic competence of a citizen.

The research goal of constitutionalism, as I see it, is to develop an account of the active forms of competence with regard to institutions, both manipulative and developmental. Generic constitutionalism restricts itself to the most *generic* forms. But this is just one aspect of a broader distinctive feature of generic constitutionalism. In every way it attempts to remake the constitutionalist tradition by raising old ideas to a higher level of abstraction and then generalizing them.

The narrowest and oldest constitutionalism centered on limiting government by legal standards. Over centuries a number of more general design principles, such as the separation of powers, were added. Constitutionalism was now, as Friedrich (1963) defined it, "an institutionalized system of effective regularized restraints on government action." But the process of limiting power is fundamentally the same in public and private organizations (cf. Selznick 1969), and thus the category to which the constitutionalist ideal applies must be broader than government itself.

Power (governmental, corporate, or otherwise) can be limited by countervailing power or by impartial standards and rules. The first of these, countervailing power, is the main source of restraint in a pure pluralist or corporatist system. Working alone it produces a shifting balance based on unstable compromises. Impartial standards, by contrast, introduce into politics both principle and the rule of law. They are a very distinct type of political resource.

We can distinguish two pure types of political resources. *Private* resources come "attached" to the parties making a decision, individuals or groups, no matter what alternative they favor. *Public* resources come "attached" to the alternatives among which a decision needs to be made, no matter who favors those alternatives—impartial standards are an example. Most discussions of political resources are about private resources, such as money, organization, connections, information, education, and weapons. But if we think of a resource as anything that can influence a collective decision, then these are not the only resources. The obviousness of an alternative, and the persuasiveness of the arguments favoring it, are resources as well; they, too, can have an effect on outcomes.

A system of collective decisions (anything from a bargaining game to the modern state) is constitutionalized when the effect of public resources is strengthened, and when the effect of private resources is weakened, or when private power is put in the service of public standards. Weakening of private resources brings the system closer to political equality among decision participants. Strengthening of impartial standards, on the other hand, increases the inequality among alternatives. The system is not neutral between them, but favors those alternatives which are either supported by persuasive justifications or are easy to agree on.

Constitutionalist Elements of Moral Competence

Constitutionalism puts power in the service of public resources, both moral and institutional. It gives maximal effect to the limited supply of virtue.[5] But daily experience indicates both how difficult this task is and how easily it deteriorates into its opposite. Moral ideals and beliefs come to be distorted and, in this distorted form, serve as simple instruments of power, manipulating human minds, legitimizing unjust regimes, and more. The literature here is long, with

---

5. For more elaboration, see Sunstein's essay in this volume.

Nietzsche, Gramsci, and Foucault among the classic sources. In light of these insights of twentieth-century social science, how could power ever be put in the service of morality? Is not morality, rather, just one more instrument of power?

Much of what people ordinarily think of as morality may be indeed a simple instrument of power, because it is distorted for instrumental use. There is not much point putting power in the service of *that* kind of morality. Constitutionalism is meaningful only if we can find moral standards that are *not* distorted in this way and that are not simply weapons of power. I have elsewhere outlined an empirical research program designed to describe the objective aspects of morality (see also Nagel 1986). It is an effort to investigate the sources of persuasive force of moral arguments (Sołtan 1987). Two hypotheses of this research are most directly relevant to a constitutionalist program, hence I will discuss them briefly here. The first concerns the diversity of the moral standards that have real force; they can be procedural and formal, not just substantive. The second concerns the self-limiting nature of moral ideals, a consequence of combining procedural and substantive standards.

Substantive moral ideals, allowing us to distinguish better outcomes based on the content of those outcomes, are not the only ideals. Some alternatives are better because of the procedures used in choosing them, independent of the content of the alternatives themselves. Outcomes of a fair lottery are the standard example. They are better than other possible outcomes simply because they were produced by a fair procedure; content has nothing to do with it. The outcome is fair, because the procedure is fair. The result is what Rawls has called "pure procedural justice" (Rawls 1971).

The association with pure procedural justice, and with some popular arguments in favor of markets (e.g., Hayek 1973–79), gives too narrow an impression of the applicability of procedural standards. They are also the foundation of all arguments from authority, arguments in favor of an alternative not because of what it is, but because of how it was chosen, or who favors it. The procedure in question may require deference to *one* authority. Thus, within a traditional monarchy, it counts in favor of an alternative that the king has commanded it, not because what the king commands is always a good idea, but because following the king's commands (whatever they may be) is a good idea.

Traditional monarchy has not stood up well to rational scrutiny, but other procedures for collective decisions do stand up well. Elected presidents and legislatures replace kings, but the form of argument remains the same. Whatever is chosen through the authoritative procedure is better (other things being equal) than other outcomes, which have not been so chosen. A good part of the self-restraint achieved in contemporary institutional design is obtained in this way: through procedural standards and by arguments from authority.[6] But procedural ideals do not have a monopoly.

One way to detect the *mixing* of procedural and substantive ideals is to observe variations in the *demand* for justification. In decisions with strong procedural justification, the demand for substantive justification will be weaker. Similarly, in decisions with strong substantive justification, the demand for procedural justification will be weaker.

In situations where the substantively right outcome is obvious, proper procedures will matter less as long as the outcome is reached. Thus in tribal societies with a strong community consensus on the relevant customs, there will be limited demand for the development of "proper" procedures. Authority systems will be weak, and there will be little chance for the development of anything like a system of liberal democracy. In that context, what Hart (1961) has called the primary rules of custom will be sufficient to constrain the power of narrow interests. There will be little demand for the articulation, or imposition, of appropriate procedural secondary rules. But when consensus on custom breaks down, the demand for procedural justification will grow, and the appropriate kind of secondary rules are likely to develop. This is, in Hart's view, the essence of the transition from custom to law.

We have a parallel situation with the demand for substantive justification. When procedural justification is strong, every chosen alternative will have strong justification, and there will be little reason to show that one alternative is better than others. Thus for a broad range of decisions little substantive moral justification is required. We are—so to speak—free to do what we want: dance in the streets, buy and eat a chocolate bar, enjoy a Beethoven symphony. We are not morally required in doing these things to show that no morally better use of our resources (time, money, dancing shoes) was available. Little substantive justification is demanded or expected.

But other actions, whose procedural justification is weak, do require substantive justification. When our actions violate the rights of others, for example, we must show that our choice is better than the available alternatives. A decision-making system that violates the rights of individuals without sufficient substantive justification has

---

6. Mainly the authority of democratic procedures and those protecting individual liberties.

been traditionally known as a tyranny. What we see here, therefore, is a moral ideal whose essential aspiration is the reduction of tyranny.

"Reduce tyranny!" is a close relative of the venerable slogan of the past, "Death to the tyrant!" but it is far broader in its application. It is not a slogan of a revolutionary mob, but the aspiration of all morality. It is meant to constrain not just the ruler, but every decision maker. It is a hypothesis about the basic structure of morality put forward by generic constitutionalism, a structure that mixes procedural and substantive ideals. But the origins of the idea are quite a bit more specific and concrete.

The conscious effort to reduce tyranny is first directed against government. Its chief instruments are the rule of law and the institution of due process, a set of procedures (including the independence of courts) which limits governments' ability to arbitrarily harm individuals. The basic idea of due process can be developed in a number of ways. First, protection from individual *acts* of government is not the only protection from coercion called for. Tyrannical laws are even more of a threat than tyrannical acts, and we need to be protected against them. This kind of generalization can be seen, for example, in the history of American constitutional law. Due process provisions of the Fifth and Fourteenth amendments have repeatedly been interpreted broadly as protecting not only against individual governmental acts but also laws. "Procedural due process" has tended to evolve into "substantive due process."

A different kind of generalization of the due process idea had its origin in the recognition that protection from government is not the only protection from tyrannical power. Private power as well as public power can be coercive, and due process or the rule of law can be used to protect against both. This recognition can be seen in some changes in American private law, including the increasing willingness of judges to interfere with privately negotiated terms of contract, using the doctrine of unconscionability and others, and the development of labor law to incorporate elements of industrial democracy and industrial rule of law into the internal workings of private corporations (Selznick 1969; Stone 1981).

One can think of generic constitutionalism as simply one further step in the generalization of the due process idea. It aims to limit power in many ways, not necessarily through law, and to provide protection from all forms of arbitrary power, large scale (as in a government or corporation) or small (as in a bargaining game). Furthermore, it is not *simply* a normative ideal and a political program. We have also a constitutionalist research program, which studies the basic skills required to constitute self-limiting institutions.

Constitutionalism applies the idea of self-limitation first to government, then to significant power wherever it may be found. But finally it applies it to morality and to other ideals; their power, too, should be self-limiting. The constitutionalist alternative to the populist slogan "all power to the people" is "all power to no one." Even the highest moral ideals are not to be trusted with unlimited power. Human nature being fallible and prone to error, it is rational (Heiner 1983) to adopt rigid rules, whether in pursuit of self-interest or in the most selfless pursuit of ideals. Thus in addition to procedure or authority, and to substantive ideals, we should accept the restraint of form.

The effort to balance substantive, formal, and procedural considerations lies at the core of the rule of law. In its most general form the legal ideal is to reduce arbitrariness (Selznick 1969) by providing persuasive, rational, and impartial justifications for public decisions. But what gives law its distinctive flavor is the combination of arguments used in this effort. Courts do not simply search for a solution that would be most fair, or that would best serve the public purpose; they are restrained in that search by the requirement of formality and generality. Case-by-case equity is sacrificed to the rigidity of legal standards. More important, courts are obligated in their decision making to use the authoritative sources of law. Decisions of the Congress or Parliament have authority not because these bodies are invariably wise, but because such are the accepted law-making procedures. Courts are thus constrained both by authority and by form. But the rule of law does not substitute authority and form for substantive standards; it requires, rather, a balance among all three.

The development of constitutional law in the United States provides an example of how this balance is maintained, and of the tensions that cannot be avoided. Form is provided by the explicit authoritative text of the Constitution. The text is determined by the constitution-making procedure, the true framer of the U.S. Constitution. And implicit in the Constitution is a constitutionalist ideal, but one not precise and visible enough to be effective on its own. The text makes the ideal effective, but also transforms it, giving it a concrete shape and identity, which the ideal could not possess (thus, e.g., the president has to be at least 35 years old). But the ideal gives moral power to the text, can guide its interpretation, and hence determine its ultimate effect.

Thus we have the three elements central to the U.S. Constitution, the ingredients out of which constitutional debates are constructed. The element of procedure or authority is represented in the guise of the "intent of the framers." It must be seen in light of the actual *text* of the legal document. But the Constitution is neither simply commands of long-dead people nor the dead letter of the law; it is a "living Constitution," whose spirit and life are given by many specific constitutional doctrines and by the more general developing notions of the constitutionalist ideal. This ideal develops in a variety of ways and in a variety of contexts, constitutions being only one. It can become over time less bound by the limitations of particular institutions and particular historical situations, less distorted by particular interests, or by the emotions and prejudices of the moment. And, finally, it can become more general. So, in the end, the constitutionalism within the Constitution and the constitutionalism within the rule of law are only special cases and particular examples, parts of a grander edifice.

A Constitutionalist Political Program

A Political Program

Any constitutionalist program of reform is likely to be centered on the rule of law. Generic constitutionalism adds only a more general and abstract understanding of the rule of law ideal, an ideal whose distinctive quality is the balance it requires among substantive, procedural, and formal considerations. On the procedural side we need effective democracy and effective markets, both instruments of popular control. On the formal side, we need more extensive codification of state institutions and functions. The combination of these amounts to a politico-economic regime akin to Lowi's "juridical democracy": strengthening rules, limiting discretion, and concentrating power in democratically elected legislatures (Lowi 1979).[7] This is a program for moral skeptics, for those who have lost faith in the possibility of achieving or approximating more substantive ideals through the operation of political and economic institutions (see Brand 1988). A more fully balanced constitutionalist program goes beyond juridical democracy to incorporate more directly substantive ideals ranging from justice and rights, to the protection of the ecological niche within which the human species can survive and prosper (cf. Dryzek 1987).

When applied to liberal and market-based democratic regimes, a generic constitutionalist program of reform is distinguished from its competitors by the aspiration to maintain a balance among substantive, procedural, and formal standards. The competitors typically de-

---

7. A constitutionalist program of reform for France is sketched by Cohen-Tanugi (1985). His focus is on building legal institutions independent of the state.

mand, by contrast, either simply more democracy, or simply more markets, or simply more general and rigid rules.

Generic constitutionalism is also distinctive in its reach. It should encourage the same process of constitutionalization in the private sphere, especially within the private corporation. Much progress in this direction has already been achieved (see Selznick 1969). We have observed an evolution in private organizations toward what Selznick has called a "common law of governance" applicable to both private and public institutions and based on the core idea of due process.

Some have claimed that further progress along these lines is blocked within capitalism (Stone 1981). A fully constitutionalized corporation is inconsistent, according to these authors, with private ownership of the means of production. Even if we admit, for purposes of argument, that the fuller constitutionalization of corporations is inconsistent with the private ownership of *corporations,* its inconsistency with capitalism does not follow. Let us grant that the arbitrary power of top management cannot be sufficiently restrained by market forces (see, e.g., Lindblom 1977; Bowles and Gintis 1986). Stronger internal controls, including perhaps election of some top officials by employees, seem the most likely alternative. This appears to be possible even within the current system of private ownership of corporations (through Employee Stock Ownership Plans [ESOPs] and other arrangements), but suppose (for the sake of argument) that it is *not* possible. State ownership or "social" ownership of corporations would still not be our only alternatives.

If we move away from private ownership of corporations, we need not adopt other forms of the ownership of corporations in its place. We can move rather toward a system in which corporations are *not legally owned* in any straightforward sense at all, where stock owners as residual claimants do not have (necessarily) the ultimate right to control. The means of production would remain privately held, and thus capitalism could be preserved. The means of production would be held by private corporations, as they are predominantly in contemporary capitalism. The corporations would be private, since they would be owned neither by the state nor by society. They would not be *owned* at all (in the current legal sense). Corporate stock could be converted to new kinds of bonds (in which the lender shares more of the risk of the enterprise and accepts more variable returns). Private ownership of productive property would be maintained (corporations would own this property), even as ownership of that abstract legal entity called a corporation would be modified or eliminated.

Beyond the sphere of private organization, constitutionalism can reach further into the small scale of social interaction, into bargaining, for example. We need simply to restrain by more objective standards the manipulative politics that take place in negotiation. In doing so we replace what Fisher and Ury (1981) have called positional bargaining with what they have called principled bargaining, a strategy that treats the bargaining situation as a common search, using objective standards, for solutions to a shared problem.

A Social Movement

A constitutionalist program can be pursued in a variety of ways. But however it is pursued, it depends for success on our willingness to sacrifice for political ideals. We need some organizational instrument that activates and makes effective human idealism. In recent political thought, participatory democracy is most commonly proposed as a means for such activation. Since participation in democratic decisions seems better suited for small-scale settings, reformers have focused on workplace or industrial democracy and participatory democracy in local politics (Barber 1984; Elkin 1987). Neither is likely to achieve the ends sought, however. Participatory democracy too often amounts to tiresome and boring committee meetings, more likely to exhaust both body and mind than to inspire idealism. But even when participatory democracy is not simply too boring, it will more often provide an education not in principled but in manipulative politics, and this could hardly encourage idealism.

As part of the generic constitutionalist idea I would like to suggest a specific substitute for participatory democracy as an instrument to preserve and enhance civic virtue: participation in social movements whose aim is to change institutions, rather than in decision-making institutions themselves. The activation and promotion of idealism has a better chance to succeed in constitutionalized, self-limiting social movements on the model of Gandhi and King, than in participatory democracy. The economic and commercial goals of governments are best pursued in markets, with the government (for the most part) out of the way. The same is true for the development and pursuit of loftier ideals. We should develop separate institutions that specialize in this function, and self-limiting social movements à la Gandhi are a very promising start.

The aims of social movements designed to exercise pressure can be restricted more radically than the aims of decision-making bodies. It is easier to exclude those tasks in which ideals can most easily be distorted and manipulated. In decision-making institutions certain things simply have to be done, whether or not they provide an occasion for manipulative politics. Thus, for example, a state must have a tax code, no matter what form of politics tax legislation occasions.

A social movement, by contrast, can more easily refrain from action entirely. A self-limiting, constitutionalist social movement does not simply refrain from violence, it can be self-limiting in other respects as well. It can limit itself, for example, to *obviously* just goals (or moral "self-evident truths"), about which moral disagreement is so minimal that manipulative politics cannot hide (as it so often does) behind a mask of moral dispute. The goals need not be large, but they must be obviously just.

Participatory democracy dissipates the energies of idealism because it is forced to attempt too much; it is unable to focus moral energies. A social movement, by contrast, can take as a model Gandhi's campaign to destroy the British monopoly on salt production, or Martin Luther King's campaign to integrate lunch counters. A limited goal, like these two, when it is part of the larger constitutionalist task of putting power in the service of morality, can both activate and focus moral energies. It is a strategy that may not work well if a movement's whole purpose is *simply* to achieve the limited goal at hand. Few will care enough, then, to be willing to sacrifice. But when the limited goal is clearly seen as a way to focus moral energies, it can be more effective.

The Goal of Limited Sovereignty

If we look at the broader historical context we can see the constitutionalist tradition as one of two possible paths away from traditional monarchy. The *populist* path transfers sovereignty (at least symbolically) to the people; the *constitutionalist* path limits sovereignty. Populism is built on an illusion. Sovereignty, in its classical sense—the unilateral habit of obedience, as Austin ([1861–63]1970) defined it—cannot possibly be transferred to the people. Both popular sovereignty and its economic counterpart, consumer sovereignty, are myths. The difficulties with the idea of popular sovereignty are now more fully clarified thanks to the work of Arrow and other social choice theorists (see Riker 1982). The idea of consumer sovereignty is simply a nonstarter, and *not* because real markets are different from the ideal markets of economic theory.

In an ideal, perfectly competitive market there is nothing like consumer sovereignty, and there should not be. If consumers were really *sovereign*, surely all goods would be free, since consumers prefer it that way. But goods in a market are not free. If consumers were sovereign we would observe them issuing *commands*. But we do not see that either. The distinctive virtue of (perfectly competitive) markets is that *no one* is sovereign. Everyone is a price taker, and no one can influence the market. Markets are built out of exchanges, not commands, and they undermine (not establish) habits of obedience. In a market, both supply and demand determine exchange rates. A system based on consumer sovereignty would require, by contrast, an economy driven entirely by demand.

Where, then, have we gone wrong? We have simply been blinded by a populist framework. Markets eliminate, or drastically diminish, tendencies toward *producer* sovereignty, which are strong when productive enterprises have monopoly powers. But the alternative to producer sovereignty is *not* consumer sovereignty, but *no* sovereignty at all. Instead of transferring the habits of obedience to new parties, we destroy them or radically limit them. Thus markets as sovereignty limiters are a vivid example of a *constitutionalist* institution, which can only be misinterpreted in a populist framework.

The ideal of limiting sovereignty provides us with another, perhaps most inclusive, angle on the political program of constitutionalism. To limit sovereignty today means to expand "interference in the internal affairs of states," since states are the sovereign entities of contemporary politics. This does not lead to tolerance of large states bullying the small. But it does support those institutions that limit state sovereignty in a way that promotes larger and less parochial goals, most notably free trade in the economic sphere and the free operation of international social movements such as Amnesty International.

One final point, possibly the most important of all, must be made, though it cannot be discussed adequately in the confines of this essay. The constitutionalist goal of limited sovereignty applies on the largest scale as well as on the smallest. It urges us to accept the *limited* sovereignty of mankind on earth, in accordance with the limited life-sustaining capacity of our natural environment. The grand constitutionalist theme of self-limitation is also (and perhaps most of all) an environmentalist theme. The politics it demands is the politics of ecological balance, recognizing and accepting mankind's limited role in the natural environment.

REFERENCES

Arendt, Hannah. 1963. *On Revolution*. New York: Viking.
Austin, John. (1861–63) 1970. *The Province of Jurisprudence Determined*. 2d ed. New York: Franklin.

Barber, Benjamin. 1984. *Strong Democracy*. Berkeley and Los Angeles: University of California Press.
Becker, Gary. 1976. *The Economic Approach to Human Behavior*. Chicago: University of Chicago Press.
Bowles, Samuel, and Herbert Gintis. 1986. *Democracy and Capitalism*. New York: Basic.
Brand, Donald. 1988. *Corporatism and the Rule of Law*. Ithaca, N.Y.: Cornell University Press.
Cohen-Tanugi, Laurent. 1985. *Le droit sans l'état: Sur la démocratie en France et en Amérique* [Law without the State: On Democracy in France and America]. Paris: Presses Universitaires de France.
Dahl, Robert. 1982. *Dilemmas of Pluralist Democracy*. New Haven, Conn.: Yale University Press.
Dryzek, John. 1987. *Rational Ecology*. Oxford: Blackwell.
Dworkin, Ronald. 1977. *Taking Rights Seriously*. Cambridge, Mass.: Harvard University Press.
Elkin, Stephen. 1987. *City and Regime in the American Republic*. Chicago: University of Chicago Press.
Elster, Jon. 1979. *Ulysses and the Sirens: Studies in Rationality and Irrationality*. Cambridge: Cambridge University Press.
Fisher, Roger, and William Ury. 1981. *Getting to Yes*. Boston: Houghton-Mifflin.
Friedrich, Carl. 1963. *Man and His Government*. New York: McGraw-Hill.
Giddens, Anthony. 1984. *The Constitution of Society*. Berkeley and Los Angeles: University of California Press.
Hacking, Ian, ed. 1981. *Scientific Revolutions*. Oxford: Oxford University Press.
Hart, H. L. A. 1961. *The Concept of Law*. Oxford: Clarendon Press.
Hayek, Friedrich. 1973–79. *Law, Legislation and Liberty*. 3 vols. Chicago: University of Chicago Press.
Heiner, Ronald. 1983. "The Origins of Predictable Behavior." *American Economic Review* 73:560–95.
Holmes, Oliver W. 1897. "The Path of the Law." *Harvard Law Review* 10:457–78.
Homans, George. 1974. *Social Behavior: Its Elementary Forms*, rev. ed. New York: Harcourt, Brace, Jovanovich.
Horvat, Branko. 1982. *The Political Economy of Socialism*. Armonk, N.Y.: Sharpe.
Kaminski, Bartlomiej, and Karol Sołtan. 1989. "The Evolution of Communism." *International Political Science Review* 10:371–91.
Lindblom, Charles. 1977. *Politics and Markets*. New York: Basic Books.
Lowi, Theodore. 1979. *The End of Liberalism: The Second Republic of the United States*. 2d ed. New York: W. W. Norton.

Luce, R. Duncan, and Howard Raiffa. 1957. *Games and Decisions.* New York: Wiley.
Margolis, Howard. 1982. *Selfishness, Altruism, and Rationality.* Chicago: University of Chicago Press.
Merton, Robert. 1957. *Social Theory and Social Structure.* Glencoe, Ill.: Free Press.
Nagel, Thomas. 1986. *The View from Nowhere.* New York: Oxford University Press.
Olson, Mancur. 1965. *The Logic of Collective Action.* Cambridge, Mass.: Harvard University Press.
———. 1982. *The Rise and Decline of Nations.* New Haven, Conn.: Yale University Press.
Parsons, Talcott. 1937. *The Structure of Social Action.* New York: McGraw-Hill.
Rawls, John. 1971. *A Theory of Justice.* Cambridge, Mass.: Harvard University Press.
Ricci, David. 1984. *The Tragedy of Political Science.* New Haven, Conn.: Yale University Press.
Riker, William. 1982. *Liberalism against Populism.* San Francisco: Freeman.
Schelling, Thomas. 1960. *The Strategy of Conflict.* Cambridge, Mass.: Harvard University Press.
Selznick, Philip. 1969. *Law, Society and Industrial Justice.* New York: Sage.
Sen, Amartya. 1977. "Rational Fools: A Critique of the Behavioral Foundations of Economic Theory." *Philosophy and Public Affairs* 6:317–44.
Simon, Herbert. 1969. *The Sciences of the Artificial.* Cambridge, Mass.: MIT Press.
Skinner, B. F. 1953. *Science and Human Behavior.* New York: Macmillan.
———. 1976. *Walden Two.* New York: Macmillan.
Sołtan, Karol Edward. 1987. *The Causal Theory of Justice.* Berkeley and Los Angeles: University of California Press.
Stinchcombe, Arthur. 1968. *Constructing Social Theories.* New York: Harcourt, Brace & World.
Stone, Katherine. 1981. "The Post-War Paradigm in American Labor Law." *Yale Law Journal* 90:1509–80.
Taylor, Frederick. 1947. *Principles of Scientific Management.* New York: Norton.
Unger, Roberto Mangabeira. 1987. *Politics: A Work in Constructive Social Theory.* Cambridge: Cambridge University Press.
Vico, Giambattista. (1744) 1948. *The New Science.* Ithaca, N.Y.: Cornell University Press.
Weber, Max. 1949. *The Methodology of the Social Sciences.* New York: Free Press.

CHAPTER FIVE

Pragmatic Liberalism, the Rule of Law, and the Pluralist Regime

CHARLES W. ANDERSON

A Critique of Pure Liberalism

CLASSIC LIBERALISM takes as legitimate only those public actions that can be derived from principles that are impartial among human wants, interests, and conceptions of the good. In another sense, to justify a public policy in liberal thought is to show that it arises from, or would logically arise from, the reflective, autonomous choices of individuals, equally considered. Straightforward as this seems, these are contentious tests of political propriety. Precisely what is required for a rule to be regarded as impartial? Or for an act of individual will to be certified as reflective, autonomous, and "equally considered"? It is in trying to interpret these criteria that all the basic conflicts of liberal thought—and liberal politics—arise.

Furthermore, classic liberalism, as a matter of method, insisted on the most strenuous ground rules for the justification of principles, or public policies. The product of a Cartesian worldview, in which any claim to knowledge, or any conception of the human good, had to be demonstrated to the complete satisfaction of the skeptical intellect, it placed an impossible burden of proof on the proponent of collective action. Taken in the strictest sense, the intellectual challenge that classic liberalism thought it had to meet was to prove the rational necessity of a unique set of principles of right order. And this it could not do. It is possible to create systems of liberalism, but liberalism has never been reduced to a system. And by setting the test of certifiable knowledge and legitimate public purpose so high, classic liberalism was in peril of suggesting that anything was plausible and, hence, anything was permitted (Spragens 1981). Once that implication was recognized, the quest began—at least in those twentieth-century forms of philosophy and political thought with which we are here concerned—for criteria of knowledge and legitimate public action that were attainable by human reason and in human experience.

There is a less demanding standard of legitimate political action that arises from the classical tradition: the simple test of rational consistency, in which we justify public decisions by invoking a universalizable rule that we are willing to apply to future cases of the same kind. In effect, we purchase our principles on a line of credit extended against future decisions. The particular content of the principles to be invoked is not specified. To many, this seems an arid formalism, but it gives us more of a foothold on the problem than one might suspect. If it is nothing else, liberalism is a long struggle against tyranny, and tyranny is authority that is self-serving, capricious, whimsical, erratic, or unexplained. As Philip Selznick (1969, 12) says, the essential purpose of law in liberal society is to reduce the degree of arbitrariness in human affairs.

This is also the essence of Hayek's (1960, 56–59) idea of "the rule of law." The task of liberal politics is the creation of a reliable, predictable, consistent framework for action in which individuals can work out their plans and projects with some assurance concerning their prospects for success. In a universe of danger, flux, and transitoriness, the task of politics is to create a rational order as a prerequisite of human freedom and intelligent action. Rational order is also a condition of justice, for if the outcomes of human choices and actions are to be deserved, they must arise from intention, effort, and plan, not random fortune or luck.

Liberalism means acting on principle. But if it is possible to construct multiple coherent systems of liberal principles, if we can, with integrity, act on diverse values to diverse ends within the liberal order, where are we then?

To act as a liberal in the classic sense is to apply some general maxim to each situation of public choice. It is to say that, at the margin and in the absence of other compelling considerations, one will adopt the policy that will best assure an outcome that reflects individual free choices registered through marketlike arrangements, or the policy that will yield the greatest aggregate social utility, or one that will best reflect the deliberate will of those concerned, or one that will be of greatest benefit to the least well-off, without infringing on individual liberties.

In effect, then, to justify a public decision, to show that our choices are grounded in impartial norms rather than in personal proclivity or interest, is to identify with some liberal program, some ideology for the gradual transformation of society toward a hypothetical idea of personal autonomy, social efficiency, or human equality.

If we cannot do this, then our public choices are to some extent arbitrary or expedient.

But if we can point to the principle that informs our judgments, other citizens will know "where we stand." They can support us or oppose us electorally according to their "preferences" concerning the rules that should be applied consistently to all issues of public concern. Politics, then, is to be played out among the adherents of clearly defined doctrines. In office, those elected adherents will do their best to put their ideals into practice. They are properly evaluated by asking whether their policies can be shown to be directed by their principles. To many, this would be the essence of responsible democratic government. Others will suspect a hint of irony.

A corollary of all of this is that we are expected to know our principles before we enter the public debate. We are not fit for political participation, for citizenship, until we have formulated a systematic philosophy, a coherent ordering of principles. Those who are uncertain or skeptical, those who entertain some doubts about matters of ultimate conviction, are in no position to evaluate the conduct of public affairs. Acting on principle means *having* principles, and all in good order before the occasion of action. At least, that seems the clear implication of all forms of classic, rationalist, liberal philosophy and political economy.[1]

For the pragmatic liberal, this seems both an unrealistic and an excessively formal approach to the problem. We do not necessarily know our principles in advance of action. Perhaps we should not. A working political philosophy is forged through the years, in successive efforts to match general norms to experience.[2] The very issue for liberal (as for scientific) reasoning is to define the nature of a configuration of circumstances by subsuming it under a general rule, to *discover* the principle that fits the case.

Liberal theory is normally written at a high level of abstraction. It is conventionally addressed to the most general questions of political order. It is as though citizens were always to be imagined as members of a constitutional assembly, perennially debating the constitutive principles of the regime. It is as though we could, at any time, start over again, on new foundations.

In fact, we normally enter public life in midstream, seldom at the

---

1. This case is often made in policy theory. See, e.g., Yates (1981, 32–51), Paris and Reynolds (1983), MacRae (1976).

2. Even Ronald Dworkin (1978, 105–30) speaks of a judge's "emerging" judicial philosophy. One does not wait until one's philosophy is complete before accepting a position on the bench.

WTDC Mansfield
Building Control

10Apr1

beginning. We are seized with responsibility for a concrete undertaking: the construction of a road, the reform of a tax, the redefinition of the rights and duties that attach to a pattern of human action. The issue for political *thought* is to appraise the project in the light of primary political values, and, to *find* the point on which the decision must turn, the crucial consideration that defines—and justifies—the appropriate course of action.

Put another way, we are concerned with the relation of theory to practice. Public problems arise in relation to some organized pattern of human action, some pattern of practice. In this society we evaluate such human endeavors in the light of liberal values. Our *political* concerns run to some deficiency, something problematic, in a pattern of practice. In one case, it may be an issue of social efficiency, in another of equity, in a third, of the arbitrariness of authority. It is in this sense that principles emerge from a consideration of practice.

A Defense of Pragmatic Liberalism

To pose the alternative to classical liberalism is to restate a conception of practical political reason that gradually emerged in the American mind in the first decades of this century. I call this *pragmatic liberalism*, to stress continuity with a philosophic tradition. (To use the term *progressive liberalism* would be to pay respects to a partisan or ideological tradition.) This is an approach to political thinking that arose both as a critique of the excessively individualist, mechanical, and atomistic logic of classical liberalism and as a response to the institutional developments of twentieth-century life, the "social facts," as Oliver Wendell Holmes would have called them, of organization and complexity. However, this is not an effort at historical reconstruction. I am not trying to be faithful to the ideas of Dewey, Commons, Veblen, and the rest. Rather, I am trying to restate and to carry forward a line of argument that we somehow lost track of, to reconstruct it and to show its pertinence to the problems of contemporary liberal politics.

Both terms in the phrase "pragmatic liberalism" are important. "Pragmatism" alone too easily connotes expedience, or, even in serious philosophical usage, a rather tough-minded relativist instrumentalism. "Liberalism," taken by itself, may suggest an arid abstract formalism, an emphasis on pure norms of impartial procedure, divorced from all substantive concerns. Taken together, however, the terms suggest a method of political analysis of peculiar rigor and subtlety.

Pragmatic liberalism is concerned with the application of liberal principles to the various forms of organized social action, the collective "ways of doing things" that emerge and evolve to give form and content to liberal society, which is otherwise no more than formal framework. We scrutinize and criticize these associations and undertakings in the light of liberal values. Here, we say, is an industry that is not as productive as it might be: it could contribute more to aggregate social efficiency. Medical practitioners, we propose, may be lax in providing patients with full information about the implications of drugs and procedures, and "informed consent" is an essential feature of contractual probity. The employment policies of that university may be in some respects arbitrary, and that offends against liberal norms of justice. Pragmatic liberalism presumes that there is a "public" dimension to institutions and associations that are generally distinguished as "private" in classic liberalism. For pragmatic liberalism, all human associations are ways of performing a public function and all are properly evaluated by the norms of public life.

This means that the governance of the enterprise is as appropriate a subject for political thought as the governance of the state. It means that the performance of such a concern is to be construed not simply as the product of market forces but is a matter of policy, a policy that arises from a process of deliberation and criticism and is essentially political in character in that it culminates, in rules of good practice, a conception of standardized performance that becomes determinative for the society. The implication is that such rules of good practice are properly subject to continuing scrutiny, not only by the practitioners or professionals but by the public generally. This does not mean that all human activities become subject to detailed regulation by the state. The process of refining the norms of practice is normally vested in the communities of practice themselves. But, as we shall see, this does provide a warrant for a more active and differentiated state role than is usually associated with classic liberalism, and it implies that the basic liberal conception of the rule of law applies to private governments as well as to the state.

All of this implies that pragmatic liberalism endorses a pluralistic conception of the legitimate regime, in the full and classic meaning of the term.

The Rational Enterprise and the Pluralist Regime

Every political theory must begin from some notion of fundamental constitutional order, a conception of the legitimate regime. For all versions of liberalism, the basic model for social organization is the idea of *contract*. Forms of collective endeavor are legitimate insofar as they can be shown to arise in response to individual will and interest. In the formative years of liberalism, the law of contract, once understood as pertaining primarily to business transactions, expanded to become the basic metaphor for all social organizations (Friedmann 1972, 120). The family, the church, the club, and the firm were all to be understood as forms of voluntary contract, as was the state itself, which was presumed to arise out of an initial bargain, a social contract, among consenting individuals.

If *contract* described the statics of legitimate order, the market described its dynamics. If a perfectly competitive market could allocate goods and services so as, ideally, to fit the expressed preferences of individuals, then, analogously, a free market for scientific, artistic, and cultural programs, for religion, for all forms of human endeavor, would reach equilibrium in a pattern of social order better expressive of the deliberate wills of individuals than any comprehensive plan could devise.

It is a first premise of any kind of liberalism that the state should not be the architect of social order. Rather, the "constitution," in the classic sense of the term, will evolve out of institutions formed through the deliberate choices of individuals.

Pragmatic liberalism, to be sure, accepted the ideas of contract and the market as "ideals of natural order,"[3] as prototypes for the appraisal and criticism of established tradition, practice, and usage. However, it also acknowledged that the primitive contractual context was a transient state of affairs. Once the bargain was made, an institution came into being (a "growing concern" in John R. Commons's [1968] language) with characteristics far different from those of the ideal contractual situation. One no longer created something new from voluntary, reciprocally calculated choice. Rather, one now *joined* an ongoing endeavor and adapted one's preferences, as consumer, employee, practitioner, to the logic of "good practice," to the rationalized "way of doing things" that was emerging within the enterprise. Such institutions were only partially responsive to individual will. They were basically justified by their capacity to provide a valued service or performance predictably, systematically, rationally.

Pragmatic liberalism was to take these rational enterprises seriously. They were very much a distinctive product of this century, and they constituted a basic anomaly for the social theory of classic liberalism, which concerns itself only with the calculated choices of

---

3. The term is Stephen Toulmin's (1961, 45). It refers to the implicit, paradigmatic assumptions in any scheme of scientific expression: such as perfect, straight-line, Euclidean motion in Newtonian mechanics. Such ideals do not explain anything: rather they identify what is problematic for the theory, what needs to be explained.

atomic individuals and defines the political problem only in terms of the relationship of the individual to the state.

Pragmatic liberalism generally took a positive view of these consciously systematized, purposive associations. They represented a process of cooperative, intelligent, evolutionary adaptation that was very congenial to pragmatic notions of knowledge and action. They echoed an older, more organic conception of the regime as a constitutional configuration of functional associations. Potentially they were moral communities that could provide a sense of solidarity to compensate for the lost affinities of traditional society (as Durkheim argued.) They were, perhaps, "intermediary associations" of the kind Tocqueville admired, a buffer between state and individual, a force for political stability, and an opportunity for personal participation in political affairs. But most significantly for our purposes, such communities of practice and their attendant vocations would provide liberal society with what MacIntyre (1981) was to call a sense of virtue, of the right and wrong way of doing things in specialized, socially significant performance. Being "professional" may be the modern American's way of being ethical.

All of this suggests, as I noted earlier, a pluralist conception of the legitimate regime. Here we must define terms carefully. In popular usage, pluralism today seems to mean no more than competitive politics, as opposed to monism or totalitarianism. In conventional political science, pluralism is normally understood as a theory of the political process in which public policy is represented as the outcome of a pattern of interest group "pressure," and the state is represented as a "broker" among interests. All of this is but a thin, archaic remnant of the classic idea of the pluralist regime that was a central concern of political science in the early decades of this century.

Various theoretical controversies are associated with the idea of pluralism. Robert Dahl (1956) argued that interest group pluralism might serve as a realistic proxy for pure, participatory democracy. Galbraith (1952) suggested that the interest group system might reach a natural equilibrium of "countervailing powers." These interest group liberals suggested that the spontaneous associational processes of an open society could, like the ideal market, meet the basic liberal norm of a political order that could be certified as effectively neutral among diverse personal life plans and interests.

Others argued that it could not. Various commentators argued an inherent "bias" in pluralism that weighted the claims of the wealthy, the organized, and the active above those of the poor, the unorganized, and the disbursed. In the end, Theodore Lowi (1969) was to assert that interest group pluralism was a corruption of the liberal system, that any special relationship between state and sector was suspect, and that only a "juridical democracy," operating on the basis of impartial, general principles, was consistent with the fundamental liberal notion of rule of law. With this, the argument seemed to have gone full circle.

However, again, all of this is but a pale residue of the concerns of classic pluralist theory. To be sure, classic pluralism was never fully stated as a theory of the regime. (The main line of this tradition seems to have come to an abrupt end about 1930, probably because Mussolini's syndicalism rather discredited the essential idea in Western liberal eyes and because of the increasing irrelevance and silliness of the related Guild Socialist movement in England; see Webb 1958, 86–87). There are indeed many arcane questions once heatedly debated in this tradition—such as the "real personality" of groups—that no longer need concern us. But there are certain themes in classic pluralist theory that need restatement if we are to comprehend this alternative version of liberalism.

The crucial point is that purposive enterprises are regarded as having a public and a political character. They are part of the political order; they are constitutive features of the regime. They are public in that they perform important social functions and the terms of "practice" are properly a matter of public concern. They are political in that they create a system of rights and duties, privileges and sanctions, and a pattern of authority, and they are thus properly understood as "private governments" (see Lakoff and Rich 1973).

There is a strong claim to the autonomy of the rational enterprise in liberal thought, based both on norms of free association and contract and pragmatism's own distinctive concern for "intelligent adaptation" through collective inquiry and action. But in pragmatic liberalism, this autonomy is always qualified and conditional. The liberal norms of legitimate authority, of the rule of law, apply not only to the state, but to any organized form of social authority. There is no radical separation of the public and private realms in pragmatic liberal thought. And in pragmatic liberalism, it is not just the power of the state that is perennially suspect. Any concentration of social power may constitute a threat to private right.

The Rational Enterprise and the Rule of Law

The essence of formal liberalism is that public decisions should rest on impartial, general principles, consistently applied. The basis for this may be an innate intuition of justice, but there is a practical reason for the rule of rational consistency as well. The real problem with tyranny, with arbitrary authority, is that it makes the world an unpredictable, strange, and treacherous place. As Hayek suggests, the ultimate liberal reason for the rule of law is that it is a condition of human freedom. The object of law is to create a stable, comprehensible framework for action, one in which the individual can work out projects with some sense of their likely consequences.

Hayek applied this Kantian test of rational consistency only to the realm of public law.[4] However, it is an ideal of rationality that has far broader application. In fact, it is probably the distinctly modern conception of what rationalism means. Some think Kant's rationalism purely formal. However, understood in a certain way, it seems the foundation of our contemporary ideas of practical reason. This is not the rationalism of indisputable Cartesian proof. It is rather more congenial to the instrumental rationalism of the pragmatic tradition. And it is a conception of rationalism that unifies the realms of scientific inquiry, politics and law, and practical endeavor.

In each of these areas, the object of analysis is to reduce the personal, whimsical, capricious and arbitrary to orderly system. The purpose of science is the generation of reliable knowledge (Ziman 1968). Its goal is to render nature comprehensible, which is to say, predictable and routine.

By the same token, in the various realms of practical endeavor, as in politics and law, the object of analysis is to render human performance knowable, systematic, orderly, disciplined, and consistent and, in that sense, predictable and routine. The virtue of rationally designed laws, scientific principles, airline networks, telephone systems, and motel chains is that they will work as they are expected to when one calls on them. In medicine as in manufacture, the object of rational inquiry is to create a standard, universal, and consistent product or performance, one that functions the same way "in all relevantly similar situations."

The conditions of freedom in modern society thus depend not only on the rational consistency of law, but on that of a variety of organized, coordinated performances. Whatever the number of competing firms, the "standard practices"—of the medical system, the housing system, the agricultural system, the educational system—are not discretionary goods and services, produced by the market in response to the varying nuances of consumer demand. They are,

---

4. On Hayek's Kantianism, see Grey (1968).

rather, structured processes, products of an evolutionary collective process of rational analysis. The justification for such rational enterprises is not so much that they reflect individual will, but more that they represent a sustained effort to reduce the degree of arbitrariness in the provision of an important service.

Such enterprises belong to the public life of liberal society, and their claim to rationality, like that of the law itself, is a proper subject for public scrutiny, in the light of basic liberal values. Thus it is appropriate to appraise the universality, the equity, the impartiality of the performance of the rational enterprise. However, the proximate value for judging the legitimacy of the enterprise is efficiency itself.

Efficiency is not the same as economy. Economy merely implies that a function is carried out with a minimum of social waste, at the least cost consistent with purpose. This is, to be sure, the paramount utilitarian virtue. Efficiency, which has a closer affinity to the pragmatic version of liberalism, rather means "fittedness to purpose." This implies that means are well suited to ends. It also means that a performance can be consistently repeated: that it is reliable. Economy, then, is but one aspect of efficiency. The efficiency of a practice is properly evaluated through critical comparison of alternatives. And, once again, this is not simply a "technical" matter, an affair of experts, but is properly regarded as a topic for public deliberation. And, for reasons that should be clear, the comparative efficiency of rival practices cannot be definitively tested by relative profitability in the market.

Rational efficiency is not a particularly popular virtue among expressive intellectuals. Even Weber spoke of "the iron cage of rationalism" and deplored the "disenchantment of the world." It is true that the disciplines of reliable performance entail a certain loss of spontaneity and expressiveness. However, conscientious service seems the condition of that community-enhanced capacity for free action that is the point and purpose of liberalism. It is thus that rational efficiency is a close cousin of the rule of law. For the triumphal overture to be heard, the audience must assemble, and that means not only that someone must direct traffic, but that the oil tankers must have left port on schedule many weeks before.

In any event, the idea of rational efficiency should connote neither the numbing monotony of the assembly line nor the unctuous rigidity of narrow-minded bureaucracy. These are perversions of rational enterprise, properly subject to public criticism and, perhaps, to publicly enforced reform. To understand this, we must consider how the value of consistent, predictable performance is related to a larger ideal of collective social action in pragmatic liberalism.

The Rational Enterprise as a Community of Inquiry

The basic model of social organization in pragmatic liberalism is neither the hierarchy nor the contract but, rather, the ideal scientific society. This image is an essential link between pragmatic philosophy and pragmatic politics: Peirce's conception of knowledge as consensus among critical investigators is reflected in Dewey's (1963) understanding of democracy as intelligent collective adaptation.[5] The idea is also pertinent to the purposive enterprise. It complements and completes the idea of rationality as systematic performance. For while rationalization may connote the routine, scientific inquiry evokes an image of an open experimental system, a community consciously questioning and reexamining established doctrine, a mode of deliberation and action that seems, in many respects, distinctively political.

The legitimacy of the rational enterprise lies, then, not in the predictable routine itself but in the claim that standard practice is "best practice" as well, that it arises from a sustained self-conscious process of critical analysis of how a particular function is properly performed. The goal of the rational system is not to standardize custom or common practice but to make the exemplary case general and routine.

In liberal society, the justification for the autonomy of rational enterprise, its right to prescribe practice, is that it arises from such a systematic process of inquiry. Liberalism properly regards as equally arbitrary those actions of public effect that arise from personal caprice and those that rest on unexamined tradition or dogma.

The rational enterprise, then, is to be understood both as a delivery system and as a community of inquiry. The professional is, on the one hand, charged with carrying out a function according to the norms of collective order. On the other hand, the professional is also understood to be a contributor, potential or actual, to the community of discourse engaged in a continuing reappraisal of practice.

The idea of the community of inquiry is distinctive to pragmatic liberalism. Since it is an image both of the broader political community and the functional association, it leads to a general theory of the regime. "Community of inquiry" applies to human understanding as well as to politics, thus linking a doctrine of practical reason to broader epistemological and philosophical concerns.

As a model of political order, "community of inquiry" implies the reconciliation of certain apparent antinomies: hierarchy and democ-

---

5. On C. S. Peirce, I would start with "The Scientific Attitude and Fallibilism" (see Buchler 1955).

racy, continuity and experimentation, the rule of law and popular will. It requires both reliable performance, and as Peirce or Popper would have put it, a system "always open to further inquiry."

The community of inquiry is an ideal of rightful order. It serves as a counterpart to the ideals of contract and the market in classic liberal thought. And as no human relationship quite meets the full conditions of a free, informed contract between equals—just as no market is ever quite perfect—so no human concern ever fulfills the prototypical conditions of the ideal community of inquiry.[6] The problem then is to establish the "degree of permissible power," as John R. Commons (1968, 31–39, 325–26) once put it, to determine the extent to which actual human undertakings may deviate from the ideal.

The role of the state in relation to the pluralist enterprise thus becomes a central concern of pragmatic liberalism. This is a question of "autonomy and control" as Robert Dahl (1982) recently described it. However, this is also an area where our public deliberations are awkward and uncertain. We do not have clear notions of when there is a public interest in the performance or political order of a pluralist enterprise and when there is not. Our political language in this area is filled with strange assumptions, inhibitions, and taboos. This is an underdeveloped part of liberal thought. The agenda of progressive and pragmatic liberalism was never quite completed. This then, as Holmes might have said, is a realm where experience counts more than logic. It is an area of political argument ideally suited, not to the invocation of a priori maxims, but to the deliberate search for the rule that fits the case.

The Public Interest in an Enterprise

Some of the most perplexing problems of applying liberal theory to practice arise when we ask whether there is a public interest in an enterprise, whether it is appropriately subject to state regulation and control. Classic liberalism set stringent limits on the state, but pragmatic liberalism belongs to a tradition that understood that the creation and maintenance of the conditions of liberalism required the active assertion of public authority. And again, in this tradition, it is assumed that the issue of arbitrary authority arises not only in connection with state power, but with private power as well. The result is an

---

6. Rousseau's general will might be one version of this prototype. So might Jürgen Habermas's conception of "Communicative Competence." Habermas, one recalls, sees himself standing in a line of descent from C. S. Peirce. See McCarthy (1978).

ambiguous doctrine. Pragmatic liberalism is neither "for" the state nor "for" private interest. It strongly supports the autonomy of the diverse associations and endeavors that arise in the pluralist regime. On the other hand, pragmatic liberalism sees such associations as subject to general norms of individual right and public interest. The resolution of this tension can never take place in the abstract but only in contemplation of the particular patterns of practice that develop in the liberal polity.

The conventional ground for public intervention in pluralist undertakings is the presence of some flaw in the contractual nexus or some form of market failure. These are not unambiguous criteria. On a narrow construction, they might apply only against force and fraud in contract or collusive monopoly in the market. Many classic liberals would have it so. However, in ideal liberal theory, any disparities of power or opportunity, information or access, raise questions about the legitimacy of the contractual nexus. Costs that fall upon those other than the contracting parties, or on the commonwealth—the "externalities" of productive activity—become proper cause for public regulation. Adam Smith's category of "useful public works," appropriately the province of state action, need not be read strictly as "public goods," where costs cannot be allocated, but can be viewed in a more inclusive way, so as to embrace any promising service or technology that private enterprise does not make generally available in a timely fashion. Such a latitudinarian reading opens the door to a more robust program of public activism, all properly justified in the name of classical liberal values.

Such are the familiar terms of the debate. To regard the purposive association as rational enterprise and community of inquiry does not displace this fundamental framework for appraising the role of the state in the pluralist regime, but it does add dimensions to it.

There may be a public interest in the terms of practice of an enterprise. It may be important for the state to secure the reliable, routine provision of a critical public service. When the issue is reliable supply of a fully "rationalized"—for example, standardized—practice, the virtues of flexibility and experimentalism, peculiar to the market, do not apply. Such public utilities are, as we suggested earlier, part of the stable frame of "rule of law" that makes expressive freedom and intelligent adaptation possible. The question of whether such services are better provided by a state agency or by regulated private firms is probably moot, but it is true that the public utility is expected to behave more like a state agency than a private business. It is not at liberty to reduce or abandon service arbitrarily or to change its mode of operation simply according to the dictates of economic interest.

There may be a state interest in the promotion, diffusion, or universalization of practices. In theory, the liberal state is neutral among the various forms of human undertaking that arise within society. In practice, it is not. For pragmatic liberalism, all rational enterprises have their roots in open, undetermined marketlike conditions. But out of this seedbed of free contract, association and exchange, collective inquiry, rational criticism, and organization will yield, in the end, dominant alternatives, which are the rational enterprises or communities of good practice. At this point, policy-making becomes an art of judgment, and we see fully what it means to say that the application of universal liberal norms depends on the particular characteristics of a form of practice. The "finding" of a public interest in a rational enterprise is a case concerning how a particular liberal quality might better be realized in a particular way of doing things.

Thus, there may be a legitimate interest in the promotion of a promising new technology or practice, a need to hasten its development faster than market forces would permit, particularly when that development is hampered by the dedication of resources and energies to existing techniques. (Consider public subsidy of alternative energy sources or of commercial air transport in the 1920s.) In other instances, the relevant public interest might lie in complementing the rationalization of emergent enterprises, as in the road-building programs and expanded police systems that accompanied the development of the "automobile system" in this century. Or there might be a presumed public interest in universalizing a form of practice, making it more comprehensively available than would be the natural result of market forces—or the public interest might even make a practice compulsory.

Thus schooling, once an optional engagement for the individual, part of the pluralist array of options available in a free society, becomes a prescribed practice as the cultivation of the habits of rational inquiry become understood as an essential foundation of the liberal polity. The state goes on to sanction, and to subsidize, the dominant modes of science and scholarship, ratifying their prescriptive methodologies, making them constitutive of the curricula both of the public universities and the public schools.

Similarly, the foundation of the American welfare state is the practice of insurance, made universal and compulsory. Again, an institution of the pluralist political economy, one that has evolved autonomously in the realm of calculated contractual choice and collective action, becomes the basis for an extension of the domain of right and constitutive order.

In each case, the rationale for public action is particular to the practice concerned. Rational consistency does not require that the principle invoked as crucial in one case be then applied to all other human endeavors. To promote the diffusion of libraries and day-care centers through public means does not entail doing the same for dry cleaners and tanning spas. Pragmatic liberalism despairs of the notion that every discrete act of policy must reflect an overarching predisposition either for market autonomy or state control. The pluralistic regime is diverse, not only in the varied forms of human activity it embraces but also in the variety of relations of these undertakings with the state. While the end in view is always to render institutions responsive to individual will and reflective intelligence, the means of achieving this cannot be reduced to a subtle maxim or model to be applied in all cases.

Though the reason for state action is often to secure the consistent, universal provision of basic service, as though by right, such arrangements need not be regarded as cast in stone. Reasons of public economy, changes in technology, or ideas of practice may counsel deregulation, a period in which market experimentation sorts out the desirable organization, quality, and distribution of service along new lines. And of course, the new patterns of rationalization that emerge from such a process are subject to fresh political scrutiny and to the contrivance of additional patterns of relationship between the state and the purposive enterprise.

The state may also legitimately find a public interest in underwriting the conditions of good practice through professional certification and licensing, building codes, governmental regulation and inspection, liability law, and the like. Usually such measures are understood to be grounded in the police power, the state's interest in health or safety, or as a corrective for flaws in the contractual nexus, the inadequacy of the rule of "caveat emptor" under contemporary conditions. However, they can also be understood as a public interest simply in rational enterprise itself, in the performance of a public function, such as medicine, construction, or food processing, according to the best available methods.

In sanctioning the rules of good practice, the state need not merely ratify the standards set by an autonomous industry or profession. The criteria of good practice are not simply internal to the character of a craft. Good practice in residential construction entails ideas of safety, reliability, and aesthetics, not all of which are necessarily inherent in the standards of the trades themselves. Good practice in medicine may come to include an economizing element, hitherto unrecognized by the professions themselves, as a result of public pressure. Good practice in forestry, and in agriculture, has never meant only efficient production but good husbandry and stewardship of resources as well. In all of these ways, the standards of practice reflect not just the inherent "virtues" of a calling, but its public character. In this sense, the definition of good practice is not a matter that can be resolved within the autonomous professional community alone.

In addition to its performance, the liberal polity will want to evaluate whether the private government of the rational enterprise conforms to its overarching premises and values. To be sure, we have a strong predisposition not to intrude in the realm that the law describes as that of "domestic tribunals." Our implicit assumption is that, in pluralist society, individuals can always leave associations that seem to them oppressive. The strong strictures of liberal political theory seem to apply only to involuntary organizations, of which, presumptively, the state is the only example.

Nonetheless, the state is the constitution maker for other forms of association. It defines the legitimate charters of the corporation, the university, the union, the family. Current arguments about marital property reform are very much about whether the state ought to sanction a paternalistic or a democratic political order within the family. As Selznick (1964, 41–86) has shown, the industrial relations legislation of the 1930s created a new form of industrial government, with sovereignty vested not in the stockholders but in the "constitutive contract" between management and labor, which established a fundamental structure of rights and duties within the firm.

In recent American law, we have seen the extension of a variety of due process rights and protections against arbitrary authority to the domain of the pluralist association. The association becomes recognized as a source of law, of rights and duties backed by coercive sanctions, and as such it becomes, like any other public agent, subject to the higher-order norms of lawful authority that regulate the system.

At this point, the question of the public interest in the enterprise understood as a community of inquiry becomes pertinent. Again, it is not systematic performance itself that justifies the rationality of an enterprise, but rather the fact that the terms of practice can be certified as arising from a sustained, open, critical, self-conscious consideration of the best way of achieving a social purpose.

Here the crucial public problem for a theory of pragmatic liberalism is that of orthodoxy. Pragmatism has great respect for the collective undertakings that have grown through a process of reflective evolution within the liberal polity. But enterprises that succeed, that work in practice, also take on enormous power. People come to depend on them. They become dominant parts of the cultural landscape. They are so pervasive, so "rational," their conception of practice becomes so well understood and accepted, that it is hard to imagine alternatives. Competing conceptions of practice are considered both comparatively "speculative" (for they do not rest on the prescribed methodology of the dominant practice) and "impractical" (for they quite obviously are *not* the most efficient way of "getting things done"). This is the problem of orthodoxy. The question of the role of alternative energy sources in a petroleum-based society, of chiropractic and similar healing arts in relation to certified, scientific medicine, of "alternative" or "experimental" education in relation to the professionalized university: all are examples of the theme.

To affirm or deny the legitimacy of a community of inquiry in the face of a charge of orthodoxy is one of the subtle problems of political judgment in pragmatic liberalism. On the one hand, established practitioners have a vested interest in excluding competitors, and, by their lights, they do so righteously, for the established way is the long product of trial and error; it has passed scrutiny and other schemes are (obviously) "untried" if not "crackpot." When this occurs, a strong norm of pragmatic liberalism can be invoked. The path of inquiry has been blocked, the possibility of further investigation has been foreclosed. There may be a public interest in the reform of the community of practice so that it more closely approximates the model of an ideal scientific society, or perhaps, a realm of open and undistorted communication.

However, the problem of orthodoxy is not that easily settled. Practitioners *are* the guardians of responsible practice. They *do* have the right to certify what counts as reliable knowledge. They do have a responsibility to suppress quackery. The fact that scientific medicine does not give full faith and credit to herbalists does not necessarily mean that doctors are a self-protective elite. This is obviously both a crucial and a complex issue. To find the elusive line that distinguishes legitimate self-discipline from corruption in a community of inquiry, one must delve deeply both into liberal political theory and the philosophy of science. But specifically, one must know much about the particular community of practice at issue.

There is an apparent affinity between the pragmatic liberal image of the community of inquiry and ideas of industrial democracy or worker's control. To be sure, pragmatic liberalism is historically cousin to most forms of twentieth-century democratic radicalism—from Guild Socialism to Prairie Populism. However, advocates of industrial democracy generally are concerned above all with the conditions of legitimate power within the firm. The end of open participation in the community of inquiry is not that the enterprise should be rendered responsive to the "workers' interests." Rather, the end of "openness" in the system is the progressive refinement and adaptation of practice. From this perspective, and it is a point that harks back to Plato, to manage a practice in the interest of the practitioners alone—whether workers or capitalists—is a fundamental corruption of the idea of practice itself.

For pragmatic liberalism, the legitimacy of the pluralist regime depends on an evolving interpretation of liberal political theory itself. The thin theory of classic liberalism tells us only of the rights of individuals against the state and of the formation of spontaneous order through contract and the market. It does not tell us, then, enough about the political and economic nature of disciplined collective action, of the rights of individuals against abuses of private power, of the role of the state in securing the autonomy of the pluralist association, and in guaranteeing that the vital public functions of these associations are efficiently, conscientiously, and reflectively performed. As I suggested, pragmatic liberalism, in its first phase of historic development, never did provide a full doctrine of how these problems were to be handled. Perhaps appropriately, it left more to experience and judgment than to logic. Nonetheless, there are important distinctions here that require a more precise formulation. Particularly, we need a clearer resolution of the dilemmas of autonomy and control, of the warrants for independent action by the community of practice, and the grounds that would justify intervention in the name of compelling public interests in its performance or system of governance.

Pragmatic Liberalism and Differentiated Political Economic Policy

In formal, classic liberalism, the state is to govern through general, impersonal laws that are impartial among the diverse interests and activities of its citizens. From this point of view, the state is to be indifferent to the performance of any specific human undertaking, and to the particular mix of goods and services generated by the economy, so long as the pattern can be assumed to arise from the revealed preferences of individuals acting through marketlike arrangements.

The state should be concerned only with the aggregate performance of economy and society, with the sum of satisfactions available to the citizenry. While the state may legislate in relation to matters of health, safety, and contractual probity, it may not define the substance of the economic product, of art and culture, science, religion, or the practice of the professions.

Orthodox liberalism regards any structured relationship between the state and the pluralist enterprises as inherently corrupt. In recent years, particularly, the decision to promote, universalize, or regulate a specific practice is interpreted as a matter of interest group politics, a tawdry exchange of privilege for political support.

Thus, liberal political theory becomes rarified and abstract as the protagonists deliberate only the constitutive principles of contextless, impersonal order.

For classical liberals, the conditions are satisfied if a minimal state provides security for person, property, and contract and leaves the rest to the market.

For Keynesians, the state's role should be limited to securing the optimum aggregate performance of the economy. If the public finances can be so arranged as to generate full employment, steady growth, relative price stability, and balanced trade, then the collective social product can be presumed to arise from individual preferences. Any "sectoral" policy will only distort the fabric of the political economy.

For a classical Great Society liberal, the aggregate performance of society is justified if it arises from manifest individual choice, but this can only be certified under conditions of relatively pure meritocratic competition. This requires that equality of opportunity be assured, that the conditions of the race be fair, and this warrants efforts against discrimination and special assistance to the most conspicuously disadvantaged.

Egalitarian liberals differ only in insisting that the aggregate outcome of liberal society can only be justified if relative equality of income and political participation are guaranteed.

The tradition of pragmatic liberalism is distinctive. It shares with formal liberalism a concern for the integrity and legitimacy of the liberal community, that the aggregate product must somehow reflect the deliberate wills of individuals, equally considered. However, it goes beyond this to presume that liberal politics is a process of sustained inquiry into the substantive character of the specific technologies, activities and processes that arise within the framework of liberal norms.

Thus, the nature of the nation's transportation system, or its energy system, or its health care system, its practices of journalism, or architecture or scientific inquiry, are all appropriate subjects of political deliberation and, potentially, law and policy. Such activities are essentially public in nature, and they are appropriately appraised in relation to the foundation values of the liberal regime, which include their own inherent "fittedness to purpose."

This suggests a more differentiated realm of public policy. It is possible for the state to have different policies toward, say, agriculture, telecommunications, construction, steel—and different intentions concerning what they should accomplish. Public debate becomes more concrete, more practical, more informed and realistic, when we get down to such cases in point. Rather than working on the absurd hypothesis that all human activities can be reduced to the same "laws of the market," we acknowledge that the pluralist political economy will be organized in different ways that reflect diverse histories of institutional development, distinctive relations of large firms, small units, and suppliers and consumers; these are industrial political cultures that are peculiar and unique and that may very well include distinctive legitimate relations between the sector and the state. We come to appreciate that the governance of agriculture is not at all like that of heavy industry and, for that matter, the governance of milk is not very much like that of wheat, beef, or soybeans.

But we have dwelt too long on the role of the state and public policy. Pragmatic liberalism is no more enthusiastic about the large intrusive state than other versions of liberalism. In fact, the whole reason for making such a point of the public character of the rational enterprise is to buttress its claims to autonomy. Pragmatic liberalism suggests that such undertakings can be guided by considerations of public responsibility rather than narrow institutional self-centeredness or simple greed. Management of the concern is seen as a form of statecraft. Conscientiousness in the practice of a profession, and as a participant in the community of inquiry of one's vocation, is a fundamental act of citizenship as important, surely, as voting or partisan affiliation. This, I suspect, is the moral significance of pragmatic liberalism, and this may constitute its most distinctive appeal within the family of liberal political theories.

REFERENCES

Buchler, Justus, ed. 1955. *Philosophical Writings of Peirce*. New York: Dover Publications.

Commons, John R. 1968. *The Legal Foundations of Capitalism*. Madison: University of Wisconsin Press.

Dahl, Robert. 1956. *A Preface to Democratic Theory*. Chicago: University of Chicago Press.

———. 1982. *Dilemmas of Pluralist Democracy*. New Haven, Conn.: Yale University Press.

Dewey, John. 1963. *Liberalism and Social Action*. New York: G. P. Putnam.

Dworkin, Ronald. 1978. *Taking Rights Seriously*. Cambridge, Mass.: Harvard University Press.

Friedmann, Wolfgang. 1972. *Law in a Changing Society*. 2nd ed. Hammondsworth: Penguin.

Galbraith, John Kenneth. 1952. *American Capitalism: The Concept of Countervailing Power*. Boston: Houghton-Mifflin.

Grey, John. 1968. *Hayek on Liberty*. New York: Cambridge University Press.

Hayek, Friedrich A. 1960. *The Constitution of Liberty*. Chicago: University of Chicago Press.

Lakoff, Sanford, and Daniel Rich. 1973. *Private Government*. Glenview, Ill.: Scott, Foresman.

Lowi, Theodore. 1969. *The End of Liberalism*. New York: W. W. Norton.

McCarthy, Thomas. 1978. *The Critical Theory of Jürgen Habermas*. Cambridge, Mass.: MIT Press.

McIntyre, Alasdair. 1981. *After Virtue*. Notre Dame, Ind.: Notre Dame University Press.

MacRae, Duncan. 1976. *The Social Function of Social Science*. New Haven, Conn.: Yale University Press.

Paris, David C., and James F. Reynolds. 1983. *The Logic of Policy Inquiry*. New York: Longmans.

Selznick, Philip. 1969. *Law, Society and Industrial Justice*. New York: Russell Sage Foundation.

Spragens, Thomas A. 1981. *The Irony of Liberal Reason*. Chicago: University of Chicago Press.

Toulmin, Stephen. 1961. *Foresight and Understanding*. New York: Harper & Row.

Webb, Leicester C., ed. 1958. *Legal Personality and Political Pluralism*. Melbourne: Melbourne University Press.

Yates, Douglas. 1981. In *Public Duties: The Moral Obligations of Public Officials*. Edited by Joel L. Fleishman, Lance Liebman, and Mark H. Moore. Cambridge, Mass.: Harvard University Press.

Ziman, John. 1968. *Public Knowledge*. New York: Cambridge University Press.

CHAPTER SIX
Constitutionalism's Successor

STEPHEN L. ELKIN

CONTEMPORARY CONSTITUTIONAL THOUGHT is flawed. It has largely been shaped by classical constitutionalism and has paid insufficient attention to other traditions of constitutional thinking. As a result, contemporary constitutionalism has an incomplete understanding of political institutions and sees them as essentially practical devices for limiting the arbitrary exercise of political power.[1]

This is understandable given the political life of the twentieth century. Little more than its historical outlines are necessary to establish that political power can be placed in the service of the greatest evil. The problem of limiting the exercise of political power must remain central to any adequate conception of political institutions—and well-understood devices for limiting power, such as the separation of powers and particularly the centrality of an independent judiciary, must be at the center of institutional design.

There are, however, two other uses of political institutions.[2] First, they are the means by which policy-making is carried on. Or, more broadly, they are devices for social problem solving. Second, political institutions work to form the character of those who act within them and, to a lesser degree, those who otherwise come into contact with

---

1. For a discussion of classical constitutional theory, its various reformulations by contemporary theorists, and other traditions of constitutional thought, see "Constitutionalism: Old and New" (Elkin, in this volume). Useful collections of contemporary constitutional theorizing can be found in the books edited by Robert Goldwin for the American Enterprise Institute series, Constitutional Studies. See, e.g., Goldwin and Schambra (1985). See also Fisher (1978), Sunquist (1986), and Robinson (1985).

2. "An institution is merely an established practice, an habitual method of dealing with the circumstances of life or the business of government" (Wilson 1908, 14).

them. Political institutions are educative and thus have an ethical dimension. An adequate constitutional theory must then look at the design of political institutions not only with an eye to controlling the powerful but also with a concern for intelligent social problem solving and the formation of the character of citizens.

A compelling constitutional theory cannot stop with delineating the purposes to which political institutions are put. It must also discuss the considerations pertinent to combining political institutions into desirable and workable political wholes. Here again contemporary constitutional thought is insufficient: no well-worked principles of combination have been developed.

Contemporary constitutional theory has an additional shortcoming. Its adherents have reacted nervously to the arguments of those who have pressed the claims of popular sovereignty as the principal basis for governmental legitimacy and who have thereby suggested that arguments for substantial limits on government are flawed. In particular, much contemporary constitutional theory is unable to decide how to assess the growth of the extensive social welfare state that has been a principal consequence of a politically expansive demos. But if constitutional theory is to remain a vital enterprise, its practitioners must actively engage these arguments for an expanded democracy. They are not only powerful arguments; they also reflect the political fact that the democratic genie has long been out of the liberal constitutional bottle.

In what follows, I will address these shortcomings of contemporary constitutional theory and sketch some of the central features of a more adequate formulation. The various pieces of my argument will come together in a sketch of contemporary constitutionalism's successor: a theory of the political constitution of a constitutional regime. I will start with a discussion of the additional purposes of political institutions over and above their employment as a way to limit the arbitrary use of political power.

Policy-Making and Social Problem Solving

Political institutions need to be designed with an eye to ensuring that the policies they make and enforce promote national well-being. There is a strong temptation to view this policy-making task as an exercise in defining goals and selecting efficient means to reach them. In a policy context, this seems to define being rational: means are to be fitted to ends. Political institutions are then to be designed so that they are adept at defining precise goals and selecting the most efficient means to achieve them. But a number of considerations militate against such a view of policy-making. Not the least of them is that, in any complex society, there is, at the start of decision making, unlikely to be agreement on ends precise enough to guide the choice of means. Moreover, it is unlikely that the large number of means-ends calculations can be made for any but a few well-defined problem areas, either because the necessary data are unavailable or the cost of getting these data are too great in the context of resource constraints. In addition, it is unlikely that human beings are sufficiently synoptically rational to carry out what are, in effect, highly complex planning tasks.[3]

Those institutional designers who work in the aggregative tradition have a more plausible view of the ends of policy.[4] The fundamental premise of an aggregative view of political institutions is that the satisfaction of the preferences of individuals is the test of good political practice.[5] Institutions are evaluated in terms of their ability to ascertain and combine preferences over the possible outcomes at stake in such a fashion that the extent of total preference satisfaction among those concerned is increased and, ideally, maximized.

We should look then, argue aggregators, to increases and decreases in total preference satisfaction to see whether policies are succeeding. Instead of positing collective ends, aggregators argue that we should start from the proposition that those affected by a policy will likely have different and conflicting evaluations of it that vary with their various interests and values. The primary task is to make the evaluations commensurable by transforming them into the costs and benefits of particular policy choices. For some aggregators this leads to viewing policy-making as an exercise in cost-benefit analysis by a single decision maker—and thus to the same impasse that impedes those who look to the achievement of substantive ends. For most aggregators, however, it leads to a consideration of the merits of decentralized, interactive decision processes—particularly as seen in markets and political bargaining—that can reveal the intensity of preferences for those affected by a particular outcome. In effect, these decision processes reveal through behavior the costs and benefits attached to the various policy alternatives under consideration.

But, however much an improvement an aggregative view represents in the design of institutions for policy-making, it has serious

---

3. The literature here is very large, but the most seminal work has been done by Hayek (1973), Simon (1976), and Lindblom (1977).

4. See "Constitutionalism: Old and New" (Elkin, in this volume) for a discussion of the aggregative tradition.

5. For a particularly clear statement of an aggregative view see Stokey and Zeckhauser (1978, esp. chaps. 13–14).

faults. It sees political institutions as complex bits of machinery that take fixed inputs—preferences—perform computations on them according to a set of operating rules, and serve up a series of "decision products" that, if the proper rules are at work, increase social efficiency. In the aggregative view, political interactions are understood as being much like gears or processors in a machine, and political institutions are understood as more or less adequate calculating machines.[6]

If nothing else, this view of social problem solving is too static. Problem solving occurs through continuous interaction, and it rarely comes to some natural resting place where totals may be rung up. Every resolution of one problem creates new difficulties and thus new costs, inefficiencies, and opportunities. In their search for more perfect social calculation, aggregators forget that political life is lived in medias res.

Along the same lines, aggregators are mistaken in their view of the value of competitive markets. They typically understand competition as a mechanism that produces efficient results. But, as Hayek argues, competition in the market is best understood as a spur to "discovery." All of the relevant facts about choices and preferences for results are not and cannot be known in advance of the choice—thus the problem is to discover a way to proceed, not to choose among existing paths. Moreover, in the process of discovery, preferences also change. The result is that we cannot know what results "ought" to come out of the market choice, and thus we cannot say that competition leads "to a maximization of any measurable results," that is, to efficiency. And what is true of the market is even more applicable to the political realm (Hayek 1979, 68).

In addition, and perhaps most tellingly of all, it is doubtful that any large body of people could continue to associate on the terms that make up the kind of political institutions that aggregators would design. For aggregators, politics does not fundamentally differ from economics since, in both, the central task is to solve a kind of investment problem. Political life is thus viewed as essentially cooperative: a conflict of views among actors is restated as a problem of how best to combine preferences.[7] The reality of political life is, however, rather different. Central to it is the temptation to use institutions designed

---

6. Consider here the view, common among economists, that perfect markets are functional substitutes for an all-rational planner. Since an all-rational planner is impossible, efficient allocation of resources can only be achieved through markets. Political institutions are understood by aggregators on the model of markets. See James Buchanan's (1978) critical comments on viewing markets as calculation machines.

7. See "Constitutionalism: Old and New" (Elkin, in this volume).

for social calculation for less pleasant purposes. In such circumstances, the central political question is not how to improve social calculation. It is instead a matter of contriving durable forms of association that will enable us to put to one another the questions necessary for social problem solving while keeping to a minimum the temptations inherent in having contrived institutions capable of wielding arbitrary political power.

What would a more compelling view of policy-making and social problem solving generally look like? Consider here the arguments of Lindblom on problem solving as a process of mutual adjustment (see Braybrooke and Lindblom 1963; Lindblom 1965, 1977). For Lindblom, political institutions provide the means through which one may seek advantage and control over others, but they are also devices for organizing social intelligence. Governments are not only organized power systems but coordination devices as well.

Lindblom's basic premise is that we cannot escape from politics into calculation. Social problem solving is and must be political. He argues that if we successfully engage in social problem solving and, more broadly, allocate our resources in effective ways, it cannot be because we are good social calculators.

As Lindblom's thinking has evolved, what he seems to be arguing is that, instead of starting with end states to be achieved, we should start with those ubiquitous features of political life: control and the struggle for political authority. In one sense, this is merely to take account of reality, since the struggle for authority and efforts to domesticate its use are the very stuff of politics. Any attempt to tie institutional design to a view of political institutions as essentially calculating devices is doomed to failure. But Lindblom's argument is also built on a recognition that if we solve social problems it must be through political interaction: problem solving can only be the other side of politics. Otherwise put, if we get better problem solving it will be because we develop better control processes, that is, better methods for controlling authorities. In democracies especially, this means that the interactions that constitute actual efforts at problem solving —the struggles and arguments over proposals and counterproposals—should not be shaped by either systematic veto of certain kinds of proposals or by the exclusion of those proposals from the public agenda.

Lindblom may be understood as arguing that we should see political institutions as simply patterns of interaction through which we attempt to alter the behavior of one another—and through which satisfactory adjustments in our common life can occur. Institutions are the forms our associations with one another take as we attempt to adjust our conflicting interests in the course of coping with the problems we face. If we do this well, it is because we have found ways to stop these associational forms from being dominated by the powerful, who will foreshorten the range of considerations that can inform our interactions. The problems that we face are never solved once and for all, and thus problem solving is more nearly a process of making repeated adjustments to existing situations. Hence our modes of association are important in themselves and are not the means to reach end states of which we can have little or no conception.

For Lindblom then, social problem solving is an exercise in coping with unknown eventualities. The dimensions and character of the policy problems we will face are uncertain, the idea of a solution to our problems is tenuous, and the very goals we pursue are unclear. Under these conditions, political institutions are effective devices for social problem solving to the degree that they provide stable forms of interaction through which proposals may be advanced, discussed, tested by argument, tried, and revised. Social intelligence depends on political organization that affords the stable patterns of association necessary for argument and revision to proceed.

Formative Institutions

Political institutions are more than devices that limit the exercise of political power and modes of association for social problem-solving. They also help form individual character. A useful beginning point for understanding this conception of political institutions is Lon Fuller's juxtaposition of pipelines and institutions.

> We should not conceive of an institution as a kind of conduit directing human energies toward some single destination. Nor can the figure be rescued by imagining a multipurpose pipeline discharging its diverse contents through different outlets. Instead we have to see an institution as an active thing, projecting itself into a field of interacting forces, reshaping those forces in diverse ways and in varying degrees. A social institution makes of human life itself something that it would not otherwise have been. We cannot therefore ask of it simply, Is its end good and does it serve that end well? Instead we have to ask a question at once more vague and complicated—something like this: Does this institution, in a context of other institutions, create a pattern of living that is satisfying and worthy of man's capacities? (Fuller 1981, 54–55)

The point is echoed by Philip Selznick (1969, 151) who, in a study of industrial justice, comments that the institution of collective bargaining is "constitutive" in the sense that it creates "new forms of responsibility" and transforms the legal requirement to bargain in good faith into a "*modus operandi* extending over the entire life of the agreement and suffusing the relationship in depth." And the meaning of institutions as formative is nicely amplified by James Boyd White (1984, 266), who remarks that the law "establishes roles and relations and voices, positions from which and audiences to which one may speak, and it gives us as speakers the materials and methods of a discourse. It is a way of creating a rhetorical community over time."

From any individual's point of view, the members of a political community are overwhelmingly "unknown others" (see Titmus 1971, esp. chap. 13, "Who Is My Stranger?"). They are neither friends nor lovers but strangers. But what sort of strangers? In what relation do they stand? As bargainers engaged in political exchange? As partisans attempting to impose their views? As deliberators in a forum? Political institutions help provide the answer by defining the forms of relation in which citizens stand.[8]

Each form of relation poses an implicit question. The forms are patterned ways of asking and answering these questions. Take two simplified cases. In an exchange relation, the question posed to each individual is, What do you want for yourself? But in certain sorts of public forums, the question is, What does an individual think the community ought to have? Concomitantly, the form of relation might emphasize the seeking of quid pro quos or the giving of reasons. Overall, institutions make available certain ways of experiencing others. The kinds of questions posed and the answers that count distinguish political institutions from one another.

In much the same way, political institutions ask us to use language in different ways. In deliberative institutions, language is used in an effort to say what something is, to name it. Is it just or efficient, for example? In exchange-based institutions, language is used not to develop collective definitions; instead, it is used as an instrument to identify and pursue the interests of individual actors. Language is essentially manipulative. In bureaucracies, language is used to interpret existing rules. Since, from one point of view a community is a network of language, how that language is used is essential to defining that community. How we talk to one another is crucial to who we are. Cicero (1928, 65) makes the fundamental point when he comments that "a people is not any collection of human beings brought together

---

8. In this and the several succeeding paragraphs I draw freely on earlier work (see Elkin 1987, chap. 6).

in any sort of way." In helping to form a people, political institutions are thus both means and ends.[9]

The idea of political institutions as formative is meant to capture that aspect of political life that can be compared to trying to build a boat on an open sea without having any clear idea of the waters to be sailed and the ports to be reached. In such a situation, it is the relationships engendered in building the boat that are central, not the boat's ability to reach a destination. In much the same way, politics is not only about where we are going—about which we can have only very limited knowledge—but about how we stand in relation to one another along the way.

Putting the Pieces Together

The design of the set of political institutions that will compose any political regime must then concern itself with their three uses: (1) to limit the arbitrary use of political power, (2) to facilitate intelligent social problem solving, and (3) to help form the character of citizens. The specific institutions and the purposes they serve are essential ingredients of what may be called the theory of the political constitution of a regime.

Such a constitutional theory specifies the particular political institutions that compose a regime and how they are to be arranged.[10] In doing so, it shapes how the individuals who carry on their lives within the regime are to stand in relation to one another as they go about coping with the difficult-to-predict possibilities and problems that arise and the conflicts attendant upon that common fate. A political constitution defines how the people of a regime are to associate together in the face of unknown possibilities and the prospect that political institutions may be used as means to arbitrary advantage and domination.

In general, the political institutions, and the political constitution

---

9. The point about institutions being formative can be restated, as Robert Lane does, in more psychological language. He comments that "the idea that governments could, even if they wanted to, fail to shape personality is vacuous. Every framework of government, every constitution, necessarily embraces and reinforces a theory of personality" (Lane 1981, 12). But such a formulation directs our attention away from the qualities of institutions themselves, which is our concern here, to what in the end is a discussion of the kinds of virtues needed by citizens. See, e.g., Galston (1988).

10. The theory applies both to the generic type of regime—e.g., one built around popular control of authority—and specific instances of such a regime, e.g., the United States.

they compose, define the essential nature of the citizenry.[11] They do this by shaping the questions that are asked about the citizenry's common life (what aspects of it they find problematic) and the kinds of answers that are likely to be given. By defining the terms on which people have access to one another in their on-going practical and passionate engagements, political institutions create the characteristic organization, habits of mind, and mores of a people. A people's constitution is in major part defined by how they solve problems, cope with the attendant conflict, and channel the temptations to use political institutions to seek advantage and domination. The political constitution as a set of on-going practical and passionate engagements defines the political way of life of a people.[12] As the Scottish Enlightenment thinker Dugdale Stewart put it in 1829, "It is by the particular form of their political institutions that those opinions and habits which constitute the *manners* of nations are chiefly determined" (as quoted in Collini, Winch, and Burrow 1983).

"Constitution" in the sense employed here is rooted in the Latin noun *constitutio*, which refers to the " 'shape,' 'composition,' or 'establishment' of a people in their political association" (Maddox 1982, 806–7; see also Cicero 1928, e.g., *De Re Publica*, book 1). The constitution of a regime, then, does not only set out offices and powers, the frame of government. It is, more generally, an "ordering" by which the organization (order) of something gives it its constitution. Thus, a constitution not only limits a government but forms a polity, enabling it to act by giving it form. A theory of political constitution defines the constitutive institutions through which a regime acts.[13]

There still remains that question of how to combine the institutions that make up the regime: What principles should guide the combining of political institutions into a workable and attractive whole? One approach is to treat political institutions as embodiments of political values—in the manner of much analytical moral philoso-

---

11. As distinct from the character of the citizens understood as the ethical and behavioral disposition of each of them separately. Here I am referring to the citizenry as a whole, *its* overall shape and disposition.

12. This view of a political constitution parallels that set out by Hannah Arendt. As George Kateb (1983, 19) characterizes her views, "A constitution is not a program or policy. . . . It has no goal; it does not make an object. Rather, it is the creation of a frame of institutions for indefinite future possibilities."

13. This emphasis on the various modes of association by which citizens may be joined makes clear that citizenship refers to a *relation*—the manner of association of those who make up the regime—and not just to bare individuals standing alone with their resources, attitudes, and other individual attributes.

phy when it concerns itself with political questions.[14] Viewed this way, the question of how to combine institutions is transformed into one concerning the logical coherence of political values. Thus, it can be asked whether liberty and equality or efficiency and equality are mutually contradictory.

Now, there is no doubt that the emphasis on competing values is a big improvement over arguments that political practice can be judged from the viewpoint of a single value: to serve a single value is not a political problem but a problem of administration. But there is still something wrong, and it is to be found in the search for logical coherence itself. In a word, a practical problem is transformed into a logical one (for an example, see Fishkin 1979). As Bernard Williams says (1983, 35), "It seems . . . to be assumed that the virtues of an intellectual theory, such as economy and simplicity, translate into a desirable rationality of social practice."

Depending on their definition, liberty and equality may indeed be contradictory values. But what is logically contradictory may, in fact, work as a practical matter—simply because, in actual practice, contradictions can be modified by, for example, periodic alterations of behavior that stop the conflicts from getting out of hand. This is quite apart from the more obvious point that whether political values are contradictory depends on the definition given them.

But most important of all, in order to take the inquiry into logical coherence as an inquiry into how the world works, it is necessary to assert that there is a more or less perfect correspondence between values conceived of as abstract rules of behavior and the actual behaviors that embody these values in the world. But it is precisely these actual behaviors that are the subject of interest. And once we get down to actual institutional behaviors the world is likely to look very different in comparison to what is assumed in the logical exercises.[15] We may find, for example, that a supposed contradiction between equality and efficiency may not only be mitigated in practice, but that, under certain conditions, efficient behavior may enhance equality and vice versa. (See Elkin 1987, chap. 9). In any case, as Bernard Crick says, contradictions may be a good thing; indeed, they are the very point of capitalist democracies (Crick 1972, esp. chaps. 1–2; see also Elkin 1985*b*).

---

14. For a wide-ranging discussion of this type of moral philosophy see Williams (1980).

15. Alasdair MacIntyre (1981, 22) says that we cannot understand the claims of any moral philosophy "until we have spelled out what its social embodiment would be."

At the risk of overstatement it might be said then that political values just *are* institutional arrangements, not the products of institutions. Thus freedom is not the result of courts; it is, rather, the availability of certain procedures that shape the interactions of members of a political community (see Oakeshott 1962).

If the preceding arguments are correct, the problem of combining values is the problem of combining the institutions that embody them.[16] It is a practical task.[17] Whether the different institutions necessary for a satisfactory political way of life can coexist can only be settled by empirical investigation into, for example, whether the maintenance requirements of the various institutions can all be met. In short, political practice is a matter of creating and maintaining a set of institutions understood as durable modes of association.[18] And thus, the sociology of institutions is more to the point than a logical parsing of political principles.[19]

Given these arguments, constitutional theory is also then a problem in practical reasoning: the theory focuses on the design of political institutions and the proper way to combine them into a workable whole. A plausible starting point for the exercise of such practical reason is that there just *are* conflicting values in the world, and no amount of ratiocination will shape them into some coherent whole. This is a description of our condition as human beings, not some evidence of our failings as philosophers.[20]

16. Mary Douglas (1986, 124) comments that "moral philosophy is an impossible enterprise" if it does not start with and take institutions as its central concern.

17. Michael Ignatieff (1986, 137) says, "These contradictions [between freedom and solidarity, and between fraternity and equality] cannot be resolved in principle, only in practice."

18. The motto of such a political sociology might be Burke's (1969, 373–74) comment on the setting up of a free government. "To make a government requires no great prudence. Settle the seat of power; teach obedience; and the work is done. To give freedom is still more easy. It is not necessary to guide; it only requires to let go the rein. But to form a free government; that is to temper together these opposite elements of liberty and restraint in one consistent work, requires much thought, deep reflection, a sagacious, powerful, and combining mind."

19. As Hayek says, "We are not fully free to pick and choose whatever combination of features we wish our society to possess, or to fit them together into a viable whole, that is, we cannot build a desirable social order like a mosaic selecting whatever particular parts we like best" (1973, 59–60). He elaborates the point by saying that "whether a new norm fits into an existing system of norms will not be solely a problem of logic, but will usually be a problem of whether, in the existing factual circumstances, the new norm will lead to an order of compatible actions" (105). And he concludes that "norms cannot be judged according to whether they fit with other norms in isolation from facts, because whether the actions which they permit are mutually contradictory depends on the facts" (106).

20. The premier modern statement is by Berlin (1969).

The essential political problem would seem to be just how to combine these conflicting values as they are embodied in political institutions. For combine them we must if we are to live together. And our living together depends on the creation and maintenance of desirable forms of relation that we might have with one another wherever we are headed. In the end, an adequate theory of the political constitution of a regime must take seriously Bernard Williams's (1985, 117) comment that "the only serious enterprise is living, and we have to live after the reflection." What Williams calls the intellectual virtues—logical coherence among them—are important, but they are not as important for constitutional theory as those that might be called the "practical virtues."

A Constitutional Regime

Having sketched the essential elements of a theory of the political constitution of a regime, I will turn to the specific regime—a constitutional regime—that concerns us here. A theory of a constitutional regime needs to specify which institutions are fundamental to the regime, why this is so, and how they are to be combined in constituting the regime.

I cannot here spell out a full theory of the political constitution of a constitutional regime. This would require explication of the various institutions that will engage in the limiting of political power to reduce arbitrariness, social problem solving, and the forming of the character of the citizenry. I will focus instead on the problem of the limitation of power, and I will consider some of the essential questions that must be addressed if political power is to be properly limited. Limiting political power is at the heart of a constitutional regime. Moreover, in considering how this may be done, the character of the citizenry will prove to be crucial, so that the formative effects of political institutions will receive attention.

As for the design of political institutions for intelligent problem solving, a constitutional regime must not only be a regime of limited powers, it must also be a regime that makes effective use of such powers: policy-making must effectively promote the well-being of citizens (see Holmes 1991). Moreover, policy-making will almost certainly involve a good deal of bargaining given the likely diversity of interests and opinions. As I have argued, social problem solving deals mostly with difficult-to-foresee problems whose solutions are extremely difficult to judge. This uncertainty will in itself produce a heterogeneity of opinions and interests, as will the social complexity of any modern society. To these sources will also be added the heterogeneity that stems from the free expression of opinion, which is the hallmark of constitutional regimes. Thus, effective policy-making must revolve around the perfection of the political bargaining that will be its driving force.[21]

It will be useful to start the discussion of the limitation of political power by extending my opening comments concerning the shortcomings of contemporary constitutional theory. A substantial portion of this theory implies or explicitly argues that the limiting of political power rests on ascertaining and enforcing standards that transcend the practice of politics. As Hartog puts it (using the term *government of laws* where I have talked about *constitutionalism*):

> In most versions, the idea of a government of laws has been said to lead to a vision of limited government. Government is legitimate only so long as it recognizes that there are things that it cannot do. . . . At the same time, the notion of a government of laws has suggested a government that must justify itself by its congruence with external standards and norms. (Hartog 1987, 1034)

In a constitutional regime, it is said, a set of external standards act as injunctions to prohibit what rulers may do. In the case of a regime built around the rule of the people, the people, acting through their representatives, are just as limited in the purposes they may legitimately pursue as kings or aristocrats would be. In particular, theorists of constitutional regimes have asserted the necessity of some line between the public and the private sphere, which is said to stem from such external standards. This line of demarcation is to be enforced in the laws of the regime: the people are to act only in public matters, and political power is not to reach into the private sphere (see, e.g., the discussion in Friedrich [1950]).

In the arguments of many contemporary constitutional theorists, the private domain is given its separate and preeminent status because it embodies and allows the exercise of moral principles: for example, rights to one's own body and the fruits of its labor, or the principles and purposes of nature and nature's God as they are revealed to human reason. In short, these are natural law theorists who believe that positive law must uphold and foster the underlying normative structure of the universe (see Weinreb 1987; Moore 1985; Finnis 1980).

A widely discussed version of such arguments is to be found in the work of Hayek. While not strictly a natural law theorist, as that

---

21. See Lindblom (1965) for an elaborate attempt to spell out the variety of what he calls mutual adjustments processes.

perspective is now understood, he uses arguments characteristic of contemporary natural law theorists, and he promises much the same sort of certainty to which they pretend.[22] For law to be law, Hayek contends, it must be general, and it must apply to unknown persons without anticipation of its effects on particular people.[23] This is a characteristic kind of natural law argument: for law to be *real* law, the statements of those in power must have a certain form or be of a certain kind. Otherwise these statements are mere commands. To this Hayek adds another kind of natural law argument: only general laws are fitted to the nature of human beings.[24]

The purpose of Hayek's argument is to deny the legitimacy of a democratized politics that aims at alleviating the burdens of particular groups in the society. Such efforts, he contends, are inconsistent with the rule of law, which is the very essence of constitutional government. Hayek's arguments reflect the ambivalence of classical constitutional thought concerning active government and the rule of the people. While contemporary constitutional theorists are, by and large, less uneasy than Hayek in these matters, their arguments still often betray an attempt to rein in a demos given to relying on state authority to cope with its problems.[25]

But there is little to be gained and much to lose in denying that popular self rule is as powerful a source of legitimation as rule according to law. Once the people admit themselves to the stage of history, no argument is likely to be compelling that denies that the consent of the governed is as important as the form government action takes. In part, this is only to fit theory to the facts, but it is also a recognition that democratic consent is a powerful source of political value.

Such indeed are the premises of those who may be called demo-

22. See Jones's (1958, 150) comment that Hayek might be accused of "falling into the pit of natural law thinking." But see Hayek, (1979, 207, n. 62). For Hayek there are natural laws—in the sense of rules that are not the product of human *design*, but which are not transcendent either. These laws are a part of human practice and can be understood by human reason. They are then neither conventional nor "natural" if by that we mean that they are above social practices in the manner argued by much contemporary natural law thinking. But in an older sense, such laws, Hayek thinks, are indeed natural. See also Hayek (1973, chap. 1, esp. 21).

23. The original statement is in Hayek (1944, chap. 6). Hayek has since modified his views, but the burden of his argument remains much the same.

24. At various points, Hayek uses such statements to formulate what are essentially utilitarian arguments: only general laws will promote material prosperity.

25. See the discussion of Lowi, Riker, and Buchanan in "Constitutionalism: Old and New" (Elkin, in this volume).

crats.[26] They imply that constitutional theory needs to accommodate the rise of the demos—with its preference for an active state whose activities blur the line between the public and the private—onto the political stage. To guard against arbitrariness, these democratic theorists suggest, must also mean removing the barriers that systematically prevent the translation of popular opinion into governmental action. Thus, popular rule is not only arbitrary when the people disregard a supposed line between public and private. Such rule is corrupted when democratic opinion is systematically distorted—for example, by a grossly unequal distribution of political resources.

Many democrats go further in pressing the case for an expansive system of democratic control of authority.[27] They argue that a compelling case cannot be made for knowable external standards that demarcate the public from the private spheres. At least as far as the United States goes, the first to enter the discussion of the basis for the public-private distinction were the legal realists. They argued that any attempt to ground this distinction in the unfolding of the neutral principles of the law was untenable. Law was not a "science," its principles were far from neutral, it mostly favored the powerful, and, most important of all, law is what judges say it is.[28]

Once the case is made that law is not the neutral arbiter of the public-private distinction, the various means of demarcating a "natural" private sphere—via private property, markets, economics, or the family—are also open to question. It has become increasingly clear that property, whatever it once may have been, is now largely a product of the choices made by the state (see Nedelsky 1990; Michelman 1988; Dahl 1985). Property can hardly then serve as a source outside of politics to delimit the proper scope of state activity. Recent feminist theory has arrived at much the same conclusion, showing that the supposed private sphere built around family and household is, to an important degree, the creation of the law, that is, of state activity. In much the same way, the effort to demarcate a private sphere bounded

---

26. For a theorist who chafes at the limits that classical constitutionalism imposes, see my earlier discussion of Dahl (Elkin, in this volume). Walzer (1981, 1983, 1987, 1988) is even more forthcoming in this respect. He (Walzer 1983, 287) says that "the proper exercise of power is nothing more than the direction of the city in accordance with the civic consciousness or public spirit of the people."

27. This section draws freely on an earlier paper of mine (Elkin 1991), and on a paper with Jyl Josephson (see Elkin and Josephson 1992).

28. See the concise discussion in Michelman (1987). See also Posner (1990 chap. 1). For one widely discussed contemporary alternative to legal realism, see Dworkin, 1986.

by free choice in the marketplace has been shown to rest on a tendentious understanding of labor. Radical economists have argued that labor is unlike any other commodity in that it cannot be separated from the person providing it. Labor therefore requires "disciplining" in a way that other commodities do not, and therefore the buying and selling of it is a deeply political matter (see Bowles and Gintis 1986, chap. 3).

If this critique of external transcendent standards is accepted, then constitutional regimes stand or fall on the ability of the people to limit themselves. Without external standards as the basis for limits on the citizens of a republic, the foundation of a constitutional regime must be a *self-limiting* popular sovereign. Where then can citizens of constitutional regimes turn in the effort to ensure that popular rule does not simply take over where tyrannies of one and the few have left off? Constitutional rule must be limited rule: a popular regime must still be a regime of law. How are the limits to be established and the laws given content, if there are no transcendent standards to offer guidance?

Finding a basis for self-limitation need not be as great a problem as it first appears, for the people, acting through their representatives, are not without guidance. The history of popular government provides some practical knowledge of how to limit the people's rule. While metaphysics may not vouchsafe knowledge, reflection on constitutional practice can. Some ways in which the people might rule simply will not work. Sooner or later they will undercut the very qualities of the regime that secure their rule and thus bring about one or another kind of authoritarianism. For example, emptying the treasury to provide benefactions for the mass of citizens will lead not only to economic chaos but, almost certainly, to civil strife and subsequently to a politics built around the arbitrary exercise of power. In much the same way, there is some practical knowledge about what limits will actually work and how they may be made to work: there is much historical experience that suggests that some combination of private property and the division of governmental powers is effective in preventing unlimited rule.

What such considerations point to is the importance of practical political reason.[29] The question of whether limitation on rule is itself

---

29. For discussion, see Salkever (1990). For a certain kind of pragmatic thought that bears a resemblance to practical political reason in the Aristotelian mode, see Anderson (1990 and esp. 1991).

justified is not separable from how and whether it can be accomplished. Thus, it is more than a matter of three separate questions: What are the appropriate limits on the people's rule? How are these limits justified? and How can limitation be made to work? The answer to one question depends upon the answer to the others. Starting from the premise that some limit on the people's rule is necessary—if only because such rule cannot survive without limits—the process is one of considering specific limits on rule, investigating how they might be accomplished, and deciding upon a reasonable set of limits in light of what is necessary to achieve them.

The means of limiting popular rule can thus be settled through a process of reasoning in which those who advocate specific limits marshal arguments and adduce evidence for their positions, and then respond to criticism. What drives the process is a commitment to the value of reason and what it can tell us about how the world may be made to work. And it is from the mix of reasoning tested against what works or seems likely to work that an understanding of the value of constitutional government can grow. Creating a limited popular regime in this understanding of practical reason does not consist of divining transcendent values and trying to implement them. If anything, the process is the reverse: what is valuable emerges from a tentative, conditional commitment to constitutional rule, and its full value only emerges in the process of trying to bring constitutional rule to fruition. It is, then, through the exercise of popular rule itself—as an exercise in collective reasoning—that both the full value of limitation and its specifics emerge: limitation is self-limitation.

Now it may seem that this is not much to go on, that limitation of popular rule cannot succeed if it is only to be guided by such practical, conditionally normative reasoning. However, it is very likely the case that the problem of giving content to the law will look much the same even if we believe that there are transcendent standards. Given the long-standing and deeply contested effort to identify and give content to transcendent limits, it is unlikely that anything specific enough to guide practice is available (Shklar 1964, pt. 1). Thus even if transcendent standards can be convincingly demonstrated, they will end up playing the same role as the pragmatist's commitment to limiting popular rule on the basis that it is unlikely to work any other way. Both are starting points—and their value can only emerge out of the process of trying to give them concrete meaning. As Leo Strauss (1953, 162) comments, "There is a universally valid hierarchy of ends, but there are no universally valid rules of action. . . . One has to consider not only which of various competing objectives is higher in rank but also which is more urgent in the circumstances."[30] In short, in both cases—with or without transcendent standards—much of the work is done by the exercise of practical reason.

It is the case then that even if there are transcendent standards, constitutional rule will nevertheless depend on self-limitation. The burden will remain very much on the people and their representatives to give content to the limits of their own rule. If this line of argument is accepted, the central problem of a constitutional regime is how to create and maintain a popular sovereign capable of limiting itself through the exercise of practical, conditionally normative reason. The constitution of a constitutional regime must seek to ensure that the people, acting through their representatives, attempt through such reasoning to demarcate and enforce the domain over which public power can legitimately be exercised. A constitutional regime *is* a regime where a private domain is secured against the exercise of political power. That domain may shift over time, its edges may be blurry, but its absence is the antithesis of constitutionalism.

The heart of a constitutional regime must then be institutions able to reason about appropriate limits to political authority that, when expressed in law, give content to self-limitation: a constitutional regime must have a deliberative core. Institutions capable of practical reasoning concerning the limits of political authority—that is, institutions capable of deliberation—must then be at the core of a constitutional regime *whether or not there are transcendent standards* that are said to limit the people's rule: the existence of such standards does not obviate the necessity of practical reasoning, and thus the institutional design must be the same.[31] Limitation rests on the proper organization of popular self-rule. There must be deliberative ways of lawmaking in either case.

Not only must the people and their representatives deliberate in lawmaking—as against engaging in deduction from transcendent standards—they must deliberate rather than bargain over the content

---

30. Salkever (1990, 42) says that theory of the kind that posits natural ends or purposes "is useful to practice in clarifying the real issues involved and exposing the false solutions, ... but not in providing answers." In my discussion here, "transcendent" should be understood as simply that which is valuable for reasons other than conventional agreement. Salkever—and Strauss (1953)—are not defending a modern natural law theory where choices are deduced from overarching standards. Aristotelian political science rests on the nature of human needs as they can be rationally interpreted by human beings who need to realize them in collective life.

31. William Galston (1991, 55) says that "philosophical reasoning is not as far removed from moral and political deliberation as is often supposed. . . . Philosophy, like deliberation, is the collective effort of preparing ourselves to recognize what is worthy of our assent."

of the law. It is hard to see how self-limitation could work if they bargained.[32] There could be no guarantee that the question of the proper dimensions of public and private spheres of activity would even arise. The result would be that such matters would be decided as a by-product of other considerations. While such a procedure is not wholly unattractive—large questions being difficult to settle through the exercise of reason—it will not be easy to demonstrate that some "invisible hand" of bargaining will produce outcomes of any merit beyond that there *is* an outcome. And even this is not guaranteed (Mueller 1989, chaps. 5–6).

Now the effort at self-limitation cannot stop with the people through their lawmakers' reasoning about the proper scope of their own power to rule. Attention must also be given to what makes deliberation possible in the first place. The institutions that make a constitutional regime possible must themselves be maintained if they exist or created if they do not. Self-limitation is then in part a reflexive exercise: it involves securing those institutions that give the regime its characteristic manner of working.

Like all institutions, those that make a constitutional regime possible—here, deliberative ones—are subject to corruption and decline and must therefore be regularly repaired. Moreover, as noted, not all the necessary institutions are likely to be in place at any given time: the regime will be in a state of becoming, incomplete and poised to move forward or to fall back. Attending to the constitutive foundations of the regime is then a recurring necessity. And unless the people act in their political, organized form—not least through their representatives—to secure and expand the constitutive foundations of the regime, it will fail. Once created, a constitutional regime—or any other regime for that matter—cannot be left alone as its citizens go about the ordinary business of getting and spending and the pursuit of limited political objectives.

Attending to the constitutive foundations of the regime is not, then, some special activity to be reserved for special constitutional occasions and special procedures. Nor is it only for supposed specialists such as high court judges, who, it is claimed, somehow know more about these matters than do others of the people's lawmakers. As Paul Brest (1988, 1628) says with regard to American constitutional interpretation, "Constitutional decision-making does *not* take place

32. Although the question cannot be explored here, the association of lawmaking with the problem of limiting public authority suggests that other activities of government—particularly the domain of "policy"—might be carried on through bargaining. How to join lawmaking as deliberation and policy-making as bargaining is thus a crucial problem in the design of constitutional regimes.

only at rare moments. . . . The Constitution is constantly being made and remade."[33] Securing and expanding the constitutive foundations of the regime is a continuous project and one in which the people in all their organized political capacities must be involved.[34] Constitutive matters arise all the time, if for no other reason than the fact that the pursuit of more limited political and economic objectives often have serious constitutive implications. Who is to pay for what—one of the mainstays of ordinary political debates and deals—is hardly irrelevant to securing the constitutive foundations of the regime. Even if no one is paying attention, "ordinary" politics, in its working and outcomes, has constitutive effects. Attending to the constitutive foundations of the regime is not something apart from "real" politics; it is a notable portion of real politics itself.[35]

Having said this does not of course mean that a constitutional regime cannot devise special procedures and institutions to address the constitutive foundations of the regime—not to mention the demarcation of the public and private spheres. It may make use of constitutional conventions and high courts. The claim here is only

33. While it is not difficult to understand how supposed constitutional expertise came to be associated with lawyers—after all they were important in formulating the idea of a government of laws and working for its implementation—it is far from clear that the association should have continued. After all, what do people who go to law schools know, for example, about the theory of political constitutions? If they have ever heard the matter discussed, it is in the context of the case law of a supreme court, which while relevant, hardly exhausts the subject. And since, as I have just suggested, the role of such a court is itself a principal subject of the theory of political constitution, the conundrum deepens. It might even be argued that ordinary training in law, as it now occurs, intellectually disables lawyers from thinking clearly about these matters. The skills they learn are ones tied to close reading, logic of a certain kind, and rhetoric. Would it not be more to the point if those who attended to the constitutive foundations of constitutional regimes knew their Locke more than they knew their Prosser? Indeed they might be able to do a splendid job if they never even heard of Prosser. For a powerful statement on why constitutive issues cannot be just left to the courts and related issues, see Brest (1988).

34. *"Constitutional discourse and decision-making are the most fundamental prerogatives and responsibilities of citizens"* (Brest 1988, 1628; italics in original).

35. "But constitutional decision-making does *not* take place only at rare moments. If modern court-centered scholarship has taught us anything, it is that the Constitution is constantly being made and remade" (Brest 1988, 1628; emphasis in original). For a powerful analysis of American constitutional history and theory that is premised on such a separation, see Ackerman (1991). In an earlier version of this whole argument I talked about attending to the constitutive foundations of the regime as an exercise of "political rationality," which I contrasted to "economic rationality" (see Elkin 1985a). Here, I am less concerned with naming the kind of reasoning that is required and considering some of its general features, and more with its substance in the context of republican regimes.

that these efforts alone will be insufficient. Moreover, even if an independent judiciary is crucial in attending to constitutive matters—more crucial than I have allowed—still the question arises, What makes it possible to *have* an independent judiciary?

We may summarize the argument to this point by saying that a constitutional regime is one in which lawmaking is, in considerable part, deliberative. It is a certain kind of popular regime, namely one that operates through law, and law properly understood must be built on reasoning. And the reasoning that is necessary cannot only be the province of courts and judges.

Now, most lawmakers, and legislators in particular, will not be inclined to deliberate out of some selfless motivation or sense of civic virtue. They are not, after all, likely to be Solons but ordinary people who will only act in deliberative ways, if at all, for the same reasons that most people do—because it is personally rewarding to do so. They will be self-interested. But their conception of their interests will be potentially expansive, and very likely will include a desire that their fellows esteem them for their knowledge of public matters. In addition, lawmakers will likely be motivated by fear of being shown up as ignorant by their legislative adversaries, by the relative ease of getting first-rate information on public matters, and by the prospects of political advancement enhanced by a reputation for being knowledgeable about public affairs.

The motives just canvassed might be harnessed by the legislature toward making lawmaking a deliberative process. The legislature can be a school, and much can be done in this way.[36] But it is doubtful that such tutelary efforts will be sufficient in themselves to engender the necessary habits and dispositions. At a minimum, if those elected to the legislature are strongly averse to deliberation and think that their task is to further their own or a group's interests through logrolling and bargaining, then it is unlikely that the legislature will act in the necessary ways. If the legislature does not have the right pupils it will fail in its teaching. Indeed, it cannot be the proper sort of school without the right teachers, and who are those teachers but lawmakers who are willing to support legislative habits conducive to lawmaking as deliberation?

Additional, and crucial, incentives for lawmaking as deliberation must come then from the citizenry. It is in the combination of the legislative school and the capacities for judgment by the citizenry that the hope for constitutional lawmaking lies. A legislature largely

---

36. See Muir's (1982) remarkable account of the California state legislature.

composed of abject mediocrities cannot by some hidden hand miraculously turn itself into a lawmaking body of great distinction.

The citizenry of a constitutional regime must be able to judge who is genuinely devoted to making good law and who is, or is likely to be, a hack. Citizens must be able to pick out those prospective lawmakers who understand lawmaking to be, at least partly, a deliberative process and who also have either the skills necessary to make it work or the inclination to learn them.

How will the citizens learn to make the necessary distinctions? The political constitution of a constitutional regime must make provision for their education as well. Citizens must, if not overcome a natural insularity, at least substantially supplement it. If the citizenry insists on looking for parochial lawmakers and cannot distinguish hacks from deliberators, the prospects for a constitutional regime are greatly dimmed.

Here then is the sense in which a constitutional regime stands or falls on the qualities of its citizenry. The question then becomes, Where and how are the citizens to get the education necessary to make them competent judges of those who will make their laws?

The answer, long posited by theorists of constitutional government, is through local government (see e.g. Mill 1991; Tocqueville 1945). A crucial component of the theory of the political constitution of a constitutional regime must then be its design for local government.

What must local political institutions look like in a constitutional regime? First and foremost, local political institutions must place citizens in relation to one another as deliberators, as those who think that a crucial feature of decision making about public choices is the giving of reasons.[37] Where possible, public choices should elicit arguments about what is beneficial to the members of the community, and not just reflect the summation of wants and interests.

By giving expression to such public-regarding sentiments, such local political institutions work to reinforce them. And by allowing the citizenry's powers of judgment to be exercised, the powers are refined. Citizens will thus be more able to judge the inclinations and capacities of their lawmakers to deliberate.

Deliberation is then the handmaiden of judgment, and it is as judges that constitutional citizens find their excellence. Madison long ago made the essential point.

37. Here I draw freely on my earlier work (see Elkin 1987, chap. 8; see also Elkin 1989, 1993).

But I go on this great republican principle, that the people will have the virtue and intelligence to select the men of virtue and wisdom. Is there no virtue among us? If there be not, we are in a wretched situation. No theoretical checks, nor form of government, can render us secure. To suppose any form of government will secure liberty or happiness without any virtue in the people, is a chimerical idea. If there be sufficient virtue and intelligence in the community, it will be exercised in the selection of these men, so that we do not depend on their virtue, or put confidence in our rules, but in the people who are to choose them.[38]

The heart of a constitutional regime is a self-limiting popular sovereign. It in turn rests on (1) deliberative ways of lawmaking that will give content to the distinction between the public and private domains and secure the constitutive foundations of the regime and (2) the institutions that help to foster a citizenry that has what might be termed constitutional virtues. The hoped-for link between the two—the citizenry rewarding actual and prospective lawmakers who act in the necessary ways—is crucial to understanding how the institutions that compose the regime are to be put together. A fully realized constitution will of course include more than these institutions and the links between them. Defining the limits of public authority and securing the foundations of the regime do not exhaust all political activities. There will be, for example, the full run of policy problems characteristic of political life in all modern popular regimes, and, therefore, there will need to be other institutions doing other things than those that have been described here. And the form of lawmaking itself will need to be adjusted to these other activities.

Conclusion

The central task of a constitutional political science is to develop the theory of the political constitution of a constitutional regime. The first step in achieving this end is to spell out the uses of political institutions and the considerations that should guide their combination into workable wholes—that is, to set out the essentials of the theory of the political constitution of any regime. With these in hand, a substantive theory of a constitutional regime may be developed. This is the second step. The intellectual terrain of a theory of the political constitution of a constitutional regime is somewhere between

---

38. James Madison, June 20, 1789 (as quoted in Diamond 1980, 38). For a modern statement, see Galston (1988).

an attempt to answer two questions—What is the best political way of life? And how we may know this?—and the empirical analysis of how political systems operate. The constitution of such a regime is not a "problem in arithmetic" (Edmund Burke as quoted in Lippmann [1943, 253]). It is a practical problem that requires, for solution, a theory of practice for a people who collectively have few substantive goals toward which their collective energies are directed.

REFERENCES

Ackerman, Bruce. 1991. *We the People: Foundations.* Cambridge, Mass.: Harvard University Press.
Anderson, Charles W. 1990. *Pragmatic Liberalism.* Chicago: University of Chicago Press.
———. 1991. "Pragmatism and Liberalism, Rationalism and Liberalism: A Response to Richard Rorty." *Polity* 33 (3): 357–70.
Berlin, Isaiah. 1969. *Four Essays on Liberty.* London: Oxford University Press.
Bowles, Samuel, and Herbert Gintis. 1986. *Capitalism and Democracy.* New York: Basic Books.
Braybrooke, David, and Charles E. Lindblom. 1963. *A Strategy of Decision: Policy Evaluation as a Social Process.* New York: Free Press of Glencoe.
Brest, Paul. 1988. "Further beyond the Republican Revival: Toward Radical Republicanism." *Yale Law Journal* 97 (8): 1623–31.
Buchanan, James. 1978. *What Should Economists Do?* Indianapolis, Ind.: Liberty Press.
Burke, Edmund. 1969. *Reflections on the Revolution in France and the Proceedings to Certain Societies in London Relative to That Event.* Edited by Conor Cruise O'Brien. Middlesex: Penguin Books.
Cicero, Marcus Tullius. 1928. *De Re Publica, De Legibus.* Translated by Clinton Walker Keyes. Loeb Classical Library. Cambridge, Mass.: Harvard University Press.
Collini, Stefan, Donald Winch, John Burrow. 1983. *That Noble Science of Politics: A Study in Nineteenth-Century Intellectual History.* Cambridge: Cambridge University Press.
Crick, Bernard. 1972. *In Defense of Politics.* Chicago: University of Chicago Press.
Dahl, Robert. 1985. *A Preface to Economic Democracy.* Berkeley and Los Angeles: University of California Press.
Diamond, Ann Stuart. 1980. "Decent, Even though Democratic." In *How*

Democratic Is the Constitution? Edited by Robert Goldwin and William Schamba. Washington, D.C.: American Enterprise Institute.

Douglas, Mary. 1986. *How Institutions Think.* Syracuse, N.Y.: Syracuse University Press.

Dworkin, Ronald. 1986. *Law's Empire.* Cambridge, Mass.: Belknap Press.

Elkin, Stephen L. 1985a. "Economic and Political Rationality." *Polity* 18 (2): 253–71.

———. 1985b. "Pluralism in Its Place." In *The Democratic State.* Edited by Roger Benjamin and Stephen L. Elkin. Lawrence: University Press of Kansas.

———. 1987. *City and Regime in the American Republic.* Chicago: University of Chicago Press.

———. 1989. "The Political Theory of American Business." *Business in the Contemporary World* 1 (3): 25–37.

———. 1991. "The Transition to Republican Regimes." Paper delivered to the International Political Science Association, Buenos Aires.

———. 1993. "Business-State Relations in the Commercial Republic." *Journal of Political Philosophy,* forthcoming.

Elkin, Stephen L., and Jyl Josephson. 1992. "The Transition to Republican Government." Department of Government and Politics, University of Maryland.

Finnis, John. 1980. *Natural Law and Natural Rights.* Oxford: Oxford University Press.

Fisher, Louis. 1978. *The Constitution between Friends: Congress, the President, and the Law.* New York: St. Martin's Press.

Fishkin, James S. 1979. *Tyranny and Legitimacy: A Critique of Political Theories.* Baltimore: Johns Hopkins University Press.

Friedrich, Carl J. 1950. *Constitutional Government and Democracy: Theory and Practice in Europe and America.* Boston: Ginn.

Fuller, Lon L. 1981. "Means and Ends." In *The Principles of Social Order: Selected Essays of Lon L. Fuller.* Edited by Kenneth I. Winston and Stanley L. Paulson. Durham, N.C.: Duke University Press.

Galston, William. 1988. "Liberal Virtues." *American Political Science Review* 82 (4): 1277–90.

———. 1991. *Liberal Purposes.* Cambridge: Cambridge University Press.

Goldwin, Robert A., and William A. Schambra. 1985. *How Does the Constitution Secure Rights?* Washington, D.C.: American Enterprise Institute.

Hartog, Hendrik. 1987. " 'The Constitution of Aspiration' and 'The Rights That Belong to Us All.' " *Journal of American History* 74 (3): 1013–34.

Hayek, Friedrich A. 1944. *The Road to Serfdom.* Chicago: University of Chicago Press.

———. 1973. *Rules and Order.* Vol. 1 of *Law, Legislation and Liberty.* Chicago: University of Chicago Press.

———. 1979. *The Political Order of a Free People.* Vol. 3 of *Law, Legislation and Liberty.* Chicago: University of Chicago Press.

Holmes, Stephen. 1991. "The Liberal Idea." *The American Prospect* 7 (Fall): 81–96.

Ignatieff, Michael. 1986. *The Needs of Strangers.* New York: Penguin Books.

Jones, Harry W. 1958. "The Welfare State and the Rule of Law." *Columbia Law Review* 58 (2): 143–56.

Kateb, George. 1983. *Hannah Arendt: Politics, Conscience, Evil.* Totowa, N.J.: Rowman & Allanheld.

Lane, Robert. 1981. "Market and Politics: The Human Product." *British Journal of Political Science* 1, no. 1.

Lindblom, Charles E. 1965. *The Intelligence of Democracy: Decision Making through Mutual Adjustment.* New York: Free Press.

———. 1977. *Politics and Markets.* New York: Basic Books.

Lippmann, Walter. 1943. *The Good Society.* Boston: Little, Brown.

MacIntyre, Alasdair. 1981. *After Virtue.* Notre Dame, Ind.: University of Notre Dame Press.

Maddox, Graham. 1982. "A Note on the Meaning of Constitution." *American Political Science Review* 76 (4): 805–9.

Michelman, Frank. 1987. "Possession vs. Distribution in the Constitutional Idea of Property." *Iowa Law Review* 72 (5): 1319–50.

———. 1988. "Law's Republic." *Yale Law Journal* 97 (8): 1493–1537.

Mill, John Stuart. 1991. *Considerations on Representative Government.* In *On Liberty and Other Essays.* Oxford: Oxford University Press.

Moore, Michael S. 1985. "A Natural Law Theory of Interpretation." *Southern California Law Review* 58 (2): 277–398.

Mueller, Dennis. 1989. *Public Choice II.* Cambridge: Cambridge University Press.

Muir, William K. 1982. *Legislature.* Chicago: University of Chicago Press.

Nedelsky, Jennifer. 1990. *Private Property and the Limit of American Constitutional Thinking.* Chicago: University of Chicago Press.

Oakeshott, Michael J. 1962. *Rationalism in Politics, and Other Essays.* New York: Basic Books.

Posner, Richard. 1990. *The Problems of Jurisprudence.* Cambridge, Mass.: Harvard University Press.

Robinson, Donald L. 1985. *Reforming American Government: The Bicentennial Papers of the Committee on the Constitutional System.* Boulder, Colo.: Westview Press.

Salkever, Stephen G. 1990. *Finding the Mean: Theory and Practice in Aristotelian Political Philosophy.* Princeton, N.J.: Princeton University Press.

Selznick, Philip. 1969. *Law, Society and Industrial Justice.* New York: Russell Sage.

Shklar, Judith. 1964. *Legalism.* Cambridge, Mass.: Harvard University Press.

Simon, Herbert A. 1976. *Administrative Behavior: A Study of Decision-making Processes in Administrative Organization.* New York: Free Press.

Stewart, Dugdale. 1829. *Outlines of Moral Philosophy for the Use of Students in the University of Edinburgh.* 5th ed. Edinburgh.

Stokey, Edith, and Richard Zeckheuser. 1978. *A Primer for Policy Analysis.* New York: W. W. Norton.

Strauss, Leo. 1953. *Natural Right and History.* Chicago: University of Chicago Press.

Sundquist, James L. 1986. *Constitutional Reform and Effective Government.* Washington, D.C.: Brookings Institution.

Titmuss, Richard M. 1971. *The Gift Relationship: From Human Blood to Social Policy.* New York: Pantheon Books.

Tocqueville, Alex de. 1945. *Democracy in America.* New York: A. A. Knopf.

Walzer, Michael. 1981. "Philosophy and Democracy." *Political Theory* 9 (3): 379–99.

———. 1983. *Spheres of Justice.* New York: Basic Books.

———. 1987. *Interpretation and Social Criticism.* Cambridge, Mass.: Harvard University Press.

———. 1988. *The Company of Critics.* New York: Basic Books.

Weinreb, Lloyd. 1987. *Natural Law and Justice.* Cambridge, Mass.: Harvard University Press.

White, James Boyd. 1984. *When Words Lose Their Meaning.* Chicago: University of Chicago Press.

Williams, Bernard. 1980. "Political Philosophy in the Analytical Tradition." In *Political Theory and Political Education.* Edited by Melvin Richter. Princeton, N.J.: Princeton University Press.

———. 1983. "Auto-da-Fé: Consequences of Pragmatism." *New York Review of Books* (April 28): 33–36.

———. 1985. *Ethics and the Limits of Philosophy.* Cambridge, Mass.: Harvard University Press.

Wilson, Woodrow. 1908. *Constitutional Government in the United States.* New York: Columbia University Press.

PART THREE

The American Regime

The papers in this section illustrate some of the themes set out in Parts 1 and 2. The final purpose of a constitutionalist political science is not the development of theory, but its application in the constitution of particular political regimes. A focus on the American regime is a natural one since its health is of prime importance to us, its citizens, and also because a designer's, or framer's, perspective is a regular component of our political discourse.

The papers by Theodore J. Lowi, Cass R. Sunstein, and Edwin T. Haefele present three different theories of the essential constitutive features of the American regime. The comparison of such different accounts, especially their implications for institutional design, is an important way through which constitutionalist theory can advance. Through such an exercise, we can sharpen our understanding of which institutions are indeed central to the kind of regime that characterizes the United States, and we can improve our understanding of the difficulties of combining institutions into a workable political whole.

In his paper, Lowi updates the argument that he first presented in *The End of Liberalism* (1979). He reaffirms his interpretation of the American regime as being dedicated to the rule of law but failing to provide it in the administrative state. Lowi thus picks up the theme, introduced by Soltan and Anderson in Part II, that the central feature of good political regimes is the reduction of arbitrariness. Soltan and Anderson can be read not only as providing some of the theoretical background for Lowi's arguments about the rule of law but also as providing some of the groundwork for the reduction of arbitrariness in the administrative state. It is the constitutionalizing of administration that, for Lowi, is the crucial feature of a fully legitimate American regime.

Sunstein's paper examines legal doctrine within a narrowly conceived constitutional discussion; much more important, however, is his analysis of the theory of political constitution found in the writings of James Madison. While others have emphasized the importance of interests and factions in Madison's thought, Sunstein also sees an emphasis on deliberation. Interests must be balanced and controlled, but if the American regime is to flourish, then interests must also be subjected to the discipline of a well-functioning deliberative process. Sunstein may be interpreted as arguing that the lawmaking that Lowi sees as central to the success of the American regime must be done in a forum where reason giving is the dominant form of behavior. From two different starting points, their arguments converge on the centrality of legislative institutions in the American regime.

Haefele expands the discussion of the American regime and presents an account of the central constitutive relationships that compose it. He adds to the list of elements that Lowi and Sunstein set out by pointing to the crucial role that the idea of the sacred plays in the American regime and how a certain kind of relationship between state and market must obtain. More important, Haefele's paper provides a conclusion to the discussion in this section by squarely facing the question of what indeed *the* crucial institutions that compose the American regime are and how they need to work.

An extremely useful exercise would be to see how Lowi's concern with the rule of law fits with Haefele's first constitutive element, self-government. If the people are to rule, must they rule according to law? And how must legislative institutions be designed to make such rule possible? Similarly, it would be revealing to consider the links between Sunstein's concern for deliberation and Haefele's second constitutive element, civic virtue. How is civic virtue to be fostered? Is it to be done through participation in the deliberative forums that Sunstein mentions? Must the people's ruling according to law entail extensive legislative deliberation on its content? And must it rest on a foundation of civic virtue?

Questions such as these are some of the fruits of a new constitutionalism. They are questions of political practice, matters of institutional design. They are the sorts of questions that reflective citizens might ask, questions that they should be encouraged to ask. And they are questions about how a good and workable regime may be constructed out of its component, constitutive institutions.

CHAPTER SEVEN

Two Roads to Serfdom: Liberalism, Conservatism, and Administrative Power

THEODORE J. LOWI

*You must first enable the government to control the governed;
and in the next place oblige it to control itself.*
JAMES MADISON

THIS IS A REVISIT to the well of delegated, discretionary power and the politics of administrative agencies. It is the same as it was twenty years ago, the same well in the same place with pretty much the same contents, only deeper and more polluted. As in the past, my concern is for the political consequences of delegated power (see Lowi 1969, 1979).

Delegation of power is an inevitable and necessary practice in any government. No theory of representative government is complete without it. An absolutist position against delegation would be utter foolishness. However, there are relatively uncontrollable spillover effects from delegated power. Delegation of power does something to the giver and to the receiver. From the very first to the very last act delegation is a calculated risk. If it is to be done rightly, its consequences must be understood.

The consequences in question are of constitutional importance. As far as I am concerned, they embody the key constitutional issue of our time—precisely in the spirit of Madison's epigraph. The intent of the framers is not what is at issue; the *concern* of the framers is. The purpose of the Constitution is the regulation or regularization of power in at least three ways. First, and foremost, the Constitution regulates through limitations on power. This is the essence of "the social contract" as understood by Americans. Second, substantive calculability is used to regulate power. This translates into "rule of law" as understood by Americans, and is embraced as the main antidote

---

An earlier version of this chapter, bearing the same title, appeared in *American University Law Review* 36, no. 2 (1987): 295–322. Reprinted with permission.

to tyranny, that being defined as arbitrariness. Third, power is regularized by procedural calculability. This means relatively rigid formalism defined as due process. This is captured very well in Richard Stewart's notion of constitutive law, which "consists of rules that make legally recognized practices possible" (Stewart 1987).

It is my contention that the delegation of broad and undefined discretionary power from the legislature to the executive branch deranges virtually all constitutional relationships and prevents attainment of the constitutional goals of limitation on power, substantive calculability, and procedural calculability. My argument, although a hypothesis about tendencies, has appeared to be absolutist to my critics (see, e.g., Gellhorn 1987; Sargentich 1987; Stewart 1987, 328). But fortunately, that is a consequence of my style rather than inherent in the proposition itself. Let me meet my critics and contribute to constructive exchange by putting forth one important point of clarification, which is that, because the delegation of power is a matter of degree, the change of relationship between giver and receiver is also a matter of degree; this holds true until some indeterminate point when the relationship can be said to be deranged. I like the way Ernest Gellhorn (1987, 352) puts it, with some slight translation to meet my needs. He states that delegations become excessive when they are "used to create private goods." My version would be that *all* discretion delegated to administrative agencies, by degree, provides the conditions for the creation of private goods. This is the very essence of patronage, in the feudal sense of the term, and therefore of serfdom—the capacity to distribute material resources or privileges on a personalized, individualized basis. This incorporates Gellhorn's theory as a clarification of my own criterion: At what point can duly constituted authority be turned into patronage? Although it would be improbable that the precise point would be the same for each agency, it may be possible to agree that the question of the relationship between authority and patronage is the right question.

This returns us to the direct connection between delegated discretion and constitutional derangement. Because I am not an absolutist, I have no rigid commitment to a particular set of constitutional forms, ours or anyone else's. But forms do exist for a purpose, and if broad delegation changes the form and interferes with the attainment of the purpose, then we can begin to speak of derangement and its attendant consequences, and we can do so not in absolute terms but empirically and as a matter of degree.

As I began arguing nearly twenty-five years ago (Lowi 1969), liberalism was undoing itself not because its policy goals would alienate the American people but because of its failure to appreciate the constitutional and political limitations inherent in broad delegation that would interfere with attainment of liberal policy goals by contributing to the impression and the reality of patronage, with privilege and private goods going not to the deserving but to the best organized. The reasoning was as follows: every delegation of discretion away from electorally responsible levels of government to professional career administrative agencies is a calculated risk because politics will always flow to the point of discretion, the demand for representation would take place at the point of discretion, and the constitutional forms designed to balance one set of interests against another would not be present at the point of discretion.

Such arguments in the 1960s were largely disregarded or ridiculed as unrealistic. The biggest horse laugh was given to the idea of considering the revival of the *Schechter* rule.[1] Consequently, government by broad and undefined delegated discretionary power was given a forty-year test. As liberal programs advanced toward completion of the New Deal agenda, so did the breadth of delegated discretion. My 1969 critique (Lowi 1969, 101–24) coincided with the first year of a five-year binge in the enactment of important regulatory policies. Depending on who is doing the counting, an argument can be made that Congress enacted more regulatory programs in the five years between 1969 and 1974 than during any other comparable period in our history, including the first five years of the New Deal. It is possible to identify 130 major regulatory laws enacted during the decade (see Lowi 1979, 115). Moreover, an even stronger argument can be made that the regulatory policies adopted during that period were broader in scope and more unconditional in delegated discretion than any other programs in American history.

What makes this epoch of policy creativity all the more significant is that the national government during that decade was headed by two right-of-center Republican administrations (Nixon, Ford) and one Democratic administration elected on an explicit anti-Washington campaign (Carter). Yet, most of the votes for these programs in the House and the Senate were overwhelmingly favorable, with dissents coming from both parties. Although there was occasional grumbling heard from the White House, no important bills passed by Congress were vetoed by these three presidents.

In other words, the goals and methods, and the broad, virtually unconditional delegations of power were supported by strong, bipartisan consensus. Moreover, no evidence can be found that opposition to any of these programs included arguments about unduly or dan-

1. A.L.A. Schechter Poultry Corp. v. United States, 295 U.S. 495, 529–50 (1935).

gerously broad delegations of power. Thus, those who rose then, and those who rise now to defend delegated legislative power, have had their way. Also, oblivious to the consequences that might flow from broad delegation, the lawyers and the policymakers would naturally search for other explanations when the collapse of regulatory government came. And it did come, at the very time of the regulation binge itself. I recognize that many factors may have contributed to the constitutional derangements observed here, but this in no way reduces the possibility of the causal linkage between these derangements and the rise of delegated power.

Constitutional Derangements and the Delegation of Power

From Congressional to Presidential Government

In the 1880s, political science professor Woodrow Wilson characterized American national government as "congressional government," and he published an important book under that title (see Wilson 1908). At some point toward the end of the 1930s, a book characterizing American national government as "presidential government" would have been equally appropriate. Recognized by virtually all, and embraced by most, the rise of presidential government has been explained by any number of factors, ranging from the growth of the large economy to the expansion of mass communication. But the factor most immediately and obviously involved in the change from congressional to presidential government was the voluntary, self-conscious rendering of legislative power to the president, thence to the agencies in the executive branch. I call the process "legiscide" (see Lowi 1985, 28–30).

The conversion to presidential government directly contributed to the transformation of national politics, broadly defined. The most noticeable aspect of that was the decline of national political parties and their loss of control of the presidency. The transition can be understood as one from party democracy to mass democracy, where consent is conveyed not merely by election but by regular plebiscite, expressed in weekly and monthly public opinion polls. The center of initiative has become the presidency, the center of gravity has become the executive branch, and the focus of expectations on the part of the American people follows accordingly (Lowi 1985, 67–92).

Undermining the Welfare State Consensus

The last of the great expansions of the welfare state, Supplemental Security Income and the indexing of social security benefits on top of a 20 percent boost in those benefits, occurred in 1972. These were followed within a year by official recognition of a fiscal crisis in the welfare state. The problem was less one of financing, however, than of political support. There had been considerable political support for Medicare and Medicaid, adopted in 1965.[2] There had been initial support for the boost in social security benefits and for indexing pegged to the cost of living. But over the years after 1965, many corporate and middle-class supporters of welfare were one-by-one jumping ship, despite the fact that many of the expansions of the welfare state had been aimed at benefiting the middle classes themselves. They were jumping ship largely because of the welfare programs of Aid to Families with Dependent Children, public assistance, welfare in kind, and other "means tested" programs associated with the War on Poverty. Why? Because these were discretionary welfare programs, in contrast to the first several social security titles adopted after 1935, which were relatively nondiscretionary (see Lowi 1979, 232–35).

The abandonment of the relatively clear categoric criteria of the original social security titles in favor of the highly discretionary, open-ended approach of the newer programs contributed to grievous insecurity among the very persons that welfare sought to assist, cut a deep wedge between the minority poor and city hall, and alienated large segments of formerly middle-class supporters (Lowi 1979, 207–17, 226). During the 1970s, it became de rigueur to attack the welfare state. Ironically, efforts to establish welfare as a right were coming just in the wake of the successful efforts to render the very concept of welfare increasingly vague.

Undermining Regulation

To a great extent, the undermining of the welfare categories contributed to the undermining of regulation because the problems with welfare were the most important reasons for the binge of regulatory programs and the vast expansion of the scope of each (see Lowi 1979, 220–36). Regulatory programs adopted in this period have been referred to as "social regulation," for the very good reason that they had to be societywide in order to control the costs of the welfare state. Cost containment in welfare can only go so far through such

---

2. Health Insurance for the Aged Act, Pub. L. No. 89–97, 79 Stat. 290 (codified as amended in scattered sections of 26 U.S.C.). Democrats in the House voted 237 for and 48 against, with Republicans voting 70 for and 68 against (H.R. 6675, 89th Cong., 1st Sess., 111 Cong. Rec. 18,393 [1965]). In the Senate, Democrats voted 57 for and 7 against, while Republicans voted 13 for and 17 against (H.R. 6675, 89th Cong., 1st Sess., 111 Cong. Rec. 18,514 [1965]).

practices as controlling rate charges and cleansing the welfare roles of chiselers. If the welfare state assumes responsibility for indemnifying all injuries and the dependencies attributable to them, then a maximum effort had to be made to reduce cost by reducing the number of injuries themselves. This meant more regulation. In each instance, the purpose was good; an ounce of prevention may be worth a pound of cure. But legislation merely ordaining a desired goal was bound to undermine the process itself. Demands for remedies escalated from demands for relief against specific conduct to demands for the general outcome itself as a collective right—not a right asserted by an individual to a specific remedy for a specified act of damage,[3] but a generalized "class action" right to the safe water, the safe machine.[4]

Interest-Group Liberalism, Continued

The long-established pattern of officially sponsored interest group access and representation in agency decision-making processes continued, but there were some new twists in the 1970s. New groups, emerging in what is now called "the new politics" or "public interest politics," achieved close coalitional relationships with some agencies, especially the new regulatory agencies with the broadest discretion. Many of the new groups adopted a "politics of rights," attempting to put their own interests in a safe position beyond the access of majoritarian politics (see Schoenbrod 1987). This was not an illogical development; it was in fact a predictable one, considering that all legislation tends to convey some rights to some and the new, broad "goals statutes" convey some rights absolutely (Schoenbrod 1987,

---

3. In "Returning to First Principles," Ernest Gellhorn (1987, 349) suggested that I have taken the extreme position of limiting all executive discretion "to a specific remedy for a specified act of damage." That was an incorrect interpretation of the passage. I use the passage here to indicate a change in what individuals are demanding. If I were to use this passage for anything more than that, I would take it as virtually the limiting extreme of what an ideal piece of legislation would contain. But I would certainly not be so extreme or unrealistic as to reject all legislation that went beyond a specific remedy for a specified act of damage. Stewart (1987, 331) attempts to discredit the nondelegation doctrine by characterizing it as "requiring that all regulatory statutes contain detailed rules of conduct." They do not have to be all that detailed to be good rules of conduct. Detailed rules also would be a limiting case.

4. An example from the Occupational Safety and Health Act of 1970 (OSHA) will suffice: "The Secretary . . . shall set the standard which most adequately ensures, to the extent feasible, on the basis of the best available evidence, that no employee will suffer material impairment of health or functional capacity even if such employee has regular exposure to the hazard dealt with by such standard for the period of his working life." Occupational Safety and Health Act of 1970, 29 U.S.C. 655(b)(5) (1982).

1983). Although this gave some agencies an adversarial environment that they had not before had, the general pattern of privileged relations between groups and agencies continued, and so did the declining consensus for regulation itself. There were no regular political forces or processes in the national government that had the capacity of regularly pushing interest groups back toward the more public and generalized legislative process, where confrontations and competition among groups might tend to contribute to the self-regulation of which Madison spoke so longingly in *The Federalist* no. 10.

Derangements in the Judiciary

Widespread and generally critical references to activist courts and the imperial judiciary are entirely misleading (see Pierce and Shapiro 1981). The federal courts have been activist, perhaps imperial, but only in regard to state actions. At the national government level, virtually the reverse is true. As national executive power has grown and federal agencies have grown larger as well as more numerous, the federal courts have acted as though they are seeking to maintain their power as a coordinate branch of government by joining, supplementing, and generally embracing agency powers—often by pushing agencies beyond where agency chiefs want to go and by pushing agencies to act more vigorously than agency chiefs wish to act. Relaxation of the rules of standing to sue (Friedenthal, Kane, and Miller) and the filing of class action suits seem to me to be as often as not motivated by a willingness to accommodate new politics groups who are seeking to push agencies more vigorously in a direction of statutory obligations.[5] There may be a few instances in which federal courts resist federal agencies, but the fact remains that this resistance has rarely been articulated at the level of constitutional discourse. The federal courts follow the rule of statutory construction that will render the statute constitutional, and then they proceed to interpret the statute in order to help dispose of the issues brought forth in the case being litigated. The logic of this situation is generally to expand agency powers because, in most instances, especially those involving social regulation, the terms of the delegation from Congress to the agency are so broad, and contain such high-flown rhetoric about the goals, that any but an expansive interpretation would be contrary to the spirit of the statute.[6] Among other things, this leads me to ask a

---

5. On filing class action suits, see Fed. R. Civ. P. 23.
6. Consider, e.g., the Clean Air Act Amendments of 1970 (Publ. L. No. 91–604, 84 Stat. 1676, codified at 42 U.S.C. 7401–7626 (1982) to effectuate the far-reaching goal of improving the quality of the nation's air "so as to promote the public health and welfare and the productive capacity of its population."

very important question of experts such as Richard Stewart: Why is a court that is competent to interpret existing statutes and to develop rules from its decisions within the context of this broad and ill-defined statute institutionally incompetent to judge the absence of enforceable rules in the statute? And why is it politically more acceptable and less hazardous for judges to create an operational statute out of an empty legislative enactment than it is for judges to state honestly and forthrightly that the original statute is too empty to permit judges to enforce it? (See Stewart 1987, 325–28.)

Derangement of Agency Professionalism

The derangement of agency professionalism takes two paradoxical forms. First, substantive specialization and the reputation for professional judgment are displaced by formula decision making, formalistic analysis, and the appearance of theoretical science. Second, law is replaced by economics as the language of the state. The delegation of power from the legislature is not merely a straightforward grant of authority to an agency. It is that and more. The language of these broad statutes is a systems language, a language that attempts to incorporate all of the variables that might tend to explain the existence of the problem and might provide a lead toward a solution of the problem. We talk about a systems analysis today as though that were an established fact and a phenomenon capable of being analyzed. In fact, a system is a figment of imagination, an artifact of someone's theory. This has become so much a part of our thinking that it takes on the appearance of reality when, in reality, a system is at best hypothetical. Embracing the system as the universe of analysis led policymakers to think of regulation as embracing that entire system. This imposed upon the perspective of the lawmaker and the administrator a complexity beyond human capacity—to incorporate for the purpose of empirical causal analysis, and then for the purpose of control, the totality of interdependent causes and effects (see Lowi 1991, 1992). Note the language of the Occupational Safety and Health Act (OSHA): "To assure so far as possible every working man and woman in the Nation safe and healthful working conditions and to preserve our human resources."[7] Or, take the language of President Nixon's message to the Congress as they were setting up the Environmental Protection Agency, in which he said that the purpose of his reorganization plan was to respond to "environmentally related activities" and

---

7. Occupational Safety and Health Act of 1970, Pub. L. No. 91–596, 84 Stat. 1590 (codified at 29 U.S.C. 651–678 (1982)).

organize them "rationally and systematically." He went on to argue that "we need to know more about the *total environment*" [emphasis added] if we are effectively to "ensure the protection, development . . . and enhancement of the total environment."[8]

In order to reach the entire system, a systems analysis is obviously called for, and that comes not from the substantive expertise of the professions around which the agency is organized, but from a more general, theoretical science or a language indicative of such a science. It seems fairly clear that the significantly expanded use of science and technology in decision making is, as a consequence, compromising or otherwise weakening substantive specialization and the reputation of agencies for substantive judgment. At the same time, and in response to the same set of forces, economics has been replacing law as the language of the state. Formula decision making and formalistic analysis are governed more by budgetary data, aggregate data drawn from a whole variety of extra-agency sources, and systems analytic cookbooks than from solid knowledge of the sector and the problem at hand that is built up over a lifetime of direct, sensory experience. In other words, the new requirements of system analysis tend to violate the long-established theory of administrative expertise on which our whole system is built. That is not necessarily a bad thing, but it deserves some examination.

Although some skeptical scholars such as Richard Nelson have tried to demonstrate the limits of formal reasoning in policy-making, the science/technology methodologies, ranging from aggregate quantitative indices and benefit-cost analysis to zero-based budgeting, are replacing the very professional judgments for which Congress claims to have so much respect when it leaves its statutes so inadequately constructed (Nelson 1977). The involvement of science/technology as a decision-making methodology can be explained in part by America's faith in science and technology. However, another important part of the explanation is that the provision for science/technology methodology *tends to compensate for the absence of legal integrity*. Once a systems concept is combined with general, aggregate, theoretical science and generalized cookbook decision-making formulas, the boundaries of agencies are surpassed or eradicated, as the case may be. At this point, who needs the agency at all? To whom is the legislative authority being delegated? Or, I should ask, to *what* is agency authority being delegated?

8. *President's Message to Congress Transmitting Reorganization Plans to Establish Two Agencies,* 6 Weekly Comp. Pres. Doc. 908 (9 July 1970).

Derangement of Procedure

There has been an important transition from procedure to proceduralism. We have had quite a fill already of what Stewart (1987) calls "constitutive law." Just as Congress has relied upon science and technology, so Congress also has used procedure as an effort to compensate for the absence of legal integrity in its legislative draftsmanship. On the eve of the 1970s regulatory policy binge, the leading student of administrative law, Kenneth Culp Davis, observed that broad administrative discretion is unavoidable, but that safeguards are available, thereby making administrative discretion desirable, as long as discretion is "guided by administrative rules adopted through procedure like that prescribed by the federal Administrative Procedure Act" (Davis 1969).[9] That is the classic rationalization for broad delegations and poor legislative drafting.

It is certainly better to have procedure than to have nothing. But a closer look at the politics of Congress's adoption of regulatory policies will reveal that there are at least four other reasons why procedures are provided and why, in the period of the regulation binge, procedures went *well beyond* the requirements of the APA. First, as already suggested, the procedural provisions that go well beyond the APA are adopted to compensate for unconstitutionally vague and unguided delegations of power. Second, certain kinds of procedures are adopted to open access to agency decision making in order to co-opt citizens and to add legitimacy to their processes. Although some observers are dubious that broad delegations of legislative power to administrative agencies endanger legitimacy, Congress and the agencies themselves operate as though that is a real problem, and both go out of their way to use procedure to shore up legitimacy with the various organized constituencies (see Mashaw 1985). Third, and this point is closely related to the second, procedures that provide for easy access and participation by citizens and groups to the rule-making process enable officials to encourage or channel citizens and groups into the administrative process rather than to pursue the same issues prematurely in a court. This procedure-laden rule-making process has had a significant impact on interest group politics, shifting more and more of it from the lobbies of Congress to the corridors of agencies. We need a new word for the administrative equivalent to lobbying. I propose "corridoring." Fourth, and finally, many of the procedural provisions that go beyond the APA are proposed by *oppo-*

9. 5 U.S.C. 551–59 (1982). The federal Administrative Procedure Act (APA) was intended to set forth requirements for three types of procedures available to agencies: formal adjudication, formal rule making, and informal rule making)

nents of the legislation in order to reduce the effectiveness of the programs themselves.

For all of these reasons, the time span of agency decision making, from the moment a rule is proposed to the point at which it is adopted and published in the *Federal Register,* is now exceeding an average of thirty-five months. This is used in the arguments against the legitimacy and efficiency of administrative agencies when in fact a good part of that decision-making span is attributable to the deliberate, strategic, antagonistic, or dilatory imposition of procedures.

Derangement of Presidential Power

Presidential government was a direct and immediate product of the 1930s delegations of power from Congress (see Lowi 1979; 1985). The development of the office in practice and in theory took longer, although it began in 1937 with the appeal of the President's Committee on Administrative Management, whose second sentence was, "The President needs help." Help was forthcoming, to such an extent that observers were very soon referring to the "institutional presidency" and to management as an essential feature of the presidency (Neustadt 1954, 1955). It did not stop there, and it has not stopped since that time. Every president has said, or has appointed a commission to say for him, that the president continues to need help; and every president has gotten virtually all the help he has asked for, without eliminating any of the innovations and additions inherited from his predecessors.

Presidential power has been given the stamp of approval by scholarly and journalistic experts and also by the Supreme Court. One of the greatest sources of derangement has been from the scholars, many of whom stepped forward in the 1940s, 1950s and 1960s to proclaim that the presidency was not only part of democratic theory, but was a superior form of democracy to democracy based upon the legislature. In effect, the presidency represents the "real majority." This view was reflected in decisions of the Supreme Court. Even in the historic steel seizure case, although the Supreme Court denied President Truman's claim that the president had inherent powers to seize the steel mills, the justices otherwise actually strengthened presidential power by the dictum that the president could very probably have succeeded in the seizure if he had claimed the authority to do so under an existing statute.[10]

---

10. Youngstown Sheet & Tube Co. v. Sawyer, 343 U.S. 579 (1952) esp. 585–86, which notes that the Selective Service Act and the Defense Production Act authorized the president to take both personal and real property under certain circumstances.

Another important case, *United States v. Nixon*,[11] also advanced presidential power while appearing to delimit it. The court rejected President Nixon's claim to executive privilege as a constitutional protection against delivery of the Watergate tapes, but at the same time, the court stated only that the claim to executive privilege did not protect documents from a subpoena in a criminal prosecution. In all other instances, such as when there is a specific need to protect military, diplomatic, or sensitive national security secrets, executive privilege for the presidency is a privilege—qualified, but nonetheless a privilege.

The constitutional basis of presidential power was advanced again in 1983 when the Supreme Court declared the legislative veto unconstitutional.[12] The purpose of this device, which Congress had applied to 295 provisions in 196 laws, was to take back in bits and pieces what Congress had given away since the 1930s in increasingly large chunks of delegated legislative power (Abourezk 1977). Although not of fundamental importance, the decision tipped the balance between the two branches still further toward the presidency. The only other case of any importance in advancing presidential power was, in 1986, *Bowsher v. Synar*,[13] which involved the constitutionality of parts of the Gramm-Rudman-Hollings law. Here again, the Court appeared at first blush to be cutting down on presidential as well as congressional power by its ruling that Congress was relying on nonexecutive offices to make executive decisions. This threw back on Congress the burden of deficit containment and left open for the future a crisis in all independent regulatory commissions. Although the Supreme Court did not adopt the circuit court's explicit argument on this point, they have left the door open to a future attack that will require Congress to put all the independent regulatory commissions directly within presidential authority.[14]

This suggests that both Congress and the Court, having granted and approved, respectively, the enormous delegations of discretion in a long series of enactments and decisions, have locked themselves into a kind of imperative to grant additional powers, constitutional validation, and ideological embrace to the presidency in order to accomplish the impossible task of meeting the obligations that the stat-

---

11. 418 U.S. 683 (1984).
12. INS v. Chadha, 462 U.S. 919 (1983).
13. 106 S. Ct. 3183 (1986).
14. The probability of this increased significantly with the presence of Antonin Scalia and Clarence Thomas on the Supreme Court.

utes impose. If lawyers would spend half as much time expressing concern over the impossibility of presidential control of administrative agencies as they do on the impossibility of Congress's formulating decent rules of law, both presidential control and congressional lawmaking would improve immeasurably.

The Conservative Reaction

As I predicted earlier (Lowi 1969), liberalism was eventually its own undoing. Liberalism's electoral collapse was due to the structure of its laws, the increasingly discretionary character of its administrative agencies, and the disappointment and indignation that arose out of frustrated expectations built on high-flown rhetoric about collective rights to statutory goals. There were actually two reactions to liberal excesses. One was libertarianism and the other conservatism (see, generally, Newman 1984; Lowi, forthcoming). Libertarians and conservatives made common cause against big national government. Both sought to make the domestic part of the government smaller, especially in the area of the regulatory agencies. The two reactions, however, are far from identical.

The libertarian reaction was a genuine demand for deregulation. Libertarians are the descendents of the nineteenth-century, free-market liberals and had been screaming, pretty much in the wilderness, against all forms of government intervention since the 1930s. The size and strength of the libertarian critique did not really begin to revive until the liberalism of the New Deal was already in a virtual shambles in the 1970s. The growth of the popularity of the libertarian position must be attributed more to the failure of New Deal liberalism than to the strength of the libertarian position itself. Because it was suspected all along of being a front for and a sycophant to important economic interests, libertarians attempted to show in the 1970s that the costs of these regulatory programs clearly outweighed any benefits they produced. The data base for this argument, however, was extremely questionable.

Much of the data came from research done in the 1970s by Murray Weidenbaum (1978), who went on to serve as President Reagan's first Chairman of the Council of Economic Advisers. Because compliance costs are so varied across the different businesses and industries, and because firm data are hard to obtain and are usually mixed with highly subjective experiences, Weidenbaum and his team took a single year, 1976, and assimilated various studies of their own and those of a variety of other scholars to arrive at a rough estimate of $62 billion for the compliance costs to businesses (Weidenbaum 1978, 4).[15] Wiedenbaum then estimated the bureaucratic costs of regulation, deriving these from the budgets of the various regulatory agencies, and came up with a figure of $3.1 billion. This gave him a total cost of regulation for 1976 as $65 billion. But more important, Weidenbaum noted the twenty-to-one ratio between compliance costs and administrative costs and used this as the multiplier for all other years. Thus, in 1979, the estimated administrative costs came to $4.8 billion and, with the application of the multiplier of twenty, resulted in an easy estimate of $97.9 billion. Adding the $97.9 billion to the $4.8 billion, he calculated an overall cost of $102.7 billion.[16] This produced an impressive absolute figure for each year and a spectacular impression of growth—55 percent in a mere three-year period. A later reevaluation (Schwarz 1988, 90–106) of Weidenbaum's figures revealed that actual regulatory costs stayed at exactly the same percentage of GNP in 1979 as they had been in 1976.[17] In other words, modern liberalism was its own worst enemy; its failings produced such a large target that it was almost impossible for libertarianism to miss.

The genuine conservatives make a much more important and interesting case because they are no more against government regulation than are the New Deal liberals. Contrary to the expectations of most people, there was more real deregulation in the four years of the Carter administration than during all the years of the Reagan administration. President Reagan only once confronted Congress with a request for legislation actually terminating any regulatory authority, that of the Interstate Commerce Commission (ICC). Instead, the Reagan administration sought and took on significant increases in managerial power to reduce the regulatory burden, not by terminating or shrinking any of the authority now held in the executive branch, but by retaining the power and using it to control the agencies so as to reduce or delay the output of rules. The difference here is quite significant and is consonant with the history of the growth of executive power. President Reagan could reduce significantly the level and intensity of government intervention while leaving the *ca-*

---

15. The study found the aggregate cost of complying with federal regulation came to $62.6 billion in 1976 or over $300 for each man, woman, and child in the United States.

16. This consists of $4.8 billion of direct expenses by federal regulatory agencies and $97.9 billion of cost of private sector compliance.

17. Schwarz's recalculation of Weidenbaum's own figures produces a total cost of federal regulation for 1979 at $27 billion *less* than Weidenbaum's public figures claim.

pacity for intervention intact for himself and his successors. The following are examples of the conservative approach to *regulation management* as distinct from deregulation.

Impoverishing the Agencies

Budget cuts such as 15 percent of the Federal Trade Commission budget and 30 percent of the Consumer Product Safety Commission budget suggest a strategy of weakening agencies into submission. But note well that there was no equivalent shrinkage of their statutory authority.

Appointing Commissioners Hostile to Their Programs

Appointing hostile commissioners to preside over agencies while leaving statutory authority intact maximizes the president's opportunity to engage in discretionary deregulation as an aspect of regulation management. And note from the scandals in agencies such as the Environmental Protection Agency that discretionary deregulation has not been an across-the-board, evenhanded, downward pressure on regulation.

Strengthening Presidential Oversight

With the demise of the legislative veto, the regulatory review power lodged in the Office of Management and Budget (OMB) gives the president substantive item veto through the back door even as he fails to get constitutional item veto through the front door. The route to substantive item veto in the regulatory field is largely through the cost-benefit review process. It extends as a mandatory process to all departmental regulatory agencies and, as a matter of strong obligation, even to the independent regulatory commissions.

This amounts to a significant increase in the centralization of the executive branch. It has actually come at the expense of the budget process, a price, however, that a conservative president is obviously willing to pay. Increased centralization has meant the reversal of traditional budgeting from "bottom-up" budgeting, in which OMB assembles all the agency requests and constructs a budget from them, to a "top-down" approach, in which the White House sets the budgetary ceilings on goals and these are reconciled by the agencies before they go to Congress for the prescribed congressional reconciliation. This puts OMB in the position to set the terms of regulatory discourse. OMB officials are quick to protest that no more than 10 percent of the proposed rules submitted to OMB are actually turned down. But there seems to be a general consensus that this review process affects a far larger number of rules by influencing the form of their drafting prior to the review process, and far more than 10 percent are probably sent back to agencies for revision prior to ultimate approval. Thus, although it is true that the Reagan administration reduced the total amount of regulation, as measured by the number and cost of rules emanating from regulatory agencies, it achieved this result through executive centralization rather than through the actual shrinkage of executive authority (Seidman and Gilmore 1986).

Regulating the Poor

The Reagan administration significantly expanded regulatory authority over welfare cases and welfare clients. Cleansing the eligibility lists, stigmatizing welfare to reduce demands, and using the conditions of welfare to teach moral lessons in work and prudence are good examples of conservative approaches to regulation. This is not small government or decentralized government, but *different* government.

Using the Deficit as Regulation Management

There are at least two different theories of deficits. One is the Keynesian theory, which treats the deficit as a fiscal instrument. The other is the supply-side theory in which the deficit is, among other things, a regulatory instrument; it works as an automatic control over domestic commitments. Never mind that the immense and growing deficits of the 1980s contributed significantly to the revival of the economy after the fairly deep recession of 1981–82. The fact is that these tremendous deficits will put very severe ceilings on what Congress can do in the domestic field long after conservatives are out of office.

Restoring Regulatory Power to the States

Although neither President Reagan nor President Bush tried as hard as their far right wing demanded, it is nevertheless an indication of the attitude of contemporary conservatism toward government power that the two administrations unqualifiedly endorsed the restoration of the many powers taken from the states by the Supreme Court since the 1950s. These include the drastic reduction of the power of the states over persons accused of crimes; the virtual elimination of the power of the states over religious observances in the public schools; the virtual elimination of the power of the states over pregnant women and their fetuses; the restriction of the authority of local and county welfare administrators over welfare clients in the determination of eligibility without entitlement; and restoration of the power of states, counties, and cities to apply their own interpretation of national voting rights laws. These demonstrate that there is almost nothing about conservative administrations at the national, state, or local levels that indicates any inclination to reverse the fifty-year tendency toward discretionary agencies and centralized executive power. On the contrary, the purpose of decentralizing powers is to restore moral hegemony to state and local governments.

The Two Roads to Serfdom

The governmental and political institutions shaped during the fifty-plus years since 1933 have not been put under siege by the first serious alternative to liberalism this century. Whatever the "Reagan revolution" may amount to in terms of a change of policy direction, it does not amount to a revolution against liberal institutions because nothing about the Reagan revolution was aimed at the overly powerful presidency, the mass base of the presidency, the peripheral (albeit occasionally pesky) Congress, the discretionary agencies, or the cooperative courts. Here are two reasons why.

First, liberal national institutions suit conservatives. Conservatism should have tried to tone down the vulgar, mass democracy of the plebiscitary presidency and the immense size and power of the executive branch. But conservatives also need a bully pulpit; if it happens to have been built by liberalism, so be it.

This points to the second reason why conservative administrations have embraced liberal institutions: conservatives are *not* libertarians. Conservatives need a solid structure, just as modern liberals do, but a structure with a different orientation. George F. Will, one of the few writers who grasps the difference between conservatism and libertarianism made the point best. Conservatives have no interest, Will points out, in dismantling the strong national government. Rather, according to Will (1983, 23), they believe in strong government, "including the essentials of the welfare state."[18] Conservatives, however, in Will's view, reject liberal "uncertainty about . . . human nature" (Will 1983, 56–57).[19] In other words, Will argues, "statecraft" must attempt "soulcraft." Let there be regulatory policy—but for the purpose of restoring moral hegemony to traditional elites. Let there

18. In this same discussion (Will 1983, 126–32), he states that if conservatism is to engage itself with present ways of living, it must address government's graver purposes with an affirmative doctrine of the welfare state.

19. In the nineteenth century, a growing uncertainty about the very idea of a known or even knowable human nature was the reason for people to desire a statecraft that made an attempt at soulcraft. Recently, however, the reason for rejecting the state's engagement in soulcraft is nervousness about the very idea of human nature.

be welfare policy—but for the primary purpose of teaching the moral lessons required to bring the poor and self-indulgent classes into the realm of proper comportment within proper authority. Justice William Rehnquist, not William Simon or David Stockman, is the correct personification of the conservative era; the free market comes second to a strong state capable of exercising moral leadership, moral education, moral mobilization, and moral authority.

Because conservatives need a large discretionary state as much as the liberals, there is at present no constituency for the rule of law. Interest group liberals have been impatient to get on with goals defined by sentiment and by the claims of the best-organized groups. New politics groups are even more concerned with getting a favorable administrative environment. Conservative groups seek their own economic goals for the national government and moral hegemony for their new federalism. But why should that be otherwise? The surprising thing is that the legal experts offer no counterpoise. In their struggle for the power they have enjoyed as a profession throughout most of their history, lawyers have joined the flow rather than fight or shape it. Defense of the rule of law by old-fashioned lawyers and older liberals was wiped away as a mask for the status quo (see Ackerman 1984). Legal realists debunked the rule of law as a mere rationalization for private values. Later, legal realists proposed essentially to exchange the rule of law for the artificial science of economics and economic reasoning. Worst of all, the largest number of mainstream legal scholars hammer more nails in the coffin of the rule of law by providing reasoned arguments for why the effort to establish the rule of law, especially in legislative drafting, is unrealistic, unnecessary, counterproductive, and, in some instances, downright undesirable.

Let us take Stewart's position as an illustrative (and illustrious) case in point. First, to make his case for broad delegation, Stewart posits a false dichotomy: Congress cannot "write detailed commands" (1987, 324) or "precise rules of conduct" (328), *therefore,* broad and undefined delegation is the only alternative. Stewart then adds to this a second false dichotomy: federal courts are not "institutionally competent" to "invalidate wholesale" congressional statutes (326), *therefore,* broad delegation to administrative agencies is not only desirable but unreviewable (327–28). That is, the judiciary, for reasons not given, would have to condemn entire statutes on the grounds that the policies are too important to be left to administrators or that such delegations are not necessary and proper, and because this would "usurp judgments which we as a nation have concluded ever since 1937 ought to be resolved through political mechanisms," *therefore,* courts must not review the propriety of a delegation at all (326).

It is inexplicably ideological not to examine any middle points or other alternatives. Stewart leaves no room whatsoever for a bad first effort to be improved by successive efforts, unless he believes that Congress cannot learn from the experience of the administrative agencies in trying to implement the vague first effort at lawmaking (Stewart 1987, 324). Good legislation ought to be a matter of successive approximations—through later amendments, and, best of all, through codification.[20] Stewart, like so many others, apologizes for congressional incompetence by telling us how busy Congress is already (doing what?), and by telling us how much more complex our society is today (Stewart 1987, 329–30). Because no data or arguments are given to support such an apology, it remains in the realm of pure ideology. In fact, to the state legislators of the 1840s, society must have seemed immeasurably more complex than ours seems to us today. They were, after all, living in the midst of the Industrial Revolution; there was not yet any established economic theory of capitalism, no clear grasp of fractional reserve banking or insurance; and, according to the legal historians I read, even the tort law was only barely emerging (Horowitz 1977). Meanwhile, there was less continuity among legislators and less education. They had fewer staff members and a smaller budget with which to buy expertise and research. There were also problems such as greater party domination and more corruption. Yet, there was much more legal integrity in the average statute produced by the state legislatures of the 1840s than in the average statute coming out of Congress today.

Turn now to that part of the apology where Stewart (1987, 328) and others argue that it is next to impossible to formulate good rules of law for such a "vast and varied nation." The fact is that *proposals* for legislation are usually very clear and provide a very sound basis for articulating a general rule. When organized interest groups come before Congress, they tend to know exactly what they want and can generalize their wants into a rule that would be clearly understood

---

20. In the first edition of *The End of Liberalism*, I left myself open to criticism that I was relying on the judiciary to solve all the problems of democracy by proposing that we revive the *Schechter* rule in order to force Congress to do its job by making decent rules of law. "Juridical democracy" was interpreted to mean "judicial democracy," despite my insistence that the two were far from identical (Lowi 1969, chap. 10). Efforts to correct that impression in the second edition and in other writings did not fully succeed. The purpose of the later efforts was to move the issue to a middle ground, recognizing the inevitability of broad "policy-without-law" in the first instance, followed by "successive approximations" of decent rules of law (Lowi 1979, 307). But there will be no such middle ground as long as legal experts tell legislators that their accomplishments are historically inevitable and the best possible under the circumstances.

and applicable to a known category of people or conduct. It is true that the rules they would have Congress adopt tend to be much too self-serving and often patently contrary to the public interest. It is the job of Congress to take these proposals and to work out compromises with the various contrary and conflicting proposals until a majority is ready to vote final passage. Thus, the burning question here is not why Congress is unable to formulate legislation with clear rules, but why Congress, in the process of compromise, takes proposals that embody clear rules and turns them into the vague and meaningless delegations of power that apologists call inevitable. All of this gives the ring of eternal verity to the observation (attributed to Bismarck) that "those who love laws and sausages would do well not to watch either one being made." Granted compromise is required in a system of majority rule and, granted also, compromise is not very pretty; but there is more than one kind of compromise. In fact, there are at least two kinds of compromise: compromise through weakness and compromise through vagueness.

The classic illustration of compromise through weakness is the compromise typical of business transactions in which the seller is asking far too much and the purchaser is willing to pay far too little. Each side weakens its initial position until the point where a transaction can be made, ordinarily to their mutual satisfaction. Bear in mind, however, that the item being exchanged (or, more generally, the point at issue) remains pretty much the same.

The second type of compromise, compromise through vagueness, is one in which two parties may start out with a clear understanding of the item to be exchanged or the point at issue between them, but they reach the compromise by altering the definition of the item or the point at issue, rendering the definition sufficiently vague so that each side can leave with its own kind of definition of what was at issue, what was exchanged, and how much was actually paid for it. In any of the numerous instances when original proposals are clear regarding the point at issue, there is absolutely no compelling reason why Congress chooses compromise through vagueness over compromise through weakness. But with apologists like law professors, why not?[21]

21. Because there are so few good examples of compromise through weakness (which is the same as saying there are so few good examples of law with legal integrity), I will offer the very imperfect example of the Civil Rights Act of 1964, Pub. L. No. 88–352, 78 Stat. 241 (codified as amended at 28 U.S.C. 1447; 42 U.S.C. 1971, 1975a–1975d, 2000a–2000h-6, (1982)). Because the major provisions were (1) fairly clear about the rule of law embodied therein; and (2) very controversial, compromises of a most delicate sort were called for. Proponents of the legislation enlisted the efforts of

Then there is the famous court defense. For years, the federal courts have been regularly displacing the judgment of administrators—and that is not seen as an interference into the political functions. This underscores once again how curiously ideological it is for the apologists merely to assert that for courts to engage in constitutional review of delegation would mean a leap into invalidating most of the regulatory statutes on the books and that this would reverse court positions over the past two centuries (see Stewart 1987, 325–27). In the first place, even if courts courted the apocalypse by making constitutional issues out of delegation, this would not immediately and patently mean that all regulatory statutes would be invalidated wholesale, nor would it mean that the courts would be forced to wipe out entire statutes. It should not be necessary to remind lawyers that cases come up one by one and that most important statutes embodying broad delegations are composed of sections and titles, with each subject to separate legal attack. Second, the courts would not have to invalidate a provision of the statute in so many words, such as "this provision is unconstitutional because it violates the separation of powers." Although not a lawyer, I do not believe my picture of the process is all that inaccurate. First, as already proposed, the court would not have to pass on the entire statute, but only on a particular section or title that is at issue. Second, the court would not have to invalidate, in the positive sense implied by that term, but could actually take a *Shelley v. Kraemer* approach—in effect, "Congress can pass an empty section 1066 or a totally opaque title V, but the courts cannot enforce them."[22] Third, courts, in the words of President Andrew Jackson, are not the only interpreters of the Constitution. If the court finds itself without sufficient guidelines to enforce a particular provision, Congress could respond by revising that section of the law, or administrators could find some means of enforcement other than court orders.

Finally, although I have utmost respect for Stewart's (1987, 335–41) proposal for resort to "constitutive law," I am unable to see this

---

the "Great Compromiser," Hubert Humphrey. For most of the provisions, the Humphrey forces did not seek majority support by redefining the point at issue into a vague goal statute such as, "let there be fair treatment by 1974." Instead, they usually kept the point at issue close to the original proposals that the civil rights forces devised and sought compromise by weakening the sanctions or lengthening the time span for implementation. For example, they even agreed to provide jury trials for contempt of court in some of the enforcement procedures. See 42 U.S.C. 2000h (1982), which allows for jury trial in criminal contempt proceedings.

22. 334 U.S. 1 (1948), esp. 13–21.

as any kind of a solution to the problem of excessive delegation or excessive centralization. First, as Stewart himself confesses, "constitutive rules necessarily have prescriptive elements . . . [and] prescriptive rules are created by constitutive processes" (336). Second, although it is true that constitutive rules "allow subsystem actors a measure of discretion that permits incorporation of subsystem interests and values in decisions about conduct" (336–37), it is very unfair to suggest that a clear rule of law cannot permit interaction with subsystem values. If a clear rule of law required absolute, lockstep obedience through which everyone "must act as federal officials direct," (Stewart 1983, 336–37) then no one in his right mind would be in favor of clear rules of law under any conditions. To be equal and opposite in my argument, I would be forced to say that we must oppose constitutive rules because we would be absolutely obliged to accept the decisions made by the constitutive process, even if those go contrary to basic values or national goals (whatever those might be). I see no need to take that position, however, because common sense tells me that for every constitutive law there is very likely to be a prescriptive rule or a set of rules, or some well-understood limit as to the permissible range of outcomes.

Conclusion

Prospect of rule of law has too often been cast as a debate between formalist and antiformalist models. As a formalist, I will close with some comments about the consequences of antiformalism. My problem with antiformalism, or informalism, is that it amounts to a rationalization for government grounded in nothing. Liberal antiformalists rationalize their position with the authority of process allegedly grounded in science—which means methodology, a process. That is a bed of sand. Conservative antiformalists rationalize their position with the authority of morality arising out of virtuous character, or "soulcraft." That is a swamp. In both cases, antiformalism is a rationalization for government by authority rather than government by rule.

For most of the twentieth century, the national government was dominated by a liberal consensus, and the antiformalist rationalization was a defense of liberal authority. With the rise of conservatism on a national scale during the past decade, we acquired a second system of authority, for which antiformalism is equally rationalization. Government being what it is, these opposite approaches come to the same end as serfdom or the moral equivalent thereof.

Serfdom is a condition of dependency on patronage. Patronage in the medieval sense, as in "to patronize," is a relationship between holders of resources (patrons) and seekers to resources (clients), where the holders have the discretion or power to share their resources—material goods or privileges—on a personal basis. This can be in response to meritorious personal claims, or on a personal basis in which the patron seeks to recruit the client's loyalty or a general reputation for virtue or goodwill. In our modern context, patronage remains the same: *The greater the discretion that accompanies the delegation of power, the greater the capacity of agencies to become patrons because discretion enables them to convert regulatory or welfare policies into resources for group or individual patronage.*

The antidote to government by patronage is not termination of the policies or the agencies, but *reduction of their discretion*. Otherwise, conservatism and liberalism speak to each other with nothing better than alternative roads to serfdom. I have said this a dozen different ways over the past years, but Charles Hamilton (1979) of Columbia University may have said it best when he expressed his concern that American blacks may have moved from the status of slavery to the status of subject to the status of recipient, without ever having enjoyed the status of citizenship.[23] It would be a great pity if that became the new equality for everybody.

REFERENCES

Abourezk, James. 1977. "The Congressional Veto: A Contemporary Response to Executive Encroachment on Legislative Prerogative." *Indiana Law Journal* 52(2):323–95.

Ackerman, Bruce. 1984. *Reconstructing American Law.* Cambridge, Mass.: Harvard University Press.

Davis, Kenneth C. 1969. *Discretionary Justice: A Preliminary Inquiry.* Baton Rouge: Louisiana State University Press.

Friedenthal, Jack H., Mary Kay Kane, and Arthur R. Miller. 1985. *Civil Procedure.* St. Paul, Minn.: West Publishers.

Gellhorn, Ernest. 1987. "Returning to First Principles." *American University Law Review.* 36(2):345–54.

Hamilton, Charles V. 1979. "The Patron-Recipient Relationship and Minority Politics in New York City." *Political Science Quarterly* 94(2):211–28.

---

23. This is a slight variation on a theme set forth in Hamilton (1979).

Horowitz, Morton. 1977. *The Transformation of American Law.* Cambridge, Mass.: Harvard University Press.

Lowi, Theodore J. 1969. *The End of Liberalism: Ideology, Policy and the Crisis of Public Authority.* New York: W. W. Norton.

———. 1979. *The End of Liberalism: The Second Republic of the United States.* 2d ed. New York: W. W. Norton.

———. 1985. *The Personal President; Power Invested, Promise Unfulfilled.* Ithaca, N.Y.: Cornell University Press.

———. 1991. "Toward a Legislature of the First Kind." In *Knowledge, Power and the Congress.* Edited by W. H. Robinson and C. H. Wellhorn. Washington, D.C.: Congressional Quarterly.

———. 1992. "The State in Political Science: How We Become What We Study." *American Political Sciences Review* 86(1):1–7.

———. 1993. "Before Conservatism and Beyond: American Ideology and Politics in the 1990s." Norman, Okla.: University of Oklahoma Press (forthcoming).

Mashaw, Jerry L. 1985. "Prodelegation: Why Administrators Should Make Political Decisions." *Journal of Law, Economics and Organization* 1(1):81–100.

Nelson, Richard R. 1977. *The Moon and the Ghetto.* New York: W. W. Norton.

Neustadt, Richard E. 1954. "Presidency and Legislation: The Growth of Central Clearance." *American Political Science Review* 48(3):641–71.

———. 1955. "Presidency and Legislation: Planning the President's Program." *American Political Science Review* 29(4):980–1021.

Newman, Stephen L. 1984. *Liberalism at Wit's End: The Libertarian Revolt against the Modern State.* Ithaca, N.Y.: Cornell University Press.

Pierce, Richard J., and Sidney A. Shapiro. 1981. "Political and Judicial Review of Agency Action." *Texas Law Review* 59(7):1175–1222.

Sargentich, Thomas O. 1987. "The Delegation Debate and Competing Ideals of the Administrative Process." *American University Law Review* 36(2):419–42.

Schoenbrod, David. 1983. "Goals, Statutes or Rules Statutes: The Case of the Clean Air Act." *University of California Los Angeles Law Review* 30(4):740–828.

———. 1987. "Separation of Powers and the Powers That Be: The Constitutional Purposes of the Delegation Doctrine." *American University Law Review* 36(2):355–90.

Schwarz, John E. 1988. *America's Hidden Success.* Rev. ed. New York: W. W. Norton.

Seidman, Harold, and Robert Gilmour. 1986. *Politics, Position, and Power.* 4th ed. New York: Oxford University Press.

Stewart, Richard. 1987. "Beyond the Delegation Doctrine." *American University Law Review* 36(2):323–44.

Weidenbaum, Murray. 1978. "The Costs of Government Regulation of Business." Study prepared for the use of the Subcommittee on Economic Growth and Stabilization of Joint Economic Congressional Commission of the United States. Washington, D.C.: Government Printing Office.
Will, George F. 1983. *Statecraft as Soulcraft*. New York: Simon & Schuster.
Wilson, Woodrow. 1908. *Constitutional Government in the United States*. New York: Columbia University Press.

CHAPTER EIGHT

The Enduring Legacy of Republicanism

CASS R. SUNSTEIN

THE TWENTY-FIRST CENTURY is approaching in a time of considerable dissatisfaction with the American scheme of governance. The dissatisfaction takes various forms, but many of the concerns have a common root in the problems produced by the existence of interest groups, or "factions," and their influence over the political process. The scheme is challenged on the grounds that it allows powerful private organizations to block necessary government action (see, e.g., Lowi 1979), that the lawmaking process has been transformed into a series of accommodations among competing elites (see, e.g., Connolly 1969; Kariel 1970), and that the rise of a large bureaucracy exercising broad discretionary power has undermined original constitutional goals by circumventing the safeguards of separation of powers and electoral accountability (see, e.g., Freedman 1978; Stewart 1975).

The problem of faction has been a central concern of constitutional law and theory since the time of the American Revolution. Madison made control of factions the centerpiece of his defense of the proposed Constitution. His Anti-Federalist opponents objected on the ground that his solution was a false one, addressing only a symptom of the underlying problem. This debate has been recapitulated in various forms throughout constitutional history.

The central purpose of this discussion is to link three seemingly disparate areas of public law theory. The first area is the Madisonian understanding of politics and the role of representatives in counteracting the problems posed by the existence of factions. The second

An earlier version of this chapter appeared as "Interest Groups in American Public Law," *Stanford Law Review* 38 (1985): 29–87. Reprinted with permission.

is legal doctrine that interprets a number of constitutional provisions, particularly the equal protection clause. That doctrine is best understood as an attempt to impose on government a particular conception of politics, with powerful Madisonian overtones. The third area is judge-made doctrine that came into existence under the Administrative Procedure Act and other statutes that govern the conduct of regulatory agencies. Much of administrative law doctrine is also intended to respond to the problem of faction by ensuring a particular sort of behavior from public officials. All three areas reflect the same basic conception of politics and of the proper role of national representatives. That conception repudiates some of the most prominent current theories about how government does and should operate.

More broadly, I also hope to help revive aspects of an attractive conception of governance—we may call it republican—to point out its often neglected but nonetheless prominent place in the thought of the framers and to suggest its availability as a foundation from which citizens, judges, and others might evaluate political processes and outcomes. Despite the ascendancy of other approaches, this conception has continued to influence the public and the judicial mind, even in circumstances in which it seems utopian. The central commitments of the republican conception are far from anachronistic, and in its belief in a deliberative conception of democracy, the republican ideal provides a basis for evaluating administrative and legislative action that has both powerful historical roots and considerable contemporary appeal.

Introduction: Virtue, Faction, and Corruption

When the proposed constitution was debated, the country faced a choice between two different conceptions of politics. The first conception was republican. Its animating principle was civic virtue. To the republicans, the prerequisite of sound government was the willingness of citizens to subordinate their private interests to the general good (Wood 1992; Storing 1981*b*, 19–23). Politics consisted of self-rule by the people; but it was not a scheme in which people impressed their private preferences on the government. It was instead a system in which the selection of governing values was the object of the governmental process. Preferences were not to be taken as exogenous; they were to be developed and shaped through politics.

To the republicans, the role of politics was above all deliberative. Dialogue and discussion among the citizenry were critical features in the governmental process. Political participation was not limited to voting or other simple statements of preference. The ideal model for governance was the town meeting, a metaphor that played an explicit role in the republican understanding of politics (see, e.g., Storing 1981a, 5:67–69).

The republican conception carries with it a particular view of human nature; it assumes that through discussion people can, in their capacities as citizens, escape private interests and engage in pursuit of the public good. In this respect, political ordering is distinct from market ordering. Moreover, this conception reflects the belief that debate and discussion help to reveal that some values are superior to others. Denying that decisions about values are merely matters of taste, the republican view assumes that "practical reason" can be used to settle social issues.

With this understanding, the problem of faction assumes a distinct form and has a distinct solution. The problem is rooted in corruption: the elimination of civic virtue and the pursuit of self-interest by political actors. If corruption occurs, groups seeking to use government power to promote their own private ends might come to dominate the political process. If private groups were permitted to subvert government in this way, political power would supplant political discussion and debate. Corruption thus threatens to undermine the republican conception of politics. The traditional solution is to instill principles of virtue in the hope of ensuring that the spirit of faction will not develop.[1] Education and prevailing morality therefore provide the principal lines of defense against the dangers of faction.

Distinct from the republican understanding of government is a competing conception that might be called pluralist (see, e.g., Bentley 1908; Dahl 1956; Truman 1963; for the economic view, see Peltzman [1976]). Under the pluralist view, politics mediates the struggle among self-interested groups for scarce social resources. Only nominally deliberative, politics is a process of conflict and compromise among various social interests. Under the pluralist conception, people come to the political process with preselected interests that they seek to promote through political conflict and compromise. Preferences are not shaped through governance, but enter into the process as exogenous variables.

The pluralist conception treats the republican notion of a separate common good as incoherent, potentially totalitarian, or both.[2]

---

1. See, e.g., Jefferson's view: "Enlighten the people generally, and tyranny and oppressions of body and mind will vanish like evil spirits at the dawn of day" (Lipscomb and Bergh 1903, 14:491).
2. See Schumpeter (1950) but cf. Madison's *The Federalist* no. 10 (this and all other numbers of *The Federalist* referred to in this discussion are found in Wills (1982),

The common good consists of uninhibited bargaining among the various participants, so that numbers and intensities of preferences can be reflected in political outcomes. The common good amounts to an aggregation of individual preferences. Moreover, efforts to alter or shape preferences—through, for example, the education so prized by the republican tradition—may assume the status of tyranny.

Under the pluralist conception, the problem of faction arises from the possibility that one group, or an alliance of groups, will dominate the legislative or executive process and subvert the bargaining and compromise on which the model is based. Factional domination effectively deprives other groups of the opportunity to assert their views. If it were permitted to occur, the political process would be undermined and freedom would be at risk.

There are several possible solutions to the problem of faction. One response would be to create a shield of "rights"—spheres of individual autonomy into which government may not enter. Such a solution would deflect factional tyranny, whether by a majority or by a minority, by declaring certain areas to be off limits to legislators. This shield of autonomy could protect a number of different interests, ranging from rights of traditional private property to protection against discrimination on the basis of race or gender.

Another response would be to accept the pluralist conception of politics as descriptively accurate, but conclude that it is no cause for alarm. This view would allow politics to consist of uninhibited interest group struggle in the expectation that the struggle will promote social welfare better than any alternative system (see Becker 1983). Political ordering is, in this view, assimilated to market ordering. Both the variety and the intensity of preferences would be factored into the political pressures imposed on representatives. The representatives would be expected to respond rather mechanically to those pressures.[3] This marketlike mechanism would promote aggregate social welfare through an "invisible hand" similar to that found in other markets. In the view of many, this understanding lies at the core of majority rule (see Downs 1957). By denying that the existence of factions poses a problem for democratic theory, this approach accepts the pluralist model not only descriptively, but normatively as well.

A third possible response to the problem of faction would modify the second by accepting large elements of the pluralist conception

---

which suggests that an effort to extirpate factions through removing their cause is a cure worse than the disease.

3. This is a familiar if controversial view of representation. See Pitkin (1967, 198–208).

and incorporating the concern that certain groups are effectively "fenced out" of the pluralist process because they are unable to participate in political bargaining.[4] Sometimes this disability is attributed to the "discreteness and insularity" of the excluded groups.[5] The attribution is questionable, for discreteness and insularity may increase rather than impair the opportunities for the exercise of political power.[6] Disability is also attributed to dispersion and lack of political organization. The critical point is that it may be possible to accept many of the elements of the pluralist model while also concluding that steps must be taken to protect certain disadvantaged groups.

Yet another response to the problem of faction would structure the processes of representation to ensure against the likelihood of factional tyranny. The structural mechanisms would insulate representatives, to a greater or lesser degree, from constituent pressures, in the hope that they will deliberate more effectively on the public good. Unlike the alternative solutions, the structural response often represents a repudiation of the premises of pluralism and, as discussed below, might be understood as a variation on the republican understanding as it has been defined here.

The Historical Articulation: Federalists, Anti-Federalists

It should come as no surprise that many of these ideas played a central role in the debates over the framing and ratification of the Constitution. In particular, the debate between the Federalists and the Anti-Federalists focused on the respective roles of civic virtue, interest groups, and political pressure in the process of governance. In tracing these themes, I make no claim to special originality, though the account offered here differs from some prominent readings in significant ways (see, e.g., Ackerman 1991; Wood 1992; Diggins 1984; Pitkin 1967, 191–96; Adair 1951; Ackerman 1984; Diamond 1977). Moreover, it will be necessary to paint with a broad brush, avoiding detailed discussion of the significant differences among both the Anti-Federalists and the framers. The major purpose is to suggest the nature and origins of the Federalist understanding of politics and

---

4. This approach accounts for large areas of modern constitutional law. See United States v. Carolene Prods. Co., 304 U.S. 144, 152 n.4 (1938); see, generally, Ely (1980), who attempts to use this principle as the basis for a conception of politics and of the proper judicial role.

5. For the classic formulation, see *Carolene Products*, 304 U.S. at 152 n.4.

6. Ackerman (1985) suggests that diffuseness is sometimes more likely to weaken political influence than "discreteness."

representation, an understanding that has played an important role in judge-made public law ever since.

The Anti-Federalist Case

In recent years, there has been a resurgence of enthusiasm for the arguments of the Anti-Federalists—opponents of the proposed Constitution, who claimed that the document amounted to a betrayal of the principles underlying the Revolution.[7] An animating principle of the Anti-Federalists was civic virtue or "public happiness." Governmental outcomes were, in this view, to be determined by citizens devoted to a public good separate from the struggle of private interests; government's first task was to ensure the flourishing of the necessary public-spiritedness. Moreover, the Anti-Federalists believed in decentralization. Only in small communities would it be possible to find and develop the unselfishness and devotion to the public good on which genuine freedom depends. Participation in government was a positive good, providing a kind of "happiness" that could be found nowhere else.[8] In these respects, the Anti-Federalists echoed traditional republican theory.

The Anti-Federalists were therefore hostile to the idea of a dramatic expansion in the powers of the national government. Only a decentralized society would allow the homogeneity and dedication to the public good that would prevent the government from degenerating into a clash of private interests. A powerful national government would create heterogeneity and distance from the sphere of power and thereby undermine the public's willingness to participate in politics as citizens.

Adhering to the traditional republican view, the Anti-Federalists argued that civil society should operate as an educator, and not merely as a regulator of private conduct.[9] Government bore the re-

---

7. For general discussion, see Main (1961), Storing (1981a), and Kenyon (1955). The position of the Anti-Federalists was hardly monolithic; there were many disagreements among them. In outlining the Anti-Federalist position, it is necessary to overlook those differences and to speak of general tendencies.

8. This is the foundation for Hannah Arendt's (1963) reading of the American Revolution and its aftermath.

9. Similarities between the Anti-Federalists' views and those of Rousseau are readily apparent. It is surprising, however, that Rousseau's name seldom appeared in the Anti-Federalist literature and is mentioned only once in *The Complete Anti-Federalist* (Storing 1981a, 7:251–52). (There, an essay by a Newport man describes Rousseau as "a republican by birth and education, one of the most exalted geniuses and one of the greatest writers of his age, or perhaps any age" and refers especially to Rousseau's suggestion "that the people should examine and determine every public act themselves." See generally Spurlin (1969).

sponsibility of inculcating attitudes that would incline the citizenry away from the pursuit of self-interest, at least in the political realm. Closely connected to this vision was the Anti-Federalists' desire to avoid extreme disparities in wealth, education, or power. Such disparities would poison the spirit of civic virtue and prevent achievement of the homogeneity of a simple and virtuous people.

It is not difficult to see why the Anti-Federalists had an ambivalent attitude toward a system in which decisions were made by representatives of the people rather than by the people themselves. In their ideal world, government decisions would be made during a face-to-face process of deliberation and debate. Such a process would inculcate civic virtue in the public at large, virtue from which the process itself would simultaneously benefit. The result would be "public happiness"—the happiness that derives from active participation in the world of governance. Thus Jefferson, though not an Anti-Federalist, proposed in this vein that the Constitution should be amended every generation, partly to promote general attention to public affairs.[10]

But the Anti-Federalists acknowledged that representation was necessary at both the state and national levels. They recognized that the size of government made it impossible to conduct political affairs on the model of the town meeting (see, e.g., Storing 1981b, 43–45). For them, representation was a necessary evil brought about by the impracticability of direct self-governance by the people (Storing 1981b, 17–18).

From this perspective, the grounds on which the Anti-Federalists based their opposition to the proposed Constitution should be clear. They believed that the Constitution would destroy the system of decentralization on which true liberty depended. The citizens would lose effective control over their representatives; they would also be deprived of the opportunity to participate in public affairs, and thus the principle of civic virtue would be undermined.[11] Rule by remote national leaders would attenuate the scheme of representation and rupture the alliance of interests between the rulers and the ruled. The Anti-Federalists foresaw a system that would effectively exclude the people from the realm of public affairs and provide weakly accountable national leaders with enormous discretion to make law.

10. Letter from Jefferson to Samuel Kercheval, 12 July 1816, in *The Portable Thomas Jefferson* (Peterson 1975, 553–58).
11. See, e.g., Storing (1981a, 2:73, 110–11; 4:94–95; and 6:160–61). Barber (1977) suggests that the exclusion of the citizenry from the processes of government was an important goal of the framers. Ackerman (1991) provides a counterpoint.

Many of the Anti-Federalists were also skeptical of the emerging interest in commercial development that had played such a prominent role in the decision to abandon the Articles of Confederation in favor of the new Constitution.[12] In the Anti-Federalists' view, commerce was a threat to the principles underlying the Revolution because it gave rise to ambition, avarice, and the dissolution of communal bonds.[13] Insofar as the proposed Constitution might be understood as an effort to promote commerce and commercial mores, it would undermine the purposes of the Revolution.

In sum, the Anti-Federalists attacked the proposed Constitution as inconsistent with the underlying principles of republicanism. The removal of the people from the political process, the creation of a powerful and remote national government, the new emphasis on commerce—all threatened to eliminate the "public happiness" for which the American Revolution had, in part, been fought.

The Federalist Response

The Anti-Federalist objections to the proposed Constitution provoked a theoretical response that amounted to a new conception of politics—indeed, a "political theory worthy of a prominent place in the history of Western thought" (Wood 1969, 615). This conception reformulated the principles of republicanism in an attempt to synthesize elements of traditional republicanism and its emerging pluralist competition.

Madison's discussion in *The Federalist* no. 10 is sometimes thought to be a conventional pluralist document, and there are indeed traces of pluralism in the analysis. To Madison, the primary problem of governance was the control of faction, understood in his famous formulation as "a number of citizens, whether amounting to a majority or minority of the whole, who are united and actuated by some common impulse of passion, or of interest, adverse to the rights of other citizens, or to the permanent and aggregate interests of the community" (Wills 1982, 43). The Anti-Federalists rooted the problem of faction in that of corruption; their solution was to control the factional spirit and limit the power of elected representatives. In their view, those close to the people, chosen locally, would not stray from

---

12. On the need for commercial development, see Alexander Hamilton in *The Federalist,* nos. 6 and 11. For the Anti-Federalist response, see Storing (1981a, 6:201).

13. More specifically, the Anti-Federalists compared the "independent feelings of ancient republics, whose prime object was the welfare and happiness of their country" with "peculation, . . . usurious contracts, . . . illegal and dishonest projects, and . . . every private vice" which might "support the factitious appearances of grandeur and wealth" (in Storing 1981a, 6:201).

the people's interests. The civic virtue of the citizenry and of its representatives would work as a safeguard against factional tyranny.

Madison and other federalists transformed the question of corruption into that of faction. They saw the "corruption" that created factions as a natural, though undesirable, product of liberty and inequality in human faculties. This redefinition meant that the basic problem of governance could not be solved by the traditional republican means of education and inculcation of virtue. Moreover, the problem of faction was likely to be most, not least, severe in a small republic. In a small republic, a self-interested private group could easily seize political power and distribute wealth or opportunities in its favor. Indeed, in the view of the Federalists, this was precisely what had happened in the years since the Revolution. During that period, factions had usurped the processes of state government, putting both liberty and property at risk. This evidence helped account for Madison's rejection of Jefferson's proposal for regular constitutional amendment on the grounds that such a proposal would produce "the most violent struggles . . . between the parties interested in reviving, and those interested in reforming the antecedent state of property."[14] Jefferson, by contrast, saw turbulence as "productive of good. It prevents the degeneracy of government, and nourishes a general attention to . . . public affairs. I hold . . . that a little rebellion now and then is a good thing."[15]

Madison viewed the recent history as sufficient evidence that sound governance could not rely on traditional conceptions of civic virtue and public education to guard against factional tyranny. Such devices would be unable to overcome the natural self-interest of men and women, even in their capacity as political actors.[16] Self-interest, in Madison's view, would inevitably result from differences in natural talents and property ownership. To this point, Madison added the familiar idea that attempting to overcome self-interest would carry a risk of tyranny of its own. Conscious shaping of preferences by government would not promote liberty, but instead destroy it.[17]

---

14. *See* letter to Jefferson from Madison, 14 February 1790, reprinted in Meyers (1981).
15. Letter from Jefferson to Madison, 30 January 1798, (Peterson 1975, 882).
16. See *The Federalist* no. 10 (Madison) and *The Federalist* no. 6 (Hamilton). "Men are ambitious, vindicative, and rapacious (Wills 1982, 22).
17. Compare Benjamin Rush's suggestion that "each citizen should be taught that he does not belong to himself, but that he is public property. Let him be taught to love his family, but let him be taught at the same time that he must forsake and even forget them when the welfare of his country requires it. . . . From the observations that have

All this justified rejection of the Anti-Federalist belief that the problem of faction could be overcome, but it supplied no positive solution to the problem. In developing a solution Madison was particularly original. He began with the notion that the problem posed by factions is especially acute in a direct democracy, for a "common passion or interest will, in almost every case, be felt by a majority of the whole" and there will be no protection for the minority.[18] But a large republic would provide safeguards. There, the diversity of interests would ensure against the possibility that sufficient numbers of people would feel a common desire to oppress minorities. A large republic thus contained a built-in check against the likelihood of factional tyranny.

This was not the only virtue of size. In a large republic, the principle of representation might substantially solve the problem of faction. In a critical passage, Madison wrote that representation would "refine and enlarge the public views by passing them through the medium of a chosen body of citizens, whose wisdom may best discern the true interest of their country and whose patriotism and love of justice will be least likely to sacrifice it to temporary or partial considerations."[19] A large republic would also reduce the danger that representatives would acquire undue attachment to local interests.

This conception of representation appears throughout *The Federalist*. Madison, in *The Federalist* no. 57, urges that "[t]he aim of every political constitution is or ought to be first to obtain for rulers men who possess most wisdom to discern, and most virtue to pursue the common good of the society; and in the next place, to take the most effectual precautions for keeping them virtuous, whilst they continue to hold their public trust" (Wills 1982, 289). Elsewhere, Hamilton suggests that wisdom and virtue would characterize national representatives.[20] Whereas the Anti-Federalists accepted representation as

---

been made it is plain that I consider it as possible to convert men into republican machines. This must be done if we expect them to perform their parts properly in the great machine of the government of the state." From *A Plan for the Establishment of Public Schools and the Diffusion of Knowledge in Pennsylvania* (Philadelphia 1786; as quoted in Hyneman and Lutz 1983, 684–87).

18. *The Federalist* no. 10 (Wills 1982, 44).

19. *The Federalist* no. 10 (Wills 1982, 46–47). Madison continued: "Under such a regulation, it may well happen that the public voice, pronounced by the representatives of the people, will be more consonant to the public good than if pronounced by the people themselves, convened for the purpose (Wills 1982, 47).

20. See *The Federalist* no. 63. An auxiliary desideratum for the melioration of the Republican form is that such a process of elections will most certainly extract from the mass of the society the purest and noblest characters that it contains; such as will at

a necessary evil, Madison regarded it as an opportunity for achieving governance by officials devoted to a public good distinct from the struggle of private interests. Representatives would have the time and temperament to engage in a form of collective reasoning. The hope was for a genuinely national politics. The representatives of the people would be free to engage in the process of discussion and debate from which the common good would emerge.[21]

In important respects, the departure from traditional republicanism could not have been greater. Madison willingly abandoned the classical republican understanding that citizens generally should participate directly in the processes of government.[22] Far from being a threat to freedom, a large republic could help to guarantee it. At the same time, Madison's understanding was sharply distinct from that of the modern pluralists. He hoped that national representatives, operating above the fray, would be able to disentangle themselves from local pressures and deliberate on and bring about something like an objective public good. Those representatives would have the virtue associated with classical republican citizens.

To be sure, Madison's sensitivity to the pressures imposed by interest groups—the problem of faction—made him unwilling to accept the Anti-Federalist conception of politics. In his view, that

---

once feel most strongly the proper motives to pursue the end of their appointment and be most capable to devise the proper means of attaining it. See Madison's *Vices of the Political System of the United States* (Rutland and Rachal 1984); see also John Jay in *The Federalist* no. 3.

21. See also *The Federalist* no. 37 (in which Madison refers to the framers' "deep conviction of the necessity of sacrificing private opinions and partial interests to the public good") and nos. 63 and 71 (Hamilton). Note in this regard that Madison attacked Congress in 1787 as "advocates for the respective interests of their constituents" (letter from Madison to Jefferson, 3 October 1785, reprinted in Rutland and Rachel 1984, 374]). In his view, "the evil is fully displayed in the County representations, the members of which are everywhere observed to lose sight of the aggregate interests of the Community, and even to sacrifice them to the interests or prejudices of their respective constituents" (Madison's *Remarks on Mr. Jefferson's Draft of a Constitution*, in Meyers [1981, 35]). Madison's preference for large election districts (Madison's speech in the Virginia Ratifying Convention, "June 1788, in Hunt [1904, 158]), fits well with this view. So too with his preference for length of service: "The tendency of longer period of service would be, to render the Body more stable in its policy, and more capable of stemming popular currents taking a wrong direction, until reason and justice could regain their ascendancy" (quoted in Meyers 1981, 508).

22. This view can be found in the literature of the Anti-Federalists, relying largely on Montesquieu. The Federalist exclusion of the citizenry from politics (see, e.g., *The Federalist* no. 63, in which Hamilton refers to the "total exclusion of the people in their collective capacity"), is stressed and deplored in Hofstadter (1948) and Nedelsky (1990, chap. 5).

conception would lead to the domination of politics by factions under the guise of civic virtue. But his solution was hardly to accept interest group struggle as a desirable part of politics that would promote social welfare.[23] Instead, he aimed to ensure against such a struggle through the mechanism of representation. The Federalists rejected the notion that political actions were inevitably self-interested. In *The Federalist* no. 55, Madison wrote, "As there is a degree of depravity in mankind which requires a certain degree of circumspection and distrust, so there are other qualities in human nature which justify a certain portion of esteem and confidence."

This was not, however, the entire story. The structural provisions of the Constitution attempted to bring about public-spirited representation, to provide safeguards in its absence, and to ensure an important measure of popular control. Bicameralism thus attempted to ensure that some representatives would be relatively isolated while others would be relatively close to the people.[24] Indirect election of representatives played a far more important role at the time of ratification than it does today; the fact that state legislatures chose senators ensured that one house of the national legislature would have additional insulation from political pressure. The electoral college is another important example; it was to be a deliberative body standing apart from constituent pressures.[25]

Perhaps most important, the distribution of national powers was designed with the recognition that even national representatives may be prone to the influence of "interests" that are inconsistent with the public welfare.[26] *The Federalist* no. 51, moreover, has a different emphasis from Madison's other work, relying on the celebrated "policy of supplying, by opposite and rival interests, the defect of better motives" (Wills 1982, 263). "Ambition," in Madison's classic formula-

23. See Meyers (1981, xxiv–xxiii), and cf. Ackerman (1984), who argues that the framers recognized pluralist bargaining as an acceptable, ordinary element of politics.

24. See *The Federalist* nos. 62 and 63 (Hamilton). For Madison's defense of the Senate on this ground, see also Farrand (1911, 422–23).

25. In *The Federalist* no. 68, Hamilton says, "The immediate election should be made by men most capable of analyzing the qualities adapted to the station, and acting under circumstances favorable to deliberation, and to a judicious combination of all the reasons and inducements which were proper to govern their choice." According to John Hart Ely (1980, 7), the increasingly "democratic" quality of American politics argues against an expansive judicial role. From the framers' point of view, however, the opposite inference might be drawn: Increasing responsiveness to constituent pressures and diminishing deliberation and "refinement" of the public view argue in favor of ensuring that some part of government take a "sober second look" at political outcomes. This perception plays a prominent role in modern public law.

26. See *The Federalist* no. 10 (Ford 1898).

tion, "must be made to counteract ambition." The system of checks and balances within the federal structure was intended to operate as a check against self-interested representation and factional tyranny in the event that national officials failed to fulfill their responsibilities. If a private group managed to achieve dominance over a certain part of the national government, or if a segment of rulers obtained interests that diverged from those of the people, other national officials would have both the incentive and the means to resist.

The federal system would also act as an important safeguard. According to Madison, the "different governments will control each other" and ensure stalemate rather than action at the behest of particular private interests.[27] The jealousy of state governments and the attachment of the citizenry to local interests would provide additional protection against the aggrandizement of power in national institutions.

The result is a complex system of checks: national representation, bicameralism, indirect election, distribution of powers, and the federal-state relationship would operate in concert to counteract the effects of faction despite the inevitability of the factional spirit. And the Constitution itself, enforced by disinterested judges and adopted in a moment in which the factional spirit had been perhaps temporarily extinguished,[28] would prevent both majorities and minorities from usurping government power to distribute wealth or opportunities in their favor.

There has been no discussion thus far of private property, whose protection was a principal interest of the framers.[29] But there is a close practical relationship between the desire to protect private property from governmental intrusion and the devices set up by the framers to guard against the dangers posed by faction. In the framers' view, the problem of faction lay partly in the danger that a self-interested group would obtain governmental power in order to put property rights at risk. The various safeguards, including representation by officials who would be able to take a broader view of the relevant issues, may be understood as having the protection of property rights from majoritarian incursion as one of their principal pur-

---

27. *The Federalist* no. 51 (Ford 1898).

28. See Ackerman (1984). Charles Beard and others, of course, have attributed the content of the Constitution to self-interested motivations. See Beard (1913). For a useful collection see Levy (1969).

29. See e.g., *The Federalist* no. 54 (Hamilton on government instituted for the protection of property). Of course, *The Federalist* no. 10 proclaims that differences in property are based on the "diversity in the faculties of men" and that such diversity cannot be eliminated without extinguishing freedom.

poses (see Nedelsky 1990, chap 5; see also Epstein 1985). In this respect as well, the Federalists can be contrasted with their Anti-Federalist opponents, whose weaker concern for private property coexisted easily with their preference for decentralized democracy.[30] Moreover, the Federalists' hospitable view—at least in some settings—toward political stalemate and government inaction may be associated with a desire to protect private property (see, e.g., Hamilton in *The Federalist* no. 22 and Madison in *The Federalist* no. 10); inaction would preserve the existing distribution of wealth.

There is in this sense a close practical relationship between the concern for private property and the Madisonian governmental structure. But the relationship is hardly one of logical necessity. It is, for example, possible to believe in the Madisonian conception of the role of national representatives, but at the same time to accept redistribution of resources as a legitimate governmental goal. (Madison himself falls in this camp, supporting as he did provision for the poor.) Under this view, the representative must deliberate rather than respond mechanically to constituent pressures; but if deliberation produces a conclusion in favor of redistribution, so be it. This is entirely consistent with the federalist conception of politics and representation, and, as we will see, it has significant parallels in current constitutional law.

Deliberative Democracy

The picture that emerges has been aptly termed "deliberative democracy" (Bessette 1980, 102).[31] The Federalists rejected the view of their adversaries on the ground that it undervalued the likelihood that local government would be dominated by private interests instead of profiting from civic virtue. Moreover, the Federalists doubted that the private interests of the citizenry could be subordinated by instilling principles of civic virtue. Finally, they thought that commercial development was crucial to the new nation and could not be achieved without a considerable degree of centralization. But the Federalists did not believe that representatives would or should respond mechanically to private pressure. Instead, the national representatives were to be above the fray of private interests. Above all, their task was deliberative. Indeed, the task of the legislator was very close to the task of the citizen in the traditional republican conception.

---

30. But see Kenyon (1955), who argues that the Anti-Federalists were not in favor of substantial redistribution.

31. See also Hamilton on the theme of deliberation in *The Federalist* nos. 27, 61, 63, and 78.

The republican elements of the Federalists' approach are captured in Hamilton's suggestion that "when occasions present themselves in which the interests of the people are at variance with their inclinations, it is the duty of the persons whom they have appointed to be the guardians of those interests to withstand the temporary delusion, in order to give them time and opportunity for more cool and sedate reflection"[32] (Wills 1982, 363).

The notion that politics might be conducted solely as a process of bargaining and trade-offs was thus far from the federalist understanding.[33] The Federalists' suspicion of civic virtue and their relatively skeptical attitude toward the possibility that citizens could escape their self-interest led them to reject the traditional republican structure without rejecting important features of its normative understanding of politics.

For the Federalists, politics was to be deliberative in a special sense. Representatives were accountable to the public; their deliberative task was not disembodied. The framers thus created political checks designed to ensure that representatives would not stray too far from the desires of their constituents. The result was a hybrid conception of representation, in which legislators were neither to respond blindly to constituent pressures nor to undertake their deliberations in a vacuum.

The Federalists thus achieved a kind of synthesis of republicanism and the emerging principles of pluralism. Politics rightly consisted of deliberation and discussion about the public good. But that process could not be brought about in the traditional republican fashion; such an effort, in light of human nature, would deteriorate into a struggle among competing factions. A partial solution lay in principles of representation. The mechanisms of accountability would prevent representatives from acquiring interests distinct from those of their constituents. Moreover, the distribution of national powers would ensure that if a particular group acquired too much power over one set of representatives, there would be safeguards to prevent that group from obtaining authority over the national government in general.

The framers' understanding cannot be fully explained in either

---

32. *The Federalist* no. 71; see also nos. 55 and 59 (Hamilton) and no. 49 (Madison); cf. Hamilton's discussion of judges in no. 78. On voluntary foreclosure of choices, see Elster (1979). There is a close parallel between this conception of representation and recent justifications for the Supreme Court's role as a provider of a disinterested second look at legislation. *See* Bickel (1962) and Wellington (1973).

33. See Hamilton referring to "a scandalous bartering of votes and bargaining for places" in *The Federalist* no. 77.

Lockean or pluralist terms (see, e.g., Ackerman 1991; Wood 1969; Wood, 1992; Katz 1969; Kramnick 1982). Republican thought played a critical and too often neglected role in the framers' understanding—notwithstanding their departure from the more conventional republicanism of Anti-Federalists. A significant element in Federalist thought was the expectation that the constitutional system would serve republican goals better than the traditional republican solution of small republics, civic education, and limited reliance on representatives. The Federalists believed that the new scheme of representation would preserve the underlying republican conception of politics without running the risk of tyranny or relying on naive understandings about the human capacity to escape self-interest. I use the term "Madisonian republicanism" to refer to the resulting scheme, which occupies an intermediate position between interest group pluralism and traditional republicanism.

Interest Groups and the Constitution: Current Doctrine

Was Madison Wrong?

It should hardly be controversial to suggest that Madison's understanding of the role of the representative has been only imperfectly realized. Few would contend that nationally selected representatives have been able to exercise the role Madison anticipated. The state of political and economic theory on this point remains somewhat crude. But there is mounting evidence that the pluralist understanding captures a significant component of the legislative process and that, at the descriptive level, it is far superior to its competitors.

There are numerous theories about legislative decision making. One theory suggests that a considerable amount of legislative behavior can be explained if one assumes that members of Congress seek single-mindedly the goal of reelection (see Fiorina 1977; Mayhew 1974). Another approach indicates that three primary conditions—achieving influence within the legislature, promoting public policy, and obtaining reelection—have more explanatory power than any single-factored approach (see Arnold 1979; Fenno 1973; see also Kingdon 1981 and the synthesis in Arnold 1988). In the economic literature, there have been many distinguished efforts to explain legislative behavior solely by reference to constituent pressures (see Peltzman 1976, 1984; Stigler 1971). Such interpretations have been attacked as too reductionist (see Maass 1983; Kalt and Zupan 1984; Stewart 1983).

What emerges is a continuum. At one pole are cases in which interest group pressures are largely determinative, and statutory enactments can be regarded as "deals" among contending interests. At the other pole lie cases where legislators engage in deliberation in which interest group pressures, conventionally defined, play little or no role. At various points along the continuum a great range of legislative decisions exist in which the outcomes are dependent on an amalgam of pressure, deliberation, and other factors. No simple test can distinguish cases falling at different points on the continuum.

This is not an appropriate place for an evaluation of existing theories of legislative behavior (see Farber and Frickey 1990). It is clear that constituent pressures play a significant role in many legislative decisions and that the Federalist ideal of national responsibility to a national constituency does not exist in practice. We are far from Madison's deliberative democracy. Indeed, the evidence suggests that the factional struggle that Madison sought to escape more closely captures politics as it is generally practiced.

The Judicial Response

Constitutional doctrine has not responded with equanimity to the prevalence of pluralist politics. Indeed, it is possible to trace much of judge-made public law directly to a concern that the Madisonian ideal has been too sharply compromised in practice. The core demand of the equal protection and due process clauses, for example, is that measures taken by legislatures or administrators must be "rational."[34] This demand has been puzzling to those who understand the political process as a series of unprincipled bargains among competing social groups (see Linde 1976; Posner 1974). Under this conception of the political process, the review of statutes for "rationality" is incoherent. It demands of statutory enactments something inconsistent with their very nature as the product of self-interested efforts by competing groups seeking scarce social resources.

The rationality requirement may, however, be understood precisely as a requirement that regulatory measures be something other than a response to political pressure. In the rationality cases, the Court requires some independent "public interest" to justify regula-

---

34. Thus, e.g., when a state enacts a statute banning the sale of milk in paperboard milk cartons, the government must show that the prohibition serves some public interest and is not merely the product of a successful imposition of pressure by the plastics industry. See Minnesota v. Clover Leaf Creamery Co., 449 U.S. 456 (1981). Or when a state prevents opticians, but not ophthalmologists, from selling certain services, it must justify its action by showing that the measure is a means of protecting consumers and not simply a reflection of pressures imposed by ophthalmologists. See Williamson v. Lee Optical, Inc., 348 U.S. 483 (1955).

tion.[35] A reference to political power is, by itself, insufficient. In no modern case has the Court recognized the legitimacy of pluralist compromise as the exclusive basis for legislation.[36] In many cases, modern and not so modern, the Court has indicated that such compromise is impermissible if it is the sole reason for the legislative enactment at issue.[37] Much of modern constitutional doctrine reflects a single perception of the underlying evil: the distribution of resources or opportunities to one group rather than another solely because those benefited have exercised the raw power to obtain governmental assistance.

The Court's perception is closely related to the Madisonian understanding of both politics and representation. Under that conception, as we have seen, the task of the legislator is not to respond to private pressures but to deliberate on and to select values. In constitutional doctrine, the judicial perception of the prohibited end—decisions based solely on private pressure—is identical to the danger that united the Federalists and the Anti-Federalists in their fears about the risks posed by factional power. In constitutional doctrine as well, the government must show that something other than private pressure accounted for its decision. In both the Federalist and the judicial accounts, representatives are supposed to stand to some degree above the struggle of private interests, deliberating on and attempting to bring about a common good.

To be sure, courts give the legislature the benefit of every doubt, and rarely invalidate laws as products of faction. But the descriptive power of this conception of politics—that legislators have a deliberative responsibility—is quite broad. It captures a theme that pervades American constitutional law certainly in its rhetoric, sometimes in its outcomes. Indeed, that conception is the most plausible candidate we have for a unitary understanding of the sorts of conduct forbidden by the Constitution.

35. United States Department of Agriculture v. Moreno, 413 U.S. 528, 535 (1973).
36. The closest case is Ferguson v. Skrupa, 372 U.S. 726, 732 (1963), in which the Court stated, "Statutes create many classifications which do not deny equal protection; it is only 'invidious discrimination' which offends the Constitution." Even this statement is ambiguous, for the label "invidious" is frequently applied to classifications based only on raw power.
37. The indication can be found in cases demanding a "public value" justification for statutory classifications. See, e.g., City of New Orleans v. Dukes, 427 U.S. 297 (1976); Daniel v. Family Security Life Ins. Co., 336 U.S. 220 (1949); Tigner v. Texas, 310 U.S. 141 (1940); Rosenthal v. New York, 226 U.S. 260 (1912); Engel v. O'Malley, 219 U.S. 128 (1911); Lindsley v. Natural Carbonic Gas Co., 220 U.S. 61 (1911); Health and Milligan Mfg. Co. v. Worst, 207 U.S. 338 (1907).

The Problem of "Reasoned Analysis"

Large elements of constitutional law are not susceptible to explanation in the terms used thus far. The Constitution creates a shield of "rights" on which government may not intrude even if the legislative process is genuinely deliberative. Those rights—including most prominently the right to free speech—are protected regardless of the motivation of the legislature.[38] Deliberation is, in this respect, a necessary though not a sufficient condition for validity. Independent constitutional constraints operate to bar government action that is properly motivated under the framework described thus far.

Another set of constraints finds its source in "heightened scrutiny" under the equal protection clause. In cases involving discrimination against blacks, women, aliens, and illegitimates, the Court has invalidated statutes even when they were not raw exercises of power in the ordinary sense.[39] For example, the Court has struck down provisions stating that wives are automatically entitled to social security benefits, but that husbands must show dependency.[40] Such statutes are not raw exercises of power; they are responsive to certain (perhaps mistaken or invidious) conceptions about the nature of female participation in the workplace. How might these developments be explained?

An intriguing possibility is suggested by the Court's own explanation of why it approaches such classifications with special skepticism. In the area of gender, the Court has said that its skeptical approach guarantees that the relevant classifications are supported by "reasoned analysis" and are not the byproduct of "traditional, often inaccurate, assumptions about the proper roles of men and women."[41] At first glance, the notion that legislation must be the product of "reasoned analysis" seems odd. That notion may be properly applied to the courts and perhaps to administrative agencies. But reasoned analysis is normally not a prerequisite of legislation.

Underlying the Court's approach is a perception that classifica-

---

38. The legislative motivation does, however, play a role in determining the level of judicial scrutiny. See Stone (1983). Moreover, the right to free speech may be regarded as an effort to protect the deliberative process. See Meiklejohn (1948). Other rights-based constraints include protection against takings of private property, protection against interference with religious liberties, and protection against the unfair administration of criminal justice.

39. See, e.g., Trible v. Gordon, 430 U.S. 762 (1977); Graham v. Richardson, 403 U.S. 365 (1971); Lee v. Washington, 390 U.S. 333 (1968).

40. See Califano v. Goldfarb, 430 U.S. 199 (1977); Weinberger v. Wiesenfeld, 420 U.S. 636 (1975).

41. Mississippi Univ. for Women v. Hogan, 458 U.S. 718, 726 (1982).

tions in this context are likely to reflect private power, even if it is possible to identify a public value that the relevant classification can be said to serve. When a statute discriminates against women, there is a special likelihood that it is not an effort to promote the public good, but is instead an unthinking reflection of existing distributions of authority as between men and women. Discrimination against women may result from the disproportionate power of men over lawmaking processes or, more precisely, from widely shared understandings about the proper roles of men and women that operate to promote the social position of men and to undermine that of women.

The basic approach is largely a version of the prohibition of decisions based on raw power, but with an important twist. Here it is insufficient to invoke a plausible, even widely held conception of the public interest as a basis for the classification. The public value justification must survive critical scrutiny designed to ensure that it is not itself a product of injustice.

The "reasoned analysis" requirement has republican dimensions. The role of the representative is to deliberate on the public good, not to respond mechanically to existing social conceptions. Under the Court's framework, such conceptions must themselves be subjected to critical review. They cannot be automatically translated into law. The result is to apply the deliberative task to social practices that had previously been accepted as natural and inviolate (Sunstein 1993).

What emerges is a jurisprudence that generally inspects legislation to determine whether representatives have attempted to act deliberatively, but there are sharp divergences in the nature and extent of the judicial inquiry in various areas. In general, the Court is extraordinarily deferential, adopting a strong presumption in favor of the legislation. Scrutiny is "heightened" only in narrow circumstances in which public value justifications are subject to critical inspection. But in both contexts, the underlying conception of representation is Madisonian, and the understanding of politics is republican.

Factions and Administrative Law

Thus far, my focus has been on constitutional law—doctrines rooted in the equal protection, due process, eminent domain, and contract clauses—insofar as they reflect a particular understanding of the prohibited end. In the area of administrative law, where the basic doctrines are non-constitutional in status, there are similar themes.

At one level, this should be expected. Since the early growth of administrative agencies, the problem of faction has been a central concern. The original constitutional scheme was intended to combat that problem with the safeguards of electoral accountability and separated powers. The creation of administrative agencies breached both of those safeguards. Agency functions do not fall easily into the conventional categories of legislation, administration, and execution; often they combine all three. More fundamentally, administrative agencies exercise broad discretionary power often without continuous control from the electorally accountable branches of the federal government. The danger is that private groups will co-opt the administrative process and exploit it to their advantage.

The initial response of the courts was predictable: they invalidated the delegation of lawmaking authority to administrative agencies.[42] *Schechter Poultry* involved a delegation of legislative power to private groups,[43] who were effectively authorized to make law with only minimal supervision from Congress or the president. For various reasons, the strategy of invalidation on constitutional grounds was ultimately abandoned.[44] After the abandonment, administrative law consisted largely of an effort to require clear authorization for government intrusions into the realm of private property. This approach paralleled developments in constitutional law that used the touchstone of private property as the basis for judicial intervention. But here—as in the constitutional area, and for the same reasons—the touchstone of property is no longer an entirely plausible basis for judicial review. The best features of modern administrative law are a means of serving the original purposes of the nondelegation doctrine, and of promoting Madisonian goals, without invalidating regulatory statutes or relying on the inviolability of private property (Sunstein 1990).

Perhaps the most important doctrinal innovation in administrative law, for example, is the "hard-look doctrine."[45] In its current

---

42. See Schechter Poultry Corp. v. United States, 295 U.S. 495 (1935): Panama Refining Co. v. Ryan, 293 U.S. 388 (1935).

43. See Schechter Poultry Corp. v. United States, 295 U.S. 495 (1935). See, generally, Jaffe (1937).

44. See, e.g., Mourning v. Family Publications Services, Inc., 411 U.S. 356 (1973); Amalgamated Meat Cutters v. Connally, 337 F. Supp. 737 (D.D.C. 1971) (three-judge district court). There have, however, been some rumblings in the Court in the other direction. See e.g., Industrial Union Dept. v. American Petroleum Inst., 448 U.S. 607, 671 (1980) (Rehnquist concurring).

45. Originally created by the District of Columbia Court of Appeals, the "hard-look doctrine" is now the generally accepted framework for reviewing the work of administrative agencies. See Greater Boston Television Corp. v. FCC, 444 F.2d 841, 851 (D.C. Cir. 1970), cert. denied, 403 U.S. 923 (1971); Leventhal (1974).

incarnation, the doctrine contains four principal features. Agencies must give detailed explanations for their decisions; justify departures from past practices; allow participation in the regulatory process by a wide range of affected groups; consider reasonable alternatives; and explain why these were rejected. Courts will also scrutinize the decision on its merits. These devices may be understood as a form of scrutiny akin to what we have seen in constitutional law. The courts examine the connection between statutorily relevant ends and the means chosen by the agency to promote those ends. If the connection is sufficiently attenuated, impermissible bases for regulatory action can be "flushed out." These bases may be impermissible because they are not relevant under the governing statute or because they are solely the product of political pressures.

Accompanying this idea is the occasional judicial attempt to discipline the administrative process with contemporary principles of "comprehensive rationality." This approach requires explicit identification of goals and careful exploration of the ways in which those goals might be achieved. It aims to ensure that agency decisions will be based on statutorily permissible factors and are neither blindly responsive to political pressures nor based on irrelevant considerations. "Comprehensive rationality" is typically associated with a belief in a more or less objective public interest and with skepticism toward the idea that the purpose of politics is simply to mediate a struggle among contending social groups. Not surprisingly, critics of this judicial role have based their critique on a perception that agency decisions ought to be understood as products of pluralist politics.[46] This perception is a recent incarnation of the notion that democratic outcomes are those reached by officials who respond to constituent pressures.

Reviving Madisonian Republicanism

The judicial initiatives explored thus far are best understood as evidence of a distrust of pluralism and a preference for a scheme that borrows from the Madisonian understanding of representation. Acceptance of the Madisonian conception of politics, however, does not necessarily imply that the courts ought to play a role in moving the political process in Madisonian directions. It is highly unlikely that the courts, acting by themselves, could accomplish very much in bringing the political process closer to the Madisonian conception

---

46. See Chevron, U.S.A., Inc. v. National Resource Defense Council, Inc., 104 S. Ct. 2778, 2793 (1984); see Scalia (1982), Shapiro (1982), Scalia (1977).

(Rosenberg 1991).[47] Changes in the nature of politics will depend far more on the practices of legislative and administrative actors (Sunstein 1990; Sunstein 1991b). Moreover, the familiar considerations of judicial authority and competence counsel against an aggressive judicial role. The Madisonian approach might be criticized on two fronts, both of which raise large and difficult issues.

The Viability of Madisonian Representation

The first criticism, substantive in nature, would suggest that it is utopian to believe that representatives can be forced into the deliberative Madisonian mold. In this view, history shows that representatives, even at the national level, are unable to carry out the relevant tasks. Madisonian republicanism may be as romantic and outmoded as the face-to-face governance promoted by the Anti-Federalists. The proposed judicial role would therefore be futile. At most, it would produce "boilerplate"—rationalizations designed to placate the courts—rather than a genuine critical inquiry into issues of value and fact.

Moreover, the failure of representatives to act deliberatively may be a positive good, for it guarantees their accountability to the electorate. One person's factional tyranny may, in the view of another, be the system of accountability in action. Requiring deliberation on the part of governmental officials might remove the salutary check of constituent pressures. The virtue of majority rule, in this view, consists precisely in relatively mechanical official responses to the desires, or power, of the citizenry. Defects in the processes of pluralism should be remedied with an effort to increase access to government authority for those who are otherwise unable to participate, rather than by requiring politics to assume a deliberative form.

A final critique would stress that in view of the limitations of deliberation, at least under conditions of widespread social, economic, and political inequality, it is necessary to supplement or replace deliberative politics with exercises of power on the part or in the interest of the disadvantaged. Requiring deliberation does little to accelerate social change and may, in fact, strengthen the unjust features of the status quo. Some people invoke this possibility to suggest that Madisonian republicanism fails to address the most important problems in contemporary democracy.

---

47. Compare Horowitz (1977), who discusses institutional weaknesses of courts in bringing about social change, and Keane (1989), who discusses changes necessary to bring about reinvigorated public life.

Institutional Problems

A different critique would focus on institutional concerns about judicial competence and authority. The first claim in this connection is that existing sources of law fail to vest courts with the power to undertake the proposed tasks. The equal protection clause and the Administrative Procedure Act—the principal sources of authority for the proposed judicial innovations—are far from open-ended grants of authority to move legislative and administrative processes in Madisonian directions. Nor, in this view, are courts well suited for the task. The job of ascertaining the extent of factional control over legislative processes involves unmanageable inquiries into legislative motivation and the drafting process. Even individual legislators almost always act on the basis of mixed motivations. Conceptions of the public good and the desire to be reelected are inseparably intertwined. The problem becomes truly intractable when the issue is the "motivation" of a multimember decision-making body. In such circumstances, the notion of motivation becomes incoherent; another basis for analysis is necessary. Nor is it clear that courts can assume a neutral standpoint from which to assess social issues. Finally, there are sharp limits to the effectiveness of social reform through courts (Rosenberg 1991).

These are formidable objections. They suggest, above all, that it is unrealistic to believe that courts might on their own make significant progress in moving legislation and administration in Madisonian directions. But the objections are not insurmountable. It will be possible to sketch only the outlines of a response here.

The first point is that the existing work in economics and political science suggests that interest groups play an important but not always decisive role in most modern regulation. There are gradations of interest group pressure; other factors contribute to legislative outcomes. In these circumstances, courts might well be able to push politics in particular directions. They might be able to complement nonjudicial strategies. The claim of utopianism is therefore overstated.

Requiring justifications does not, to be sure, guarantee "reasoned analysis" on the part of the legislature. Boilerplate, representing not the actual process of decision but instead a necessary bow to the courts, is hardly an unambiguous good. But requiring justifications does serve an important prophylactic function. The history of administrative and constitutional law is filled with examples. Identification of the legitimate public purposes purportedly served by statutory classifications should improve representative politics by ensuring that the deliberative process is focused on those purposes and the extent to which the classifications serve them. In any event, procedural requirements occasionally have substantive consequences.

There is an apparent anomaly in relying on principles of Madisonian republicanism as a basis for a vigorous judicial role. Those principles are rooted in a conception of politics that does not easily accommodate judicial intrusions. But those intrusions become defensible when they are based on constitutional and statutory provisions whose purpose and effect are to improve a political process that amounts, in the circumstances, to lawmaking by powerful private groups. The judicial role outlined here is hardly desirable in the abstract, and it should hardly be exclusive; it is justified by the need for many institutions of government to incline politics in Madisonian directions.

Perhaps more fundamentally, the original constitutional framework was based on an understanding that national representatives should be largely insulated from constituent pressures. Such insulation, it was thought, would facilitate the performance of the deliberative functions of government. That system of insulation has broken down with the decline of the electoral college, direct election of senators, and, most important, developments in technology, travel, and communications that have enabled private groups to exert continuing influence over representatives. In these circumstances, it is neither surprising nor entirely inappropriate that the judicial role has expanded and that at least a few of the deliberative tasks no longer performed by national representatives have been transferred to the courts.

The final and perhaps most important question deals with the viability of Madisonian republicanism. Was Madison correct in his rejection of pluralist approaches to politics in favor of an understanding that relies on the existence of a common good distinct from the aggregation of private interests? Would it be more desirable to perfect the processes of pluralism than to adopt a deliberative model of politics? To answer these questions would require an elaborate statement, but some of the relevant considerations may be outlined here.

A pluralist approach to politics views private preferences as exogenous variables and will not subject them to critical scrutiny and review. Under a pure version of the pluralist understanding, the representative responds mechanically to constituent pressures. Those pressures are in turn a product of the existing distribution of wealth, the existing set of entitlements, and the existing structure of preferences. But all three may be objectionable to some degree or another;

the task of political actors, either representatives or citizens, is to reflect critically on them, not necessarily to accept them.

Two premises are implicit in this claim. The first is that some preferences are either objectionable or, more generally, the product of distorting circumstances. The second is that through the process of deliberation and debate, objectionable or distorted preferences might be revealed as such (Sunstein 1991a; Sunstein 1993, ch. 6). Preferences are of course shaped by the available opportunities and the existing allocation of rights and income. The phenomenon of "sour grapes" (see, generally, Elster 1983) reflects the fact that, in some circumstances, people reject opportunities because they perceive them to be unavailable. Preferences adapt to the available options; they are not autonomous.[48] In these circumstances, politics properly has, at the heart of its functions, the selection, evaluation, and shaping of preferences, not simply their implementation. For this reason, the Madisonian ideal may well result in better laws than an approach that takes for granted the existing distribution of wealth, power, and entitlements as well as the existing set of preferences. There is, in this sense, something like a "common good" or "public interest" that is distinct from the aggregation of private preferences or utilities.

Legislators operating in Madisonian fashion are not prohibited from deciding that in some settings their role is to maximize aggregate utility as it is defined by reference to public desires. A considered utilitarian judgment on the part of the legislature is hardly impermissible in all contexts. But it would require a singularly optimistic view of politics to suggest that there is an identity between the result that would be reached by the considered utilitarian legislator and that which would result from responses to constituent pressures as they are generally imposed. There is a significant difference between the legislator responding mechanically to constituent pressures and the legislator who, deliberating in Madisonian fashion, acts as a considered utilitarian. And even if, as seems most likely (see Arrow 1963), aggregation of preferences could be obtained through pluralist politics, the appeal of pluralism is undermined by the fact that the legislator should reflect on constituent preferences—a principle embodied in familiar efforts to transform preferences through representative government, as in the case of environmental and antidiscrimination laws.

48. The phenomenon of endogenous changes in preferences is one with which public choice theorists have only begun to come to terms. See, e.g., Von Weizsacker, (1971) and Yaari (1976).

In the pluralist understanding, the notion of a distinctive common good becomes tyrannical or mystical: tyrannical, because pluralists see the change of preferences, or the subordination of private interests to the public good, as inevitably coercive and rarely the product of reasoned argument; mystical, because pluralists take private preferences as exogenous variables. But those who regard the deliberative or transformative function of politics as a central feature will have sympathy for Madisonian conceptions of governance.

The second point is that a deliberative politics will make it less likely that official decisions will be produced solely for private regarding reasons. Such reasons are, by hypothesis, an insufficient basis for legislation; citizens and officials must appeal to a broader public good.[49] This requirement should in turn increase the likelihood that the public good will in fact emerge from politics. The requirement that measures be justified rather than simply fought for has a disciplining effect on the sorts of measures that can be proposed and enacted (cf. Pitkin 1981). At the same time, this requirement will make it more likely that citizens and legislators will act for public-regarding reasons.

Both of these consequences are far from certainties. To a substantial degree, citizens and representatives will generate public-regarding justifications that are largely a mask for self-interest. Moreover, social, political, and economic inequalities will have significant consequences for the potential of rational deliberation. Under current conditions, a deliberative politics is an imperfect guarantee of public-regarding outcomes (Elster 1983). But by disciplining the kinds of reasons that may be offered in support of legislation, it should increase the likelihood that they will come about.

All this is hardly to argue for the existence of a unitary public

---

49. See Tocqueville's somewhat overstated claim that, "When the public is supreme, there is no man who does not feel the value of public good-will, or who does not endeavor to court it by drawing to himself the esteem and affection of those amongst whom he is to live. Many of the passions which congeal and keep asunder human hearts, are then obliged to retire, and hide below the surface. Pride must be dissembled; disdain does not break out; selfishness is afraid of itself. Under a free government, as most public offices are elective, the men whose elevated minds or aspiring hopes are too closely circumscribed in private life, constantly feel that they cannot do with the population which surrounds them. Men learn at such times to think of their fellow-men from ambitious motives, and they frequently find it, in a manner, [in] their interest to be forgetful of self" (from *Democracy in America*, as quoted in Mill [1976]; see also Nelson 1980). This conception of public life parallels the conception emerging from some feminist writing. See Hartsock's (1983) critique of pluralism and Pitkin, (1984), who discusses "Machiavelli at his best."

good, especially in a society consisting of disparate groups with competing interests. The requirement of deliberation does not exclude compromises among those with different conceptions of appropriate government ends. But it does demand that representatives engage in some form of discussion about those ends, rather than responding mechanically to political power or to existing private preferences.

These considerations suggest that an occasionally active judicial posture in pursuit of republican goals may be both desirable and legitimate. That posture has firm roots in history and existing law; and it might sometimes help move politics in appropriate directions. It would indeed be utopian to suppose that courts can bring about a political process like that anticipated by Madison and his Federalist allies. But they are capable of generating movement in that direction.

Conclusion

The Federalist understanding of politics, though not pluralist, represented a sharp break from the thrust of previous republican thought—especially in its hostility to the small republic, in its hopes for public-spirited representation, and, perhaps above all, in its skepticism about the likelihood that civic virtue would be a significant remedy for the problem of faction. At the same time, the Federalists accepted the republican belief that private and public interests are distinct and that the structure of government should lead political actors to pursue a general public good. The Federalist solution to the problem of faction relied on control of the governmental process by a group of public-spirited representatives who would be subject to electoral supervision and to various other safeguards.

Much of modern legal doctrine focuses on the same theme. In particular, large areas of constitutional and administrative law are concerned with the problems raised by the influence of powerful private groups over legislative and administrative processes. Modern rationality review attempts to ensure that representatives have acted to promote the public good and not solely in response to political pressure. Stricter constitutional review can be understood, at least in part, as an effort to subject public value justifications to critical scrutiny. In administrative law, judge-made doctrines may be seen as an attempt to diminish the authority of powerful private groups over the regulatory process, and to ensure that regulatory decisions are reached through a process of deliberation about statutorily relevant factors. These requirements amount to an effort to promote the Madisonian conception of politics and representation without according absolute protection to private property or private ordering.

It would be a mistake to suggest that courts should play an exclusive role in performing these tasks, and it would be fanciful to believe that, on their own, courts could successfully respond to the problem of factional power over lawmaking processes. Nonjudicial institutions must be encouraged to respond to that problem as well (Sunstein 1990, 1991). But the role for courts might be justified on the grounds that judicial insulation provides an opportunity for critical scrutiny of citizen preferences—in Madison's terms, refinement and enlargement of the public view—rather than their mechanical implementation. In this respect, an occasionally active judicial role is designed to fulfill the purposes of the original constitutional system, which attempted to insulate national representatives in order to facilitate the performance of their deliberative tasks.

All of these suggestions are subject to formidable objections. The considerable trust they repose in the federal judiciary may be misplaced. At the same time, acceptance of the Madisonian conception would perpetuate the understanding, fundamental to the constitutional scheme, that the Anti-Federalist view of politics and human nature is romantic and anachronistic. That view was based on belief in the possibility that citizens as well as representatives would be able to engage in the essential tasks of politics. Much was lost—even if much was also gained—with the adoption of the Federalist skepticism about the deliberative capacity of the citizenry at large. Views resembling those of the Anti-Federalists have enjoyed something of a revival in recent years, and such views would imply a conception of politics and of the judicial role that is as distinct from the Madisonian understanding as the Madisonian understanding is distinct from modern pluralism. To those sympathetic to the Anti-Federalist conception, the Madisonian approach will seem at most a second-best substitute.

From another direction, it might be suggested that the Madisonian conception of politics, and especially its republican roots, have themselves become anachronistic. The notion that representatives might engage in the deliberative task of which the Federalists spoke seems increasingly romantic with the declining belief in civic virtue and with the mounting authority of powerful private groups over the processes of government. But as the twenty-first century approaches, it is especially important to appreciate the grounds on which Madison and his peers stopped short of pluralist approaches and sought a system in which private preferences are subjected to critical evaluation.

REFERENCES

Ackerman, Bruce. 1984. "The Storrs Lectures: Discovering the Constitution." *Yale Law Journal* 93(6):1013–72.
———. 1985. "Beyond Carolene Products." *Harvard Law Review* 98(4):713–46.
———. 1991. *We the People, Vol. 1: Foundations.* Cambridge: Harvard University Press, 1991.
Adair, Douglas. 1951. "The Tenth Federalist Revisited." *William and Mary Quarterly* 8(1):48–67.
Arendt, Hannah. 1963. *On Revolution.* New York: Penguin Books.
Arnold, R. Douglas. 1979. *Congress and the Bureaucracy: A Theory of Influence.* New Haven, Conn.: Yale University Press.
———. 1988. *The Logic of Congressional Action.* New Haven, Conn.: Yale.
Arrow, Kenneth. 1963. *Social Choice and Individual Values.* 2d ed. New York: Wiley.
Beard, Charles. 1913. *An Economic Interpretation of the Constitution of the United States.* New York.
Becker, Gary. 1983. "A Theory of Competition among Interest Groups." *Quarterly Journal of Economics* 98(3):371–400.
Bentley, Arthur. 1908. *The Process of Government.* Chicago: University of Chicago Press.
Bessette, Joseph. 1980. "Deliberative Democracy: The Majority Principle in Representative Government." In *How Democratic Is the Constitution?* Edited by R. Goldwin and W. Schambra. Washington, D.C.: American Enterprise Institute.
Bickel, Alexander. 1962. *The Least Dangerous Branch.* Indianapolis, Ind.: Bobbs-Merrill.
Connolly, William, ed. 1969. *The Bias of Pluralism.* New York: Atherton.
Dahl, Robert. 1956. *A Preface to Democratic Theory.* Chicago: University of Chicago Press.
Diamond, Martin. 1977. "Ethics and Politics: The American Way." In *The Moral Foundations of the American Republic.* Charlottesville: University Press of Virginia.
Diggins, John. 1984. *The Lost Soul of American Politics: Virtue, Self-Interest, and the Foundations of Liberalism.* New York: Basic Books.
Downs, Anthony. 1957. *An Economic Theory of Democracy.* New York: Harper.
Elster, Jon. 1979. *Ulysses and the Sirens: Studies in Rationality and Irrationality.* New York: Cambridge University Press.
———. 1983. *Sour Grapes: Studies in the Subversion of Rationality.* New York: Cambridge University Press.

Ely, John Hart. 1980. *Democracy and Distrust: A Theory of Judicial Review*. Cambridge, Mass.: Harvard University Press.
Epstein, Richard A. 1985. *Takings: Private Property and the Power of Eminent Domain*. Cambridge, Mass.: Harvard University Press.
Farber, Daniel and Frickey, Philip. 1990. *Law and Public Choice*. Chicago: University of Chicago Press.
Farrand, Max, ed. 1911. *The Records of the Federal Convention of 1787*. New Haven, Conn.: Yale University Press.
Fenno, Richard. 1973. *Congressmen in Committees*. Boston: Little, Brown.
Fiorina, Morris. 1977. *Congress: Keystone of the Washington Establishment*. New Haven, Conn.: Yale University Press.
Freedman, James. 1978. *Crisis and Legitimacy*. Cambridge: Cambridge University Press.
Hartsock, Nancy. 1983. *Money, Sex and Power*. New York: Longman.
Hofstadter, Richard. 1948. *The American Political Tradition and the Men Who Made It*. New York: Vintage Books.
Horowitz, Donald. 1977. *The Courts and Public Policy*. Washington, D.C.: Brookings Institution.
Hunt, Gaillard, ed. 1900–1910. *The Writings of James Madison*. New York: G. P. Putnam's Sons.
Hyneman, Charles, and Donald Lutz. 1983. *American Political Writing during the Founding Era, 1760–1805*. Indianapolis, Ind.: Liberty Press.
Jaffe, Louis L. 1937. Law-making by Private Groups. *Harvard Law Review* 51(2):201–53.
Kalt, Joseph B., and Zupan, Mark A. 1984. "Capture and Ideology in the Economic Theory of Politics." *American Economic Review* 74(3):279–300.
Kariel, Henry, ed. 1970. *Frontiers of Democratic Theory*. New York: Random House.
Katz, Stanley. 1969. "The Origins of American Constitutional Thought." *Perspectives in American History* 3:474–90.
Keane, John. 1984. *Public Life and Late Capitalism*. Cambridge: Cambridge University Press.
Kenyon, Cecelia. 1955. "Men of Little Faith: The Anti-Federalists on the Nature of Representative Government." *William and Mary Quarterly* 12(1):3–43.
Kingdon, John. 1981. *Congressmen's Voting Decisions*. New York: Harper & Row.
Leventhal, Harold. 1974. "Environmental Decision-making and the Role of the Courts." *University of Pennsylvania Law Review* 122(3):509–55.
Levy, Leonard. 1969. *Essays on the Making of the Making of the Constitution*. New York: Oxford University Press.
Linde, Hans A. 1976. "Due Process of Lawmaking." *Nebraska Law Review* 55(2):197–255.

Lipscomb, A., and A. Bergh, eds. 1903. *The Writings of Thomas Jefferson.* Washington, D.C.: Thomas Jefferson Memorial Association of the United States.
Lowi, Theodore. 1979. *The End of Liberalism: The Second Republic of the United States.* 2d ed. New York: W. W. Norton.
Maass, Arthur. 1983. *Congress and the Common Good.* New York: Basic Books.
Main, Jackson Turner. 1961. *The Anti-Federalists.* Chapel Hill: University of North Carolina Press.
Mayhew, David. 1974. *Congress: The Electoral Connection.* New Haven, Conn.: Yale University Press.
Meiklejohn, Alexander. 1948. *Free Speech and Its Relation to Self-Government.* New York: Harper.
Meyers, Marvin. 1981. *The Mind of the Founder: Sources of the Political Thought of James Madison.* Hanover, N.H.: University Press of New England.
Mill, John Stuart. 1977. *Essays on Politics and Society.* Edited by J. M. Robson. Toronto: University of Toronto Press.
Nedelsky, Jennifer. 1990. *Private Property and the Limits of American Constitutionalism.* Chicago: University of Chicago Press.
Nelson, William. 1980. *On Justifying Democracy.* Boston: Routledge & Kegan Paul.
Peltzman, Samuel. 1976. "Toward a More General Theory of Regulation." *Journal of Law and Economics* 19(2):211–40.
———. 1984. "Constituent Interest and Congressional Voting." *Journal of Law and Economics* 27(1):181–210.
Peterson, M., ed. 1975. *The Portable Thomas Jefferson.* New York: Viking Books.
Pitkin, Hanna. 1967. *The Concept of Representation.* Berkeley: University of California Press.
———. 1981. "Justice: Relating Public to Private." *Political Theory* 9(3): 327–52.
———. 1984. *Fortune Is a Woman.* Berkeley: University of California Press.
Posner, Richard. 1974. "The Defunis Case and the Constitutionality of Preferential Treatment of Racial Minorities." *Supreme Court Review* 1–32.
Rosenberg, Gerald. 1991. *The Hollow Hope.* Chicago: University of Chicago Press.
Rutland, R., and W. Rachal, eds. 1984. *The Papers of James Madison.* Charlottesville: University Press of Virginia.
Scalia, Antonin. 1977. "Two Wrongs Make a Right: The Judicalization of Standardless Rulemaking." *Regulation* 1(4):38–41.
———. 1982. "Separation of Functions: Obscurity Preserved." *Administrative Law Review* 34(1):5–14.
Schumpeter, Joseph. 1950. *Capitalism, Socialism and Democracy.* New York: Harper.

Shalhope, Robert. 1972. Toward a Republican Synthesis: The Emergence of an Understanding of Republicanism in American Historiography. *William and Mary Quarterly* 29(1):49–80.

Shapiro, Martin. 1982. "On Predicting the Future of Administrative Law." *Regulation* 6(3):18–25.

Spurlin, Paul Merrill. 1969. *Rousseau in America*. University: University of Alabama Press.

Stewart, Richard. 1975. "The Reformation of American Administrative Law." *Harvard Law Review* 88(8):1667–1813.

———. 1983. "Regulation in a Liberal State: The Role of Non-commodity Values." *Yale Law Journal* 92(8):1537–90.

Stigler, George. 1971. "The Theory of Economic Regulation." *Bell Journal of Economics and Management Science* 2(1):3–21.

Stone, Geoffrey R. 1983. "Content Regulation and the First Amendment." *William and Mary Law Review* 25(2):189–252.

Storing, Herbert. 1981a. *The Complete Anti-Federalist*. 7 vols. Chicago: University of Chicago Press.

———. 1981b. *What the Anti-Federalist Were For*. Chicago: University of Chicago Press.

Sunstein, Cass R. 1990. *After the Rights Revolution*. Cambridge: Harvard University Press.

———. 1991a. Preferences and Politics. *Philosophy and Public Affairs* 20:3–34.

———. 1991b. Democratizing America Through Law. *Suffolk University Law Review* 25:949–80.

———. 1993. *The Partial Constitution*. Cambridge: Harvard University Press.

Truman, David. 1963. *The Governmental Process*. New York: Knopf.

Wellington, Harry. 1973. "Common Law Rules and Constitutional Double Standards: Some Note on Adjudication." *Yale Law Journal* 83(2):221–311.

Wood, Gordon. 1969. *The Creation of the American Republic, 1776–1787*. Chapel Hill: University of North Carolina Press for the Institute of Early American History and Culture.

———. 1992. *The Radicalism of the American Revolution*. New York: Knopf.

Von Weizsacker, Carl Christian. 1971. "Notes on Endogenous Change in Tastes." *Journal of Economic Theory* 3(4):345–72.

Wills, Garry, ed. 1982. *The Federalist Papers*. New York: Bantam.

Yaari, Menahem E. 1976. "Endogenous Change in Tastes: A Philosophical Discussion." In *Decision Theory and Social Ethics*. Edited by H. Gottinger and W. Leinfellner. Boston: D. Reidel Publishing.

CHAPTER NINE

What Constitutes the American Republic?

EDWIN T. HAEFELE

The Case Presented

WHAT CONSTITUTES the American republic? Americans have been unable to articulate a wholly satisfactory answer to the question, yet find the explanations of foreigners to be very wide of the mark. F. Scott Fitzgerald came close, perhaps, when he contrasted France, England and America in a short story, "France was a land, England was a people, but America, having about it still that quality of an idea, was harder to utter.... It was a willingness of the heart" (Fitzgerald 1989, 512).[1]

The idea we have "still" is self-government, and historians and political theorists have traced the idea back to the forests of Germany and to classical Greece, depending upon their tastes and purposes. The willingness of the heart is civic virtue, which gives self-government purpose beyond self-will. Civic virtue has likewise been traced to whatever source most appealed to successive generations of political philosophers.

Had Fitzgerald written after the October 1929 market crash instead of before it, he might have had to confront another part of the constitutive puzzle—the relations between the government and the economy. Had he lived in a different era he might have pondered about a fourth constitutive question. Is America, as our pledge of allegiance asserts, a nation constituted under God?

This essay will argue that the question of what constitutes the American republic is answered by these four elements, properly understood: (1) self-government, (2) civic virtue, (3) state-economy relations, and (4) secular-sacred distinctions.

---

1. This story first appeared in *Saturday Evening Post,* 9 October 1929.

Self-government

The idea of self-government is now so freighted with history, experience, and ideological rationalization that its core is almost impossible to discuss. The recent events in Eastern Europe do, however, provide Americans with a new canvas on which to project the idea clear and fresh, without the varnishes that obscure the understanding we once had.

Self-government, properly understood, is composed of majority rule by territorial representatives meeting in open congress, the rule being constrained by individual liberties previously agreed to by supermajorities and accepted by all as a condition of citizenship.

If these simple constitutive relationships cannot be agreed upon, then self-government cannot exist and the polity sinks into a dictatorship of one, the few, or the mob. Self-government is, therefore, almost wholly about process. Outcomes and policies are not its principal province.

The U.S. Constitution is thus mostly about process, although it includes, particularly in its amendments, much in the way of constraints to protect individual liberties. The processes specified are not sacrosanct; they can be changed and some have been without harm. Changing the manner of electing senators, while it broke the tie between state legislatures and the Senate and thus broke the constitutive relationship between the two levels of government, has not crippled the republic.[2]

We could, of course, change process in ways that would do damage, pervert, or destroy the American republic. Periodic calls for "strong democracy," "responsiveness," and "citizen empowerment,"—code words all for particular outcomes—would, if heeded, strain representative government beyond its capacity. Representation is a simple concept; it is a kind of democracy practiced at every level of government and in most membership organizations. Of course it can be corrupted—by limiting the franchise, by buying elections, by all sorts of evil practiced by evil persons. The trick then is to purify the process because the one thing representative government cannot be is replaced. Other methods cannot set an agenda, cannot balance competing demands, and cannot protect minority interests. Only representative governments can do these things.

In the over two hundred years since the republic was founded, we have put great strains on our representative governments. At the

---

2. Amendment 25, secs. 3 and 4 (relating to presidential incapacity), is, however, a complete muddle. Here we must continue to rely on civic virtue or trust in the Lord, for these words will not help us.

local level we have so fragmented the general purpose governments (city and county councils) with the creation of special purpose governments (e.g., school districts, sewer boards) that representative governments cannot speak to questions of priority or fiscal responsibility. At the state level we have removed, through constitutional limitations and federal transfers of funds directly to state executive agencies, the capacity of state representatives to govern. At the federal level our representatives are so hedged about by committee rule that the grand trading arena envisioned by Madison is greatly attenuated.

Moreover, as our parties have been weakened, we seem unable to organize Congress so that it can act coherently. Instead, we show signs of drifting into a kind of plebiscitary democracy in which only the president has legitimacy.

Self-government, however, requires that "the Executive be under the law and that the law be made in parliamentary deliberations" in Justice Robert H. Jackson's famous phrase.[3] Hence legislative representation is at the core of the republic (see Pole 1966, pt. 3). A representative, as the ancient text puts it, "has the power to bind you." The representative has power of attorney, but power of attorney for people, not for specific interests or points of view.

Territory as the basis of representation became very early the only way to insure that people, who have many and varied interests that change over time, were the objects of representation. Interests were represented through people, not the other way round. Proportional representation, which uses lists to force people to vote only for an ideology, while popular in Europe, cannot be a substitute for territorial representation in this country. No one interest can hope to capture the many and varying interests of any person, nor can list voting reflect the intensities of preferences that people have over a broad range of issues. Territorial representation of people is a constitutive element in the American republic.

Majority rule, constrained by individual liberty guarantees, works in a large republic much as Madison said it would. It works because there is seldom one majority on any two issues. A heterogeneous population confronted with a variety of issues usually insures that the majority on each issue is different from the majority on any other issue. In this way a tyranny of *the* majority is avoided, as Madison predicted. A social choice theorist would say that intensities of preferences insure that minorities of all stripes have a pretty good chance of getting what they want on issues most important to them. The Democratic party of the twentieth century is, after all, a coalition of

---

3. Youngstown Sheet & Tube Co. v. United States, 343 U.S. 579 (1952).

minorities. Majority rule, so understood, is a constitutive element of the American republic.

Guarantees of individual liberties is another constitutive element of the American republic, but the quality of the guarantee is not often understood. It is not that the guarantees are written down in a constitution that is important: otherwise Russia would have been a free society since 1921 and England could have been enslaved long ago. What is important is that there be a rule of law undergirding what is said by the words. The rule of law is not another set of words but a habit of the mind and a set of processes and institutions.

America inherited the English common law and incorporated it by inference and direct reference in all original constitutions. American courts sat without hindrance from English colony to American state. Daniel Webster argued the sanctity of English charter law in the Dartmouth case,[4] and those who sought to impeach Richard Nixon did so guided in part by John Rushworth's account of the trials of Wentworth and Charles I.

We have, in the twentieth century, expanded individual liberties far beyond those envisioned by the founders and have extended their reach almost beyond the foundations on which they rest. Yet we are, not quite, beyond the rule of law, and it remains a constitutive element of the American republic.

In brief then these elements of self-government—a neutral process, territorial representation, majority rule, and the rule of law as reflected in the common law—make up one part of the answer to the question of what constitutes the American republic.

Civic Virtue

Burke said it best in 1791: "Society cannot exist unless a controlling power upon will be placed somewhere, and the less of it there is within, the more there must be without. It is ordained in the eternal constitution of things, that men of intemperate minds cannot be free. Their passions forge their fetters" (Burke 1834). Fitzgerald (1989, 512) talked of sacrifice. "It was the graves at Shiloh and the tired, drawn, nervous faces of its great men, and the country boys dying in the Argonne for a phrase that was empty before their bodies withered. It was a willingness of the heart." A modern political theorist ends his book, "But what is virtue, you ask? Perhaps it is the perfection of the soul—not an easy thought in these times, but bracing, refreshing, restorative" (Mansfield 1989, 297).

Such diverse notions can all be identified in some sense as civic

---

4. Dartmouth College v. Woodward, 17 U.S. (4 Wheat.) 518 (1819).

virtue, a notion best described as Justice Potter Stewart did of pornography, "I don't know how to define it, but I know it when I see it." Fitzgerald described it in terms of sacrifice. Burke saw it as political temperance, a befitting modesty towards one's own goals, while Mansfield and most modern theorists do not see it very clearly at all. Indeed, MacIntyre (1981) says virtue itself no longer exists.

Given the difficulties of definition I will proceed by example and start with temperance. In the 1960s, as now, those whose minds could perceive only one public issue at a time stood with Goldwater (although on the opposite side of the room) in believing that extremism in the pursuit of virtue was no vice. They may have been in pursuit of what they considered a virtuous public policy, but they did not possess civic virtue.

The woman who cried out as the Minnesota National Guard broke up a picket line, "That's not the way it is supposed to be," possessed no law on her side, but she did have civic virtue. Civic virtue was sacrificed in the Tiananmen Square tragedy in China. Civic virtue resulted in massive change in Eastern Europe, although it is not to be confused with popular uprisings. Civic virtue sometimes stands against the mob, as was the case anytime Senator Wayne Morse of Oregon rose to speak in the Senate. Civic virtue was in the words of old Senator Carl Hayden of Arizona when he advised a colleague, "There comes a time when you have to rise above principle."

It is fashionable nowadays for both the left and the right to decry the loss of civic virtue; the left on such issues as industry rape of the environment and the right because of the loss of patriotism. Both sides are undoubtedly right, as civic virtue belongs to no single party or creed. It is simply a quality of caring about public purposes and public destinations. Sometimes the public purpose is chosen over private purposes. A young Israeli economist investigating a kibbutz came across the following case. The kibbutz had money to spend. The alternatives were a TV antenna and TV sets for everyone or a community meeting hall. The economist found that everyone preferred the TV option but that, when they voted, they unanimously chose the meeting hall. Call it enlightened self-interest, a community preference, or something else, it is civic virtue in action.

If civic virtue is defined as a caring about public purposes and public destinations, then concerns about the long-term good of the polity are concerns rooted in civic virtue. Anyone who for any reason is willing to destroy that polity does not possess civic virtue. Civic virtue possessed by any people who practice self-government is sufficient for any polity that has not gone mad. (Such madness has not been unknown.) The definition probably will satisfy no political theorist but it is that definition of civic virtue that is a constitutive element of the American republic.

State-Economy Relations

It is almost but not quite the case that state-economy relations could be relegated to the subordinate position of being a policy issue of little importance to the question of what constitutes the American republic. It is not the case, for example, that the American republic could exist only with a completely free market. Indeed it is questionable whether we have ever had one (see Bourgin 1989). Most of the arguments over the market during the last two hundred years have been about the degree of control the government should exercise over the economy and not over any more fundamental question.

Certainly we have had monumental policy disputes over the question of control. They seem to break out every fifty or sixty years, beginning with the Jacksonians in the 1830s (see Schlesinger 1989, 48–51). Recent scholarship has documented the other two eras of policy dispute in the 1890s and the 1930s (Lustig 1982; Sklar 1988; Brand 1988). Notwithstanding the momentous changes effected by these three upheavals in state-economy relations, the underlying constitutive relationships between the state and the economy were not called into question.

It was left for Charles E. Lindblom to raise the issue of state-economy relations that is, indeed, the constitutive question. He said, "The large, private corporation fits oddly into democratic theory and vision. Indeed, it does not fit" (Lindblom 1977, 356). Lindblom raises the issue of the corporation per se as a political actor. Corporations are different from real people, presumably. They have different preferences; they have more resources than most people; they have longer lives than most people. Having them as players in the political process might well totally change the outcomes of public processes.

One way to examine the differences between corporations and real people is by comparing their preference functions. If we can for the moment assume, contrary to Lindblom, that our individual preferences remain sufficiently uncorrupted by corporate influences so as to have some residual of intrinsic value, then we might meaningfully compare them to the preferences of the fictive people—the corporations. Is it the case, for example, that corporate preferences are more narrowly restricted than those of real people? Do corporate preferences change at a different rate and for different reasons? Are corporate preferences entered into the aggregative process at a different time or place such that their weighting is changed relative to real people? Are there more, or fewer, interactive terms in corporate preferences? What are the statistical characteristics of corporate preferences when aggregated, that is, what kinds of distributions, means, and variances occur on given policy issues? Do they match closely those of the human polity or are they skewed in some important dimensions or are they totally different?

These questions are all amenable to empirical research, which has, to date, not been done. The research is overdue, as recent changes have thrown corporations more deeply into politics. The first change was the intrusion of public power into commercial production processes for environmental and safety purposes. That intrusion had the predictable, though unintended, consequence of provoking corporate countermeasures in the political arena. Two other events provided the corporation with increased leverage in that arena. One was a very confused Supreme Court decision—*First National Bank v. Bellotti*[5]—which had the effect, if not the intent, of granting corporations free political speech (as contrasted with commercial speech) as fictive persons. The other was the so-called reform of the election laws in 1974, which allowed corporations to sponsor political action committees or PACs.

The Court interpretation and election "reform" provide a suitable environment for new corporate influence. In particular, the expansion of First Amendment rights of the corporation as a fictive person allows corporations to play political roles not open to them before. The 1990 Court ruling in *Austin v. Michigan Chamber of Commerce* (494 U.S. 652) did allow limits to be set on direct corporate spending in political campaigns but did not otherwise change corporate political speech.

As corporations participate, can we observe differences in outcomes in public policies? For example, is the savings and loan (S&L) debacle the result of the new power of corporations in electoral politics? If it is, then real people have their work cut out for them. In the long term, however, a more hopeful scenario is possible. As corporations act out their role as good citizens they may, willy nilly, be forced to become good citizens. It is a commonplace observation that things tend to become what they pretend to be. While we cannot hope that all managers and owners of private corporations will become public-spirited, we cannot hope that about real people either. There is a sense, however, in which it is and always has been in the self-interest of private corporations to concern themselves with the long-term public purposes and public destinations of locality and country. Gaining the right of political speech, with its requirement to give

5. 43 U.S. 765 (1978).

reasons that attach to common political dialogue, may well make the fit between corporations and democracy better rather than worse. This sort of state-economy relations can, therefore, be a constitutive element of the American republic.

Secular-Sacred Distinctions

In a major work on art, language, music, and literary criticism George Steiner (1989, 3) starts by asserting "that any coherent account of the capacity of human speech to communicate meaning and feeling is, in the final analysis, underwritten by the assumption of God's presence." He concludes that "major art in our vexed modernity has been, like all great shaping before it, touched by the fire and the ice of God," and ends with an apology, "I know this formulation will be unacceptable not only to most of those who will read a book such as this, but also to the prevailing climate of thought and of feeling in our culture" (Steiner 1989, 223 and 228, respectively).

Steiner's assertions about the presence of God would have been considered commonplace by all the founders of the republic, their predecessors in England, and by most citizens today. They clearly are not commonplace to academics in the humanities, hence his apology, and emphatically not commonplace in essays in political science.[6] Indeed, the unease of intellectuals at associating the sacred and the secular, outside of the Divinity School, is ridiculous to the point of absurdity when the question is, What constitutes the American republic? If it is the case that civic virtue makes us inarticulate, then religion, seriously considered, makes us embarrassed. Yet much is explained by secular-sacred distinctions as originally made and as now made in this land. To lessen the unease, I will discuss the issue in the abstract and remind the reader that even Jefferson wrote that the inalienable rights were endowed by a Creator.

The issues are not, as might be supposed, the policy questions of prayer in public schools, aid to parochial schools, or religious displays on public property. These are trivial issues over which the justices of the Supreme Court may breathe heavily and make their ponderous decisions. The real issues concern teleology, theology, and ethics.

The teleological issue is simply put: Is there a divine purpose in the world? If there is, then the Whig interpretation of history—the inevitable progress and perfection of human institutions—may be right after all. If there is no divine purpose, then secular goals are all we have. The founders generally believed the former; practically

---

6. For two rather feeble exceptions see Grant (1985) and Diggins (1984).

all intellectuals now believe the latter. What the American public believes is unclear to me and probably to the public itself.

The distinction between the two points of view is important. To the extent that a divine purpose is not accepted, the highest secular power—the state—must bear all the responsibility for human happiness. Justice, fairness, equality, and all other human aspirations must be gained through the state by the efforts of its citizens. It is evident that this is now the role of the state as envisioned by at least those most active in public affairs. It is a mighty burden to put on secular institutions.

The theological issue—a belief in a personal afterlife—reinforces the teleological issue in the following way. When individuals believe they are of two worlds, the secular and the sacred, they spend some time on the latter, whether it be to "work out their own salvation with diligence" as the Buddha suggested (salvation being a release from the wheel of life) or just being "in the world but not of it." Secular matters are of less importance. Public matters are even less important than private matters, deserving of less attention than the examination of one's own soul. Nothing much in the way of good is expected from human institutions.

How far we have come from that attitude is evident all around us. No doubt people have always wanted to live long and prosper. Only recently have we decided that public institutions are responsible for making it happen. With the soul of no importance, the body becomes all important—witness the focus on prolonging life at all costs. Earlier members of this society might have considered such practices blasphemous. Even today some view them as obscene.

The ethical dimension of the secular-sacred distinction cuts in a different way. At the simplest level, what one can get away with is a far different proposition in a world possessing an all-seeing and interested God than in a secular world. While ethics can be secular, they were developed in religious contexts in most cultures and are remarkably the same. Murder is almost universally proscribed, not because one might be caught in the here and now, but because of divine retribution in the there and then. Most interpersonal relationships were ordered by one faith or another, and the resulting social order took much strain off civil governments.

The essence of ethics in this religious context is that a person must be personally responsible for individual actions. As Kipling put it (in his poem "Tomlinson"), "The sins ye do two by two ye must pay for one by one." Moreover, the definition of sin is not a matter of individual conscience, as are most secular ethical standards, even Kant's, but rather a fairly rigid and specific code many centuries old.

Codes of divine provenance, even if not of divine origin, have more "bite" than do the cultural norms we talk about today.

All in all, the secular-sacred distinctions that command individual responsibility for individual actions, that provide comfort outside secular activities, and that assign a purpose to human existence were all constitutive elements in the American republic. They probably still are, no doubt to the bewilderment of most academics.

Conclusion

These things constitute the American republic: self-government, civic virtue, some secular-sacred distinctions, and a certain sort of state-economy relations. They may be considered as necessary conditions for the American regime. Are they sufficient? Will they endure?

Judge Learned Hand can answer for self-government. Speaking at a wartime rally in Central Park on 21 May 1944, he said, "I often wonder whether we do not rest our hopes too much upon constitutions, upon laws, and upon courts. These are false hopes, believe me, these are false hopes. Liberty lies in the hearts of men and women; when it dies there no constitution, no law, no court can save it" (Hand 1952, 190).

So Fitzgerald was right, a willingness of the heart underlies self-government and provides the basis for civic virtue, a caring for public purposes, and public destinations. That willingness of the heart is sustained by some manner of secular-sacred distinctions. Those alone enable many to endure the hardships on this mortal plane. Can that virtue be exercised by the men and women who own and manage the private corporations that now are wholly public in their consequences? I would like to think so.

The Case Considered

One may disagree about the constitutive elements of the American republic either by suggesting additions and deletions or by maintaining that the constitutive elements have weakened or disappeared over time. My list may reflect more of the past than of the present. In this section I will examine these constitutive elements as they might be currently viewed by all those not overly impressed with what might have once been.

Self-Government

The most damning indictment of self-government is that of Ted Lowi (1979). Lowi documents in exquisite detail how representative government has failed in the midtwentieth century, turning over power to executive agencies who produce "policy without law." Politics becomes administration, and America flounders in a bureaucratic sea as do all modern governments. Max Weber foretold all this long ago and far away. It all came true.

And yet a number of curious things have happened. The Reverend Martin Luther King, Jr., took up the cross for civil rights. Rachel Carson (1962) wrote *The Silent Spring.* Lyndon Johnson tried to fight a land war in Asia without the benefit of a declaration of war. And we were blessed with the presidency of Richard Nixon. All four occurrences gave new vigor to self-government and retaught the living generations how to use this "machine that would go of itself."[7]

For our purposes the important thing about King's efforts is that he forced the machinery of government to go against the prevailing opinion and rectify its own mistaken notions. *Brown v. Board of Education* was,[8] by itself, insufficient. Representative government had to have its feet held to the fire of racial injustice. King accomplished that and representative government responded, albeit slowly and grudgingly.

The environmental movement, which may be dated from Carson's book, accomplished the same feat. Here the attack was focused directly on the bureaucracy, starting with the Corps of Engineers and the Bureau of Public Roads. Technical solutions to social problems were rejected by citizens everywhere. While representative government tried its best to hide behind the bureaucrats, in the end they were called to account and a series of environmental laws were passed. The important thing relearned here was that while bureaucrats can resist public pressure indefinitely (they simply hire more staff and hold more public hearings), elected officials cannot resist public pressure. Sooner rather than later they must get ahead of the protest and lead it.

Protests against the Vietnam War were, for a long time, totally misdirected, as they focused on the White House and the Pentagon. It was only when the protests began to focus on the Congress that change occurred. The change may be dated from the day in early 1974 that the New York State Bar chartered a train to Washington, D.C., and, eschewing sign waving in front of the White House and the Pentagon, instead fanned out from Union Station to all the House and Senate office buildings. The Congress rediscovered the war-making power and the power of the purse. The battle to end the war was soon over.

7. The phrase is James Russell Lowell's from a speech made to the Reform Club of New York in 1988. Cited in Kammen (1985, 17).

8. 347 U.S. (1954).

The greatest rediscovery of legislative authority over the executive came about, however, because Richard Nixon was elected president. Two things occurred during his administration that are of interest to this argument. First, he so scared the Congress that they retracted the enormous amount of discretionary authority they had been giving presidents (which had become so extensive that most of my undergraduates at that time believed presidents had the power to make laws) and, second, the Congress relearned how to impeach a president. Both lessons were long overdue. Richard Nixon accomplished both. (Perhaps biblical plagues were equally efficacious.)

It can be argued that none of the foregoing disasters should have occurred. In a perfect world, none of them would. Yet they did allow us to recapture some sense of how representative government works. The machinery of self-government can work only if it is used by folks who remember how to run it. Joseph Sax, a law professor at the University of Michigan, used the common law to change environmental policy in that state. Some citizens in Michigan felt that the bureaucrats responsible for state-owned resources were allowing those resources to be exploited. They sued. The courts in Michigan threw out their case, saying that the plaintiffs had no standing (i.e., could show no personal damages) and that, besides, the bureaucrats in charge were responsible to the governor and the state legislature. Let the plaintiffs use the electoral process if they wished change, said the judges.

Sax recast the issue under the common law doctrine of a public trustee. The judges were transfixed. Trustees have a duty not to waste the assets of the trust. Along that well-defined path the bureaucrats were called to account by the courts.

Self-government surely depends on the imaginative use of tools such as the common law to survive. Does it also need political parties? After all, they have been with us almost from the beginning. Even Madison, no friend of faction (which had been given a bad name in England by that time) says in the penultimate paragraph of *The Federalist* no. 50, that "an extinction of parties necessarily implies either a universal alarm for the public safety, or an absolute extinction of liberty."

In nineteenth-century America, the golden age of parties, Frederick Grimke could accurately say, "parties take the place of the old system of checks and balances. The latter balance the government only, the former balance society itself" (quoted in Hofstadter 1969, 266).

The argument is well known to readers of this essay. The "bland, enveloping coalitions" that are American political parties were capable of channeling the inarticulate and the passionate alike into supporting platforms that could, or hoped to, attract a majority in this diverse land. They were not, except on rare occasions, parties of principle because to be so was to lose the election.[9]

It is also well known to the reader that, for many reasons, the American party system is falling apart. Court orders against patronage, primary rule changes, the rise of single-issue constituencies and their lobbies, and election "reform" have all helped to destroy the standard American party. It is being replaced at the national level inside the Beltway by hundreds of special interest lobbies who honestly believe that they have the warrants to speak for the public. Moreover, they are succeeding—not in the sense they all win; obviously some oppose others—but in the sense that the national domestic agenda and the resulting political dialogue are shaped by them.

One must go back to seventeenth-century English parliamentary history to find the equivalent in self-righteous belief in one's own doctrines. Then it was religion, with the truth possessed only by one's own faction; now, it seems, it is everything from abortion to zoning, and the factions are no less convinced of their truths than were the factions of three centuries ago.

As a constitutive problem, the loss of the "bland, enveloping coalitions" and their replacement by narrowly focused interest groups operating independently of party and having no responsibility for governing might seem to be a major challenge to self-government. One can envision a legislator becoming a bland, enveloping coalition within a single skin, as each legislator tries to form responsible positions from conflicting special interests. Perhaps this is the final test of an educational system that eschews teaching substance in favor of working and playing well with peers and finding out how one feels about things. Certainly it will be a severe test.

Legislatures, surprisingly enough, are well suited to develop public policies from many voices. If the disintegration of the parties goes forward, other means may be necessary for the organization of business, including committee assignments, but that is no great task. Legislative rules and parliamentary procedure antedate parties by several centuries. One need go back no farther than to Jefferson's *Manual of Parliamentary Practice*, composed in 1800 by Thomas Jefferson from House of Commons precedents and still reprinted in the House Rules (but no longer, alas, in the Rules of Senate for which it was intended),

---

9. This is not the occasion to expand on why a two-party system, fostered by single-member districts and winner-take-all rules, is superior to a multiparty system and proportional representation. See Haefele (1971, 350–67).

to find a method of organization of business that is not dependent on parties. Moreover, Jefferson's rules come closer to being able to determine what he called "the true sense of this deliberative body" than do the current rules. Specifically, there would be, under his rules, more direct control of the legislative agenda by the members and more sophisticated bill drafting with wider member participation. Any member's right to divide a bill on a point of order would stop unwanted omnibus bills and, of course, all separation of spending and revenue decisions could easily be avoided.

It is not the case that all the unfortunate changes made since Jefferson's day were the result of parties, but it is the case that the House and Senate could function efficiently without parties using the modern equivalent of Jefferson's rules.

Choosing a president in the absence of political parties might seem to pose additional problems, but they would occur only if we change our present method of choosing a president. Under the present system the race must, perforce, become a two-person race. By the present system I mean an electoral college voting state by state, winner take all in each state. The electors themselves are, of course, an anomaly and should be abolished. The electoral vote is crucial, however, as it focuses and magnifies the necessity of achieving a majority in each state while discounting all votes larger than a majority in any state, thus guarding against mere regional popularity. Unfortunately, the understanding of the value of the present electoral system continues to diminish, despite the recent example in Israel that demonstrates just how much power is thrown into the hands of small splinter parties by so-called fairer systems. If we do, finally, fall into the fatuity of one-person, one-vote in the election of the president, then we will sail into uncharted seas with neither the compass of theory nor the map of experience to guide us.

Civic Virtue

It is entirely possible that the greatest danger threatening American civic virtue was created by a sleight of hand in economic theory performed around the turn of the century. It was then that economists "solved" the vexed question of value by consigning it to the dustbin, replacing it with the concept of individual preferences as the only source of values. By doing so, great advances were made in microtheory as a self-contained rational system. Once this system was fully developed, say with the publication of Paul Samuelson's (1947) *Foundations of Economic Analysis*, economics reemerged and began to define the rest of the social world in terms of rational choice models. That effort brought about a diminution of any and all ideas of civic virtue since all preferences, at least all legal preferences, were considered equally valued, a disaster only now being addressed as economists work with philosophers, political theorists, and law professors.

Civic virtue must, of course, address values and, in particular, public values—that is to say, shared values about public purposes and public destinations. If these are to be determined, willy-nilly, by the unconsidered preferences of the citizenry, then civic virtue is at best a sometime thing. While that ultimate rationalist, the libertarian, strives mightily to show that untrammeled individual preferences could result in a just society, it is clear to most that it could also result in total disaster.

We must, however, ask two things. The first is, Does it matter any more whether or not we possess civic virtue? And the second is, If it matters, how can we measure the ineffable so as to assess persistence or absence of civic virtue? The first question asks whether or not the process of self-government is sufficient in and of itself to sustain the American republic in an acceptable way. It has always been a deep question in political theory if the practice of self-government was an education in civic virtue. Jefferson thought so and hoped that the introduction of the old English hundred (a small unit of self-government) would allow every adult American to hold public office and that the holding of public office would itself teach civic virtue. Stephen Elkin (1987, esp. chap. 6) suggests the same thing in a contemporary urban setting.

While the thought is appealing, we must conclude that Jefferson and Elkin are in the same posture as the libertarian. Acting in a public fashion can teach civic virtue, but there are too many counterexamples for us to replace "can" with "will."

Nor can we rely on education, at least not as currently practiced. The present focus on peer relationships is the educational equivalent of Sam Rayburn's "to get along, go along," and the emphasis on feelings is too introspective—valuable, no doubt, in a safe, well-regulated world. Neither emphasis breeds civic virtue nor, indeed, civic anything.

It does matter whether or not we possess civic virtue. The reason is almost primitive. We are a tribe. Whether one focuses on a town, a nation-state, or on humankind itself, the need to consider public purposes and public destinations is essential if we are to survive. We may strive for different purposes and different destinations, but the striving must be about public purposes and public destinations.

Awareness of this need is submerged in the American republic chiefly because we have been so successful as a tribe. We have prospered in material terms and hence socially and politically. It has been only in the last two decades or so that our material prosperity, which fueled our political and social well-being (an earlier generation would have termed it "our many providences"), began to fail us. World competition and environmental degradation have revealed us to be second-rate in many areas. Great inequalities in material success have also brought us social breakdowns that hover just below the crisis stage in large urban areas.

The challenge of a second-rate economy and social breakdowns on the domestic side (to say nothing of foreign policy challenges) may well provide the incentive for rediscovery of the need to focus on public purposes and public destinations. Adversity has always been the father of civic virtue.

The second question (Can we measure the presence or absence of civic virtues?) requires that we define more closely what it is we are to measure. Surely we are not concerned with participation rates, voter turn-out, or other quantitative measures of political activity. We are rather concerned with the presence or absence of a certain mind-set or belief about the public's business. Since this is resolutely normative in nature, the trick is to define the concern in ways that distinguish concern from mere political activism that seeks specific outcomes.

We may at once dismiss the ignorant and the indifferent. Civic virtue is absent in both. We may, upon reflection, dismiss those with inflexible demands, as they are the enemy of civic virtue. Civic virtue adheres only to those who are engaged upon the public's business and who possess empathy and strive for creative resolutions of public problems. A creative resolution is one that results in a larger degree of consensus and leaves more friends than enemies. It is usually not a simple compromise, which leaves the underlying issue unresolved. It usually is a solution outside the narrow frame of reference of the contesting parties that redefines the issue in broader terms rooted in deeper and more generally shared principles. Sax's solution is an illustration, as he redefined the issue according to widely respected (and deeply embedded) doctrine and law about the duties of a trustee.

Civic virtue as thus defined is an alien concept to political scientists who view politics as a struggle for power. It is alien to rational choice theorists who are still unwilling to look behind expressed preferences. Such civic virtue is, however, meat and drink for some politicians, particularly those who never seem to take the firm stand so beloved by political activists and partisans. It could even be effectively argued that the person most possessed of civic virtue is the one who has no firm stand on any issue but does have a few principles; the one who labors in the entrepreneurial task of finding the highest level of agreement that is rooted in and connected to the highest ideals of the country. Martin Luther King, Jr., possessed unusual civic virtue precisely because he combined nonviolence and the Declaration of Independence, both deeply embedded and cherished ideals in most American psyches. He opposed deeply held social conventions, but they could not stand against Jefferson's words and Gandhi's methods. No finer example of true civic virtue exists in all our history, nor one that so clearly delineates civic virtue from "to get along, go along" or from mere advocacy and compromise.

Having defined civic virtue more closely, can we measure it? The simple answer is no. It is enough if we can recognize it when we see it, as it is always a rare bird whose markings often deceive us.

State-Economy Relations

Surely it is time to move beyond Lindblom who asserted that the private business corporation does not fit with democratic theory. Consider that the special position of business in America is as much an obligation as it is a privilege. Of course, governments must defer to business because of the capital investments business makes and for which it alone is at great risk. Business is held responsible for employment levels, technological advancements, and economic growth. Governments embrace business in a tight and loving grip, encouraging them to be efficient, to retrain workers, build a half-million alternative fuel autos even before there is a market for them; governments also sue businesses, with deeper pockets (those of the taxpayers) than any business has, for transgressions of all sorts. There are no remaining arguments about untrammeled capitalism, which does not exist and possibly never did. Nor is there any serious argument against market systems as the closest thing we have to make efficient allocations of resources (given an initial distribution of income about which more later). Socialist regimes have failed all over the world, with or without the word *democratic* in front of the word *socialist*. Conditions in the former Soviet Union and in Eastern Europe have demonstrated that we can have inefficient economies and great income inequalities. Market economies demonstrate we can have moderately efficient economies and great income inequalities. No one has shown how we can have, in practice, both economic efficiency and income equality because the economic efficiency depends on individual liberty and individual liberty results in income inequalities. This much can be asserted without argument.

No one should suppose, however, unless dedicated to the construction of a straw man, that any civil society should be content with a permanent, socially disabled underclass. It is the presence of that socially disabled underclass in the American regime that poses the problem for state-economy relations. One could, arguably, add environmental concerns, but it is now clear that the state and business are equally culpable in that area. While policy problems abound in the environmental field that are nowhere near solution, no constitutive problem of state-economy relations is present.

There is no panacea for the problem of a socially disabled underclass. Its problems were addressed by the labor movement in the late 1800s and by the New Deal in the 1930s; it was a major component of civil rights legislation in the 1960s and of Lyndon Johnson's Great Society, which showed that throwing money at the problem was not a solution. The reason for this has even reached common fiction: "There's money in poverty, all right, but it ain't the poor that git it" (Schenck 1990, 147). Senator Daniel Patrick Moynihan said the same thing in more elegant language in a speech some years ago.

As always, there are individual acts that help. A black woman in Washington, D.C., shows that public housing can be managed successfully by its tenants and job skills learned in the process. A black woman in Milwaukee demonstrates that poor parents can turn a public school system around. Myriads of self-help groups show how dependencies of all sorts can be conquered without professional guidance. But, overall, one cannot find aggregate data that offer promise.

One is tempted to conclude that the socially disabled can only be lifted up one by one, and the farther government stays from them the better. That is, indeed, the view of some of the most articulate of the underclass. Yet that will not do and cannot be tolerable in a civil society. Governments at all levels are involved and will remain so. Some things that governments do, however, would be better not done, and other things they do not do should be done. These include such diverse things as plant closings, the provision of public safety, and the use of the state as an actor in the economy.

The facts of plant closings are well known. A large corporation, driven by economic rationality calculations, closes a plant that is the mainstay of a locality. The corporation is better off, the locality is devastated. Protests are mounted, people march around with signs. Television runs stories of family lives shattered. Local politicians decry the situation and promise investigations and new laws. The sixty-day advance warning legislation is an example of the latter.

Most of this pain and misdirected political posturing could be avoided if people would simply use the tools of self-government available to them, in this case, contract law. At the time a company decides to locate a plant that requires community investment, a contract should be drawn up between the company and the public corporation (city, county, state) that sets out under what conditions the plant may be closed and what obligations the company has to the public corporation should closing occur.

Local economic development officers reading this account are now shaking their heads and wanting to explain to me how things are really done, and the kinds of incentives localities offer—like tax rebates—to get companies to locate plants in their localities. That has, indeed, been the rule. Corporations have played one locality against another in order to get concessions by places eager for economic growth. Corporations will not willingly change.

In recent years, however, governments in the most desirable locations have been able to exact concessions from companies. As environmental and "no-growth" advocates join in, more and more communities will be in a position to contract with private corporations rather than bribing those businesses to locate in their community.

Objection: Poor communities will always be at the mercy of rapacious private corporations.

Answer: That is why there are states and a national government, both of which can set standards and provide technical support to help poor communities. The Legal Services Corporation is an example of this kind of assistance.

The provision of public safety is an elemental necessity for the functioning of civil society, yet it is one utterly lacking in portions of our major urban areas. Why that is so remains a matter of contention among the people who minister to these areas. Is the answer more police, more trial judges, more social workers, more jobs? Without denying that more of something might help, let me argue that there is a precondition to supplying more of something if that "more" is to have any hope of helping. The precondition is simple safety for the residents of these areas. The precondition assumes that there is no greater percentage of evildoers in urban slums than anywhere else; it is just that the criminals control the neighborhood. That must be stopped before more of anything will be useful. At the present time, ordinary citizens in these areas are helpless, excepting the few brave and honorable individuals who resist and are usually shot for their trouble.

Such a situation is not only disgraceful in any civil society, it also breeds contempt for civil authority and hopelessness for the residents. How public safety is to be achieved will vary from place to place, but two elements will have to be present. First, involve the state government; second, increase neighborhood support on the streets. Simply increasing police saturation is not a solution; sometimes it even exacerbates the problems.

With public safety insured, other options can be implemented. Of these, the one offering the most hope combines elements of the negative income tax with job training directly in private businesses. Under this scheme individuals would be paid by the state to work and earn, and the state would pay the business to employ and train the worker. The scheme allows the individual to bring something valuable to the business from the beginning, namely money.

The final option is also a state initiative, one that has from time to time worked reasonably well. That is to use the state as the employer of last resort. During the 1930s, both the Works Progress Administration and the Civilian Conservation Corps were effective tools that not only accomplished much public good of a sort the market economy had no interest in, but also were effective in job training with all the ramifications for social order that such training implies.

Both of these options are methods by which the state can enter into the economy in noncoercive ways to aid the underclass. They are policy options that do not change the constitutive relationships between the economy and the state. More draconian measures, which do alter the constitutive relationship, involve putting more limits on the freedom of private capital. Put simply, they will not work, unless, to achieve their ends, the advocates are willing to risk losing not only liberty but the capital itself. There is, after all, no need to replay early postwar Britain.

Secular-Sacred Distinctions

We live in a time of marvelously diverse religious phenomena, much of which has secular implications. Consider this small sample of groups: cults that advocate communal living and withdrawing from society, combinations of mainstream Protestant faiths engaged in lobbying and other good works in support of every liberal cause ever thought of both here and abroad (they are having a little trouble thinking through Nicaragua right now), fundamentalist sects whose ministers seem hell-bent on demonstrating that Jesus really does love sinners, a revitalized Judaism stemming from the creation of the State of Israel, (while at the same time another Jewish sect condemns its creation), evangelical churches growing rapidly, and liberation theology created by Roman Catholic priests delivering Latin America to U.S. Protestant sects.

Serious theological scholarship under Jewish and Christian auspices (oftimes combined, as in the Anchor Bible series) is at an all time high both in quantity and quality.[10] Religious strife does not

---

10. Including Barth (1975–77), which qualifies on both counts.

diminish, particularly in the Bible lands of the Near and Middle East and in India and beyond. Serious academic journals of opinion about religion and politics are reemerging both here and in England.

Clearly something is going on beyond the ken of Lifton and Strozier (1990), although their recent review does illustrate the fatuity with which most academics view any religious experience. The something is the postwar reemergence of the sacred in American public and private lives. It has implications for the secular-sacred distinctions in the American republic.

In the black experience the church did not have to reemerge; it has been there all along as a sustaining force. From those churches have come political leaders from Martin Luther King, Jr., to Jesse Jackson and a host of others. Moreover, the black church remains, in many urban areas, the single cohesive force, struggling against great odds to hold neighborhood and community together in civil society. It still plays the role that many churches, black and white, played in earlier days of the republic, teaching and demanding private morality and public virtue in lawless eras.

We have not yet had a replacement for Reinhold Niebuhr, our first postwar minister who spoke on public issues, although we have never escaped the voice of the evangelist telling us that the country is going to hell in a hand basket. We have few public figures who can invoke the sacred in public affairs in the manner of the signers of the Declaration of Independence, "with a firm reliance on the protection of Divine Providence, we mutually pledge to each other our Lives, our Fortunes, and our sacred Honor."

The idea of the sacred as an upholder of the American republic has, perhaps, gone the way of Fourth of July oratory, whose reprise was sung by Archibald MacLeish in his radio verse commemorating the 200th anniversary of the Declaration of Independence. Two fragments of the verse go as follows:

> *Little Girl:* I want to see the USA.
> *Second Little Girl:* We can't see the USA.... Nobody has seen the USA.
> *Little Girl:* My grandfather saw it.
> *Second Little Girl:* Where?
> *Little Girl:* In France.
> *Second Little Girl:* He couldn't in France.
> *Little Girl:* He did. He told me.
> He was in France in the Great War and they stood retreat in a field and he saw it.
> He cried.
> *Second Little Girl:* Why?
> *Little Girl:* I don't know.
> The bugle blew at sunset and he saw it.

Second Little Girl: I've never seen it.
Little Girl: Neither have I.

. . .

Voices: The mass of mankind has not been born saddled and bridled for rulers to ride but to govern themselves by the grace of God and they will by the grace of God
>   they will!
>   by the grace of God they will!
>   they will![11]

I quote these fragments because they illustrate how closely love of country (here appropriately centered in the World War I soldier), belief in self-government, and the sacred ("the grace of God") are entwined. MacLeish sings here no sentimental song; the verse is a bitter commentary on America two centuries after the Declaration.

I pretend to no sentiment either, but rather have a suspicion that the Fourth of July orators were on to something, that the something was the metaphor linking the country to the sacred, and the link was (is?) firmly established in the American psyche as well as in its rhetoric. There is a dated aphorism that "the Lord looks after fools and drunkards." In the nineteenth-century version, "the Lord looks after fools, drunkards, and the United States of America." Surely he was thought to have done so in both world wars, and if he deserted us in the Vietnam War it was because we may have been fighting on the wrong side.

The link between the country and the sacred, if it is still present or could be rekindled as a serious proposition, could provide some much needed help. I hasten to deny that such a link clothes the state's actions in a mantle of holiness; that is the pose of charlatans of which we have, always, more than a sufficient supply. Quite the contrary, the link offers harsher and more rigorous critiques of the state and its actions and inactions, and on less partisan grounds, than we have seen since it was evoked by Martin Luther King, Jr. Even the faint echo of King present in the rhetoric of Jesse Jackson, muddled as it sometimes can be, is enough to bring thoughtful citizens to rethink some of their own rationalizations.

I argue no policy options here. I merely wish to stress the fact that conscience informed by some idea of the sacred has words to

---

11. MacLeish 1975, 29–30, 50. The first three lines spoken by "Voices" are Jefferson's, but he took them from a seventeenth-century Englishman, Richard Rumbold. See Cobbett (1809–29, 11:881).

speak to the citizens of this republic, words that awake old hopes and old dreams. They might awaken us from the Slough of Despond. They might tell us that we are at war, not just with the madmen of the Middle East, but against our own lethargy and despair, against politicians who think only of winning the next election, against greed and complacency that suppress all public feeling of responsibility for our fellows, and against the cynicism that whispers that nothing we do will matter.

Secular rhetoric, even that massaged by the cleverest image makers, fails to inspire. It does not touch deep roots of belief and conviction. The best that Ronald Reagan—the Great Communicator—could do was to lull us with old images, not inspire us to set to work.

Lest this seem too old-fashioned for verisimilitude, consider what the environmentalists (at least those not in the movement for yet another round of America bashing) are up to. They argue, with a few exceptions, no narrow self-interest; they evoke a necessity to save beauty, diversity, and wonder because it is there. It is, in a word many choose not to use, sacred. In other words, nature is a gift of God. Were they able to argue that case forthrightly they might win more support than they have yet mustered and they would likely throw confusion into the camps of their present enemies. Mainstream Christian ministers have begun to argue good health habits as a moral issue, finally catching up with the Boy Scouts, who got "the body as a temple of the Lord" from early nineteenth-century Christian doctrine.

We may be about to see a resurgence of a number of policy issues argued with overtones of an earlier notion of the sacred. The public scolds who irritate those of us who just want to be left alone with our private vices are called New Puritans for a reason. They are precisely that, and they may find that their scolding will, in time, have unintended consequences. The battle for separation of church and state may well be fought again, this time with some confusion about which side is which. If the state can define morality and the courts can overturn religious conviction, where, then, is the separation of church and state and which, then, the church?

As the twentieth century comes to an end, we continue to forget, and relearn, what it is that constitutes this Republic. Old people continue to worry that too much is being forgotten, but old people have always had that worry. Young people continue to believe that whatever appeals to them is worth more than what happened before they appeared on earth. So young people have always reasoned. As a representative of the older generation, let me remind those younger and more confident souls of the words of Carl Sandburg (in his poem

"Government"): "A Government is just as secret and mysterious and sensitive as any human sinner carrying a load of germs, traditions, and corpuscles handed down from fathers and mothers away back."

REFERENCES

Barth, Karl. 1975–77. *Church Dogmatics*. Edinburgh: T & T Clark.
Bourgin, Frank. 1989. *The Myth of Laissez-Faire in the Early Republic*. New York: George Braziller.
Brand, Donald R. 1988. *Corporatism and the Rule of Law*. Ithaca, N.Y.: Cornell University Press.
Burke, Edmund. 1834. "A Letter from Mr. Burke to a Member of the National Assembly in Answer to Some Objections to His Book on French Affairs." In *The Works of Edmund Burke*. New York: George Dearborn.
Carson, Rachel. 1962. *The Silent Spring*. Boston: Houghton Mifflin.
Cobbett, William. 1809–29. *State Trials*. London: N.p.
Diggins, John Patrick. 1984. *The Lost Soul of American Politics*. New York: Basic Books.
Elkin, Stephen L. 1987. *City and Regime in the American Republic*. Chicago: University of Chicago Press.
Fitzgerald, F. Scott. 1989. "The Swimmers." In *The Short Stories of F. Scott Fitzgerald*. Edited by Matthew J. Bruccoli. New York: Charles Scribner's Sons.
Grant, George Parkin. 1985. *English-Speaking Justice*. Notre Dame, Ind.: University of Notre Dame Press.
Haefele, Edwin T. 1971. "A Utility Theory of Representative Government." *American Economic Review* 16 (June): 350–67.
Hand, Learned. 1952. *The Spirit of Liberty*. New York: Alfred A. Knopf.
Hofstadter, Richard. 1969. *The Idea of a Party System*. Berkeley: University of California Press.
Kammen, Michael. 1985. *The Problem of Constitutionalism in American Culture*. Constitutionalism in America Series. Irving, Tex.: University of Dallas.
Lifton, Jay, and Charles B. Strozier. 1990. "Waiting for Armageddon" *New York Times Book Review* August 12.
Lindblom, Charles E. 1977. *Politics and Markets*. New York: Basic Books.
Lowi, Theodore. 1979. *The End of Liberalism*. 2d ed. New York: W. W. Norton.
Lustig, R. Jeffrey. 1982. *Corporate Liberalism: The Origins of Modern Political Theory, 1890–1920*. Berkeley: University of California Press.
MacIntyre, Alasdair. 1981. *After Virtue*. Notre Dame, Ind.: University of Notre Dame Press.

MacLeish, Archibald. 1975. *The Great American Fourth of July Parade.* Pittsburgh: University of Pittsburgh Press.

Mansfield, Harvey C., Jr. 1989. *Taming the Prince.* New York: The Free Press.

Pole, J. R. 1966. *Political Representation in England and the Origins of the American Republic.* New York: St. Martin's Press.

Samuelson, Paul. 1947. *Foundations of Economic Analysis.* Cambridge, Mass.: Harvard University Press.

Schenck, Hilbert. 1990. "A Down East Storm." *Fantasy and Science Fiction* 79 (4).

Schlesinger, Arthur, Jr. 1989. "The Ages of Jackson." *New York Review of Books* (December 7).

Sklar, Martin J. 1988. *The Corporate Reconstruction of American Capitalism, 1890–1916.* Cambridge: University of Cambridge Press.

Steiner, George. 1989. *Real Presences.* Chicago: University of Chicago Press.

CONTRIBUTORS

CHARLES W. ANDERSON is the Glen Hawkins Professor of Political Science at the University of Wisconsin—Madison. He is the author of *Pragmatic Liberalism* (1990).

JAMES W. CEASER is professor of government and foreign affairs at the University of Virginia. He is the author of *Liberal Democracy and Political Science* (1990).

STEPHEN L. ELKIN is professor in the Department of Government and Politics at the University of Maryland. He is the author of *City and Regime in the American Republic* (1987) and chair of the executive board of the Committee on the Political Economy of the Good Society (PEGS).

EDWIN T. HAEFELE is professor emeritus of political science at the University of Pennsylvania. He is the author of *Representative Government and Environmental Management* (1973).

THEODORE J. LOWI is the John L. Senior Professor of American Institutions at Cornell University. He is the author of *The End of Liberalism: The Second Republic of the United States* (1979).

KAROL EDWARD SOLTAN is associate professor in the Department of Government and Politics at the University of Maryland, where he is also associate director of the Center for the Study of Post-Communist Society. He is the author of *The Causal Theory of Justice* (1987).

CASS R. SUNSTEIN is the Karl Llewellyn Professor in the Law School at the University of Chicago. He is the author of *After the Rights Revolution: Reconceiving the Regulatory State* (1990) and *The Partial Constitution* (1993), and the editor of *Feminism and Political Theory* (1990).

INDEX

Ackerman, Bruce, 178n.6, 180n.11, 185n.23
Administrative Procedure Act (APA), 158–59, 175, 197
Aid to Families with Dependent Children (AFDC), 153
Almond, Gabriel, 41, 46n.5, 47, 54
Amalgamated Meat Cutters v. Connally, 194n.44
Amendments to the Constitution, 87, 208n.2, 213
American Political Science Association, 48
American Revolution, 75n.4, 174, 179, 181
Anchor Bible series, 226
Anderson, Charles W., 8n.1, 39–40, 145–46
Anti-Federalism, 174, 178–87, 189, 191, 196, 202. *See also* Federalism
APA (Administrative Procedure Act), 158–59, 175, 197
Aquino, Corazon, 79
Arendt, Hannah, 76, 125n.12, 179n.8
Aristotle, 42n.1, 72
Arizona, 211
Army Corps of Engineers, U.S., 217
Arrow, Kenneth, 2, 11, 27–28, 30–31, 92
Articles of Confederation, 181
Austin, John, 92
Austin v. Michigan Chamber of Commerce, 213

Barber, Benjamin, 180n.11
Beard, Charles, 186n.28
Bentham, Jeremy, 27n.9
Berlin, Isaiah, 127n.20
Bible, 226
Bolshevik Revolution, 74, 76

Bowsher v. Synar, 160
Boy Scouts of America, 229
Brasidas, 62
Brest, Paul, 135
Brown v. Board of Education, 217
Buchanan, James, 10–12, 14, 22–23
Buddha, 215
Bureau of Public Roads, 217
Burke, Edmund, 172n.18, 210
Bush, Gerald, 164

Carson, Rachel, 217
Carter, James Earl, Jr., 151, 162
Cartesianism, 96, 104
Catholicism, 226
CCC (Civilian Conservation Corps), 226
Ceaser, James W., 14, 39
Central Park rally, 21 May 1944, 216
Charles I (king of England), 210
Chevron, U.S.A., Inc. v. National Resource Defense Council, Inc., 195n.46
China, 211
Chomsky, Noam, 8
Christianity, 226–27, 229. *See also* United States, secular-sacred distinctions in
Cicero, Marcus Tullius, 123
City of New Orleans v. Dukes, 191n.37
Civic Culture (Almond & Verba), 47, 54
Civilian Conservation Corps (CCC), 226
Civil Rights Act of 1964, 168–69n.21
Clean Air Act Amendments of 1970, 155n.6
Cohen-Tanugi, Laurent, 89n.7
Columbia University, 171
Commons, John R., 99, 101, 107
Communism, 42–43, 76. *See also* Guild Socialism; Marxism; Union of Soviet Socialist Republics
Complete Anti-Federalist (Storing), 179n.9

Congress. *See* United States Congress
Constitution. *See* United States Constitution
Consumer Product Safety Commission, 163
Council of Economic Advisers, 161
Crick, Bernard, 126

Dahl, Robert: applied to liberalism, 107; on behavioralism, 47n.7, 49n.8; on control of power, 24–26; on democracy, 46n.5, 102; and normativism, 54, 55; *Politics, Economics, and Welfare* (Dahl & Lindblom), 9; *Preface to Economic Democracy* (Dahl), 25n.6
Daniels, Norman, 7
Daniel v. Family Security Life Ins. Co., 191n.37
Dartmouth College v. Woodward, 210
Davis, Kenneth Culp, 158
Declaration of Independence, 223, 227. *See also* American Revolution
Defense Production Act, 159n.10
Democracy in America (Tocqueville), 66
Democratic party, 151, 153n.2, 209
Department of Agriculture v. Moreno, 191n.35
Derrida, Jacques, 16
Dewey, John, 99, 106
District of Columbia Court of Appeals, 194n.45
Douglas, Mary, 127n.16
Durkheim, Émile, 102
Dworkin, Ronald, 7, 14, 81, 98n.2

Easton, David, 47n.7
Elkin, Stephen L., 1, 2, 40, 41, 221
Elster, Jon, 73
Ely, John Hart, 178n.4, 185n.25
Employee Stock Ownership Plans (ESOPs), 90
End of Liberalism (Lowi), 167n.20
Engel v. O'Malley, 191n.37
England, 103, 210, 214, 219, 227. *See also* Great Britain; House of Commons; Parliament, English
Enlightenment, 71, 74, 78, 125
Environmental Protection Agency (EPA), 156–57, 163
EPA. *See* Environmental Protection Agency

ESOPs (Employee Stock Ownership Plans), 90

Federal Communications Commission (FCC), 194n.45
Federalism: and deliberative democracy, 187–89; in Federalist/Anti-Federalist debate, 178–88; and interest groups, 191, 201; modern application of, 190, 201–2. *See also* Anti-Federalism
Federalist: general constitutional theory in, 15, 22; Hamilton's writings in, 185n.25; Madison's writings in, 155, 181, 183, 185, 186n.29, 218; no. 10, 155, 181, 186n.29; no. 50, 218; no. 51, 185; no. 55, 185; no. 57, 183; no. 68, 185n.25
Federal Register, 159
Federal Trade Commission (FTC), 163
Ferguson v. Skrupa, 191n.36
Fifth Amendment, 87
First Amendment, 213
First National Bank v. Bellotti, 213
Fisher, Roger, 82, 91
Fitzgerald, F. Scott, 207, 210–11, 216
Ford, Gerald, 151
Foucault, Michel Paul, 16, 85
Foundations of Economic Analysis (Samuelson), 220
Fourteenth Amendment, 87
France, 65, 74–76
French Revolution, 74–76
Freud, Sigmund, 3–6
Friedrich, Carl J., 9, 83
FTC (Federal Trade Commission), 163
Fuller, Lon L., 122

Galbraith, John Kenneth, 102
Galileo, 72
Galston, William, 134n.31
Gandhi, Mohandas Karamchand, 79, 91, 92, 223
Gellhorn, Ernest, 150, 154n.3
God, 207, 214, 215, 229
Goldwater, Barry, 211
Gorbachev, Mikhail, 62
"Government" (Sandburg), 230
Gramm-Rudman-Hollings law, 160
Gramsci, Antonio, 52, 53, 85
Great Britain, 65, 226. *See also* England; House of Commons; Parliament, English

Greater Boston Television Corp. v. FCC, 194n.45
Great Society, 224
Grimke, Frederick, 218
Guild Socialism, 103, 112

Habermas, Jürgen, 4, 6–8, 107n.6
Haefele, Edwin T., 30, 146–47
Hamilton, Alexander, 34, 183, 184n.22, 185n.25, 188
Hamilton, Charles V., 171
Hand, Learned, 216
Hart, H. L. A., 86
Hartog, Hendrik, 129
Harvard University, 54
Hayden, Carl, 211
Hayek, Friedrich A. von: applied to public vs. private law, 129–30; classical theory in, 22–24; on constructivism, 4; general theories of, 14; on institutional design, 34n.23; on law and liberalism, 97, 104; on political practice, 127n.19
Health and Milligan Mfg. Co. v. Worst, 191n.37
Health Insurance for the Aged Act, 153n.2
Holmes, Oliver Wendell, 99, 107
Horowitz, Donald, 196n.47
Horvat, Branko, 10–12
House of Commons, English, 219
House of Representatives. *See* United States House of Representatives
House Rules, 219
Hume, David, 21
Humphrey, Hubert, 169n. 21

ICC (Interstate Commerce Commission), 162
Ignatieff, Michael, 127n.17
India, 227
Industrial Revolution, 167
Industrial Union Dept. v. American Petroleum Inst., 194n.44
Interstate Commerce Commission (ICC), 162
Israel, State of, 226

Jackson, Andrew, 169
Jackson, Jesse, 227, 228
Jackson, Robert H., 209
Jacksonians, 212

Jefferson, Thomas: applied to civic virtue, 221, 223; applied to secular-sacred distinctions, 214; applied to self-government, 219–20; and Federalism vs. Anti-Federalism, 180, 182; in MacLeish's poetry, 228n. 11; *Manual of Parliamentary Practice* (Jefferson), 219–20; on tyranny, 176n. 1
Jesus, 226. *See also* Christianity
Johnson, Lyndon Baines, 217, 224
Joseph, Lawrence, 47n.6
Judaism, 226–27

Kant, Immanuel, 27n.9, 71, 104, 215
Kateb, George, 125n.12
Keane, John, 196n.47
Kenyon, Cecelia, 187n.30
Keynesians, 114, 164
King, Martin Luther, Jr.: in development of social movements, 79, 91, 92, 217, 228; as example of civic virtue, 223; and secular-sacred distinctions, 227, 228
Kipling, Rudyard, 215
Knowledge and Human Interests (Habermas), 6–7
Kotarbiński, Tadeusz, 9

Lakatos, Imre, 8
Lane, Robert, 124n.9
Laswell, Harold, 50, 66, 67
Latin America, 226
Legal Services Corporation, 225
Lenin, 61, 74
Lifton, Jay, 227
Lindblom, Charles Edward: applied to new normativism, 55; applied to problem solving, 121–22; critiques of political economy by, 9–12; on improving control of power, 24–26; *Politics, Economics, and Welfare* (Dahl & Lindblom), 9; *Politics and Markets* (Lindblom), 11; state-economy relations, 212, 223
Lindsley v. Natural Carbonic Gas Co., 191n.37
Lippman, Walter, 22n.1
Lipset, Seymour Martin, 46n.5
Locke, John, 136n.33, 189
Lowi, Theodore J.: applied to political practice, 89; classical theory in, 22, 23; *End of Liberalism,* 167n.20; on plu-

Lowi, Theodore J. (*continued*)
  ralism, 78, 102–3; on self-government, 216–17; summary of paper by, 145–46

McIlwain, Charles, 9, 21
MacIntyre, Alasdair, 102, 126n.15, 211
MacLeish, Archibald, 227–28
Madison, James: applied to administrative law, 194; applied to equal protection, 175; applied to self-government, 209, 218; on citizen participation, 138–39; compared to Dahl, 26n.8; on control of power, 149; on deliberation, 146; and factions, 155, 174, 189–91, 193; in Federalist/Anti-Federalist debate, 181–87; influence in communist countries, 76; revival of ideas of, 195–202; writings in *The Federalist*, 155, 181, 183, 185, 186n.29, 218
Mansfield, Harvey C., Jr., 210–11
Manual of Parliamentary Practice (Jefferson), 219–20
Margolis, Howard, 73
Marx, Karl Heinrich, 3–6, 34, 74, 75
Marxism, 10, 52, 61, 74. *See also* Communism; Guild Socialism
Medicaid, 153
Medicare, 153
Michigan, 213, 218
Middle East, 227, 229
Minnesota National Guard, 211
Minnesota v. Clover Leaf Creamery Co., 190n.34
Mississippi University for Women v. Hogan, 192n.41
Model Parliament of 1295, 21
Montesquieu, Charles Louis de Secondat, 42n.1, 76, 184n.22
Morse, Wayne, 211
Mourning v. Family Publications Services, Inc., 194n.44
Moynihan, Daniel Patrick, 224
Mussolini, Benito, 103

National Guard, Minnesota, 211
Nazism, 78
Near East, 227
Nelson, Richard R., 157
New Deal, 151, 161, 162, 224
New Puritans, 229

Newton-Smith, W. H., 8
New York State Bar Association, 217
Niebuhr, Reinhold, 227
Nietzsche, Friedrich Wilhelm, 3–5, 34, 85
Nixon, Richard Milhous, 151, 156–57, 160, 210, 217, 218

Oakeshott, Michael J., 22–23
Occupational Safety and Health Act (OSHA), 154n.4, 156
Office of Management and Budget (OMB), 163
O'Malley, Engel v., 191n.37
OMB. *See* Office of Management and Budget
Oregon, 211
OSHA. *See* Occupational Safety and Health Act

Panama Refining Co. v. Ryan, 194n.42
Parliament, English, 21, 88, 219
Parsons, Talcott, 73
Pentagon, 217
Pierce, C. S., 106, 107
Plato, 32, 113
Podgórecki, Adam, 9
Politics, Economics, and Welfare (Dahl & Lindblom), 9
Politics and Markets (Lindblom), 11
Popper, Karl, 4, 107
Prairie Populism, 112
Preface to Economic Democracy (Dahl), 25n.6
President of the United States, 151, 152, 159–61, 163–64, 217, 220. *See also names of specific presidents*
President's Committee on Administrative Management, 159
Protestants, 226

Rawls, John, 7, 11, 28n.13, 85
Rayburn, Samuel Taliaferro, 221
Reagan, Ronald, 161–65, 229
Rehnquist, William, 166, 194n.44
Republican party, 151, 153n.2
Ricoeur, Paul, 4
Riker, William, 31
Roman Catholicism, 226
Rosenthal v. New York, 191n.37
Rousseau, Jean-Jacques, 107n.6, 179n.9
Royal Writ of 1295, 21
Rules of Senate, 219

Rush, Benjamin, 182–83n.17
Rushworth, John, 210
Russia, 74, 76, 210. *See also* Communism; Marxism; Union of Soviet Socialist Republics
Russian Revolution, 74, 76
Ryle, Gilbert, 6

Salkever, Stephen G., 134n.30
Samuelson, Paul, 220
Sandburg, Carl, 229–30
Sax, Joseph, 218, 222
Scalia, Antonin, 160n.14
Schechter Poultry Corp. v. United States, 151, 167n.20, 194
Schelling, Thomas, 82
Schwartz, John E., 162n.17
Sciences of the Artificial (Simon), 9
Selective Service Act, 159n.10
Selznick, Philip, 78, 90, 97, 111, 122–23
Sen, Amartya K., 31, 73
Senate. *See* United States Senate
Senate Rules, 219
Shelley v. Kramer, 169
Silent Spring (Carson), 217
Simon, Herbert, 9
Simon, William, 166
Skinner, B. F., 71
Smith, Adam, 108
Social Choice and Individual Values (Arrow), 27
Sołtan, Karol Edward, 1–2, 39–41, 145–46
Sorel, Georges Eugène, 75
Soviet Union. *See* Union of Soviet Socialist Republics
Sparta, 62
SSI (Supplemental Security income), 152
Steiner, George, 214
Stewart, Dugdale, 125
Stewart, Potter, 211
Stewart, Richard, 150, 154n.3, 156, 158, 166–67, 169–70
Stockman, David, 166
Storing, Herbert, 179n.9
Strauss, Leo, 133–34
Strozier, Charles B., 227
Sunstein, Cass R., 146–47
Supplemental Security Income (SSI), 152
Supreme Court. *See* United States Supreme Court

Taylorism, 71
Taylor of Caroline, John, 25n.7
Thomas, Clarence, 160n.14
Thompson, Edward Palmer, 34–35
Tiananmen Square massacre, 211
Tigner v. Texas, 191n.37
Tocqueville, Alexis de, 33, 66, 102, 200n.49
"Tomlinson" (Kipling), 215
Toulmin, Stephen, 101n.3
Truman, David, 47n.7, 49n.8
Truman, Harry S., 159
Twenty-fifth Amendment, 208n.2

Unger, Roberto Mangabeira, 75
Union of Soviet Socialist Republics, 62, 76, 208, 211, 223. *See also* Communism; Marxism; Russia
United States: administrative law and factions in, 158, 175, 193–95, 201; civic virtue in, 207, 210–12, 216, 220–23; conservatism in, 161–66, 170; deliberative democracy in, 175–76, 187–89, 196, 200–202; dissatisfaction with government of, 174; in general constitutional theory, 124n.10; general reconstruction of law in, 7; importance of study of, 15; liberalism in, 65, 111, 165, 166, 170; libertarianism in, 161–62, 165; as litigant, 151, 160, 167, 191n.35, 194, 209n.3; presidential power in, 152, 159–61, 163–64; public vs. private law in, 131; regulatory laws in, 151–65, 175, 193–95; reviving Madisonian republicanism in, 195–202; revolution and constitutionalism in, 75n.4; secular-sacred distinctions in, 207, 214–16, 226–29; self-government in, 207, 208–10, 216–20; state-economy relation in, 207, 212–14, 216, 223–26. *See also* American Revolution; United States Congress; United States Constitution; United States Supreme Court
United States Army Corps of Engineers, 217
United States Bureau of Public Roads, 217
United States Congress: and administrative law, 194; basis for authority of,

United States Congress (*continued*) 88; in Federalist/Anti-Federalist debate, 184n.21; and general delegation of power, 166–69; and interest groups, 189; and liberalism, 165; and presidential power, 159–61; and regulatory laws, 151, 155–58, 162, 164; in revival of Madisonian republicanism, 196, 197; and rules of law, 167n.20; and self-government, 209, 217, 218. *See also* United States House of Representatives; United States Senate

United States Constitution: amendments to, 87, 208n.2, 213; and the American Revolution, 75n.4; and civic virtue, 175–88; and deliberative democracy, 175–76, 190–92; distribution of power by, 185, 186; and factions in current doctrine, 174, 189–93; Federalism vs. Anti-Federalism in framing of, 174, 178–88; general delegation of power in, 149–52, 165–71; general development of, 88–89; importance of study of, 15; interpretation of, in general, 135–36, 169; and liberalism, 151, 154–55, 161, 162; and presidential power, 152, 159–61, 163–64; and regulatory laws, 151–65, 190–91; in relation to the term *constitution*, 43; in revival of Madisonian republicanism, 198; and self-government, 208; summary of purpose of, 149–50

United States Department of Agriculture v. Moreno, 191n.35

United States House of Representatives, 151, 153n.2, 217, 219–20. *See also* United States Congress

United States Senate: and civic virtue, 211; and regulatory law, 151, 153n.2; and self-government, 208, 217, 219–20. *See also* United States Congress

United States Supreme Court: and administrative law, 194n.44; and interest groups, 190–92; and legislation in general, 188n.32; and power of the states, 164; and presidential power, 159, 160; and secular-sacred distinctions, 214; and state-economy relations, 213

United States v. Nixon, 160
University of Michigan, 218
Ury, William, 82, 91

Veblen, Thorstein Bunde, 99
Verba, Sidney, 46, 47, 54
Vietnam War, 217, 228
Vile, M. J. C., 9
Virginia school of political economy, 12, 14

Walden Two (Skinner), 71
Wałęsa, Lech, 79
Walzer, Michael, 131n.26
War on Poverty, 153
Watergate affair, 160
Weber, Max, 45, 46n.4, 73, 105, 217
Webster, Daniel, 210
Weidenbaum, Murray, 161–62
Wentworth, Thomas, 210
Whigs, 214
White, James Boyd, 123
White House. *See* President of the United States
Will, George F., 165
Williams, Bernard, 126, 128
Williamson v. Lee Optical, Inc., 190n.34
Wills, Garry, 176–77n.2
Wilson, Woodrow, 152
WPA (Works Progress Administration), 226

Youngstown Sheet & Tube Co. v. Sawyer, 159n.10
Youngstown Sheet & Tube Co. v. United States, 209n.3